Education Beyond School

Education Beyond School

Higher Education for a Changing Context

edited by NORMAN EVANS

First published in 1980 by
Grant McIntyre Ltd
39 Great Russell Street, London WC1B 3PH

British Library Cataloguing in Publication Data

Education beyond school.
1. Education, Higher—Great Britain
I. Evans, Norman
378.41   LA636.8

ISBN 0-86216-022-7
ISBN 0-86216-023-5 Pbk

Text set in 10/12 pt Linotron 202 Bembo, printed and bound in
Great Britain at The Pitman Press, Bath

Contents

NORMAN EVANS

Introduction

Higher education is in an unenviable condition. It is changing, that much is obvious. It is bound to change more in the future but there are no policies worked out – let alone agreement – for what it could best become. This book is an attempt to carry the discussions to a further stage as a contribution to the formulation of policy.

Many people have high expectations of higher education; others are disillusioned. Some are not at all sure that students, individuals and the country collectively are getting good value for the money that goes into it. If what is being provided does not seem convincing or sufficiently satisfying to taxpayers who finance it, the students who study and the employers who later employ those students, then questions arise as to what it ought to be doing in the future.

Furthermore, there is a somewhat uneasy relationship between higher education and the world of work. Overall, an uncomfortable mixture of fact and unreliable prediction pervades. Faced with what appears to be the near certainty of less money and the probability of fewer students, this lack of any reliable sense of direction is a prescription for crisis.

It is this uneasy relationship between higher education and the world of work which lies at the heart of the uncertainty. For behind every issue concerning the future role of higher education comes the same question: what kind of response can universities, polytechnics and colleges make to the changes individuals experience themselves and in industry and commerce where they earn their living? How willing and, indeed, how able are institutions to take the cue for their teaching and courses of study from the minority who wish to use their services and from the needs of the population at large which

produces the necessary funds through taxation? The contributions in this book are all concerned – in various approaches –
with the overriding question of the quality of institutional
responses. What changes are likely to promote the development
of a responsive relationship between higher education and the
earning world?

Three immediate issues predominate: the numbers of
students; the courses of study which are offered; and the use of
the money made available. All three interlock. If the number of
students drops, and funds are reduced proportionately, courses
will suffer, because it is impossible to adjust academic provision
of tuition as fast as money can be withheld. If the academic
provision is adjusted as a means of reducing expenditure, on
assumptions about students' interests which prove inaccurate,
then again the student numbers can drop. If the funds are
reduced while numbers of students remain steady, teaching and
learning may suffer. It is not surprising that uncertainty
abounds.

These issues and the many others they raise have to be seen in
a context wider than that of educational provision. Approaches
to any of them are bound to be affected by political, social and
philosophical views. Politically there is the major issue of
the distribution of opportunities for higher education and of the
means of enabling those opportunities to be used by those for
whom they are intended. At present some eighty-six per cent of
the population never go near it. That touches on the question of
the capacity of individuals for learning, signalling the need and
possibilities for what is known now as 'Continuing Education'
which could turn different categories of people into potential
students. This is something which is likely to become ever more
important as the demographic graphs record the changing
composition of the population, with increasing numbers of
older rather than younger men and women. In its turn that raises
questions about what may be appropriate fields of study for
older students, and what are the most satisfying ways of
facilitating that study. The implication of considering different
categories of students, finding 'new' (older) students to replace
the disappearing 'old' (younger), and the traditional predomi-

nance of the 18+ undergraduates, is simply another way of confronting the greatest uncertainty: that is, what is the future of the existing institutions – can they all survive, are they all required? And, distasteful though it may be to import commercial criteria to educational discussions, to a large extent those questions of survival are going to depend on what the accountants have taught everyone to talk about – cost effectiveness. Specifically that means trying to ensure that the best use is made of the money provided, measured in terms of numbers of students and courses. But that is powerfully affected by a more general assessment made on entirely subjective grounds, by employers, by the public and so by politicians, and indeed by former students themselves, about the value of courses studied, both in obtaining employment in occupations which are satisfying and, in even more general terms, in contributing to some sense of well-being in individual lives.

Uncertainty about all these matters is affected by the more widespread uncertainty about the education system as a whole. During the last few years of the 1970s a mood developed in the general public which was expressed in various kinds of dissatisfaction. From primary schools' methods of teaching children at one end of the age scale, to remarks about lazy layabout students at the other, complaints were voiced overall. The impression gained ground that whatever the benefits of brighter, lighter school buildings, more interesting, engaging work in schools, longer periods of compulsory schooling for all, and increasing numbers of young men and women in universities, polytechnics and colleges studying for degrees, nevertheless schools were allowing standards in the basic skills to decline, and it was perhaps a mistake to require all young people to remain in school until they were sixteen. Somehow what the schools were doing did not seem to be what parents wanted for their children. And higher education did not seem to be benefiting the country as it should through preparing the young to reverse the national economic decline. After their very extensive period of study, graduates were not coming up to the expectations of employers. 'Accountability' came to frequent the vocabulary of ordinary conversation about education just as it did in other spheres of life. Whether these views were formulated on verifiable fact or not is irrelevant. They were held, and made themselves felt. Education began to learn that it was part of a wider world.

From the early 1970s, the idea seemed to gain ground that education ought to have first call on resources, but that social services, health and housing had prior claims. It was almost as if the connections between home conditions and educational performance, proclaimed by the sociologists of education, had been heard and understood. Whatever the reasons for the distribution of resources, it seems that in the eyes of the politicians who ultimately control these expenditures through Parliament, social services were becoming more important for the general public than schooling and education. That was an ominous sign.

There was also a more dramatic sign: a Prime Minister made a major speech about education. James Callaghan is nothing if not a politician. And it was a sensitive politician faithfully reflecting a public anxiety about education who as Prime Minister did an almost unheard of thing: he made a speech about education. At Ruskin College in 1976 he called for a full discussion by all concerned about the school curriculum. Parents and employers were encouraged to talk with experts about what they were doing. The internal preoccupation of administrators and Her Majesty's Inspectors (HMIs) and the Department of Education and Science with concerns about standards of attainment being reached in schools, in relation to the timing of this speech or any other public pronouncements, are irrelevant, though intriguing. The vital point is that political assessment of the public's disquiet about education prompted the Prime Minister to talk about it in terms which sought to engage the public in what subsequently came to be called, somewhat unfortunately, 'The Great Debate'.

Since then the complications have multiplied for higher education, as have the dissatisfactions. The statistical evidence is disturbing. The percentage of those who are qualified to enter higher education leading to a degree has dropped to around thirteen per cent (some even now say eleven per cent) from 14·2 per cent in 1973 and its high point in the late 1960s. Predictions of any kind about numbers of students are notoriously unreliable, if not dangerous. But just setting that figure against the progressive decline in the number of 18 year olds in each age group from 941,000 in 1982 to 622,000 in the mid 1990s, establishes one factor of uncertainty and of considerable anxiety too. For one of the reasons why some young people reject the opportunities for study at degree level as a matter of deliberate calculation must be some sense that whatever higher education can offer them over the long term, it is not sufficiently attractive or valuable to outweigh the more immediate benefits of beginning a job.

The significance of these developments is shown by the doubts now widely expressed about the projected numbers (produced by a variety of sources) in higher education reaching 560,000 in 1981, with assumptions of about 310,000 in universities and 250,000 in polytechnics and colleges. For 1978 the figure was 512,000 on full-time and sandwich courses, with 285,000 in universities and 227,000 in polytechnics and colleges. For 1979, 530,000 is the number talked of now. And for the mid-1990s, the total is now thought to be about 450,000.

Finance is now equally uncertain. Facts jostle with uncertain prediction. Since the early 1970s steady economic decline has consistently and proportionately reduced expenditure. The Conservative Government's measures in 1979 are only a sharper version of what happened before. A Labour victory in the General Election in May 1979 might have reversed this tendency along the lines of its last White Paper on public expenditure, which looked for some steady if slight growth up to 1983/84. Even that would have produced additional strains on higher-education budgets, since there was also an assumption that universities would accept an additional 185,000 students. But with substantial reductions already made, and institutions beginning academic years with a full commitment to academic programmes without having their budgets finally settled, and with further reductions in funding predicted, everyone concerned in and with higher education has been plunged into a nightmare world, where intelligent guesswork is having to do service as informed financial and managerial judgement.

There was an abortive attempt to find a way through this morass. In February 1978 the DES and the Scottish Education

Department published their discussion document *Higher Education into the 1990s* and a follow-up document in March 1979, entitled *Future Trends in Higher Education*. Various approaches were sketched for dealing with what then was assumed to be an increasing number of students for the next few years, followed by a sharp decline running on to the mid-1990s. The one which has a certain appeal to the Labour Government was what was called Model E. This looked forward to using the empty places left over from the reduced numbers of traditional 18+ students, for a more popular and widely based role within what is now known as continuing education, to take account of many different kinds of students who had not featured much within higher education provision. A combination of evidence that student recruitment for higher education places may be lower than expected with the financial policies of a Conservative Government, and its apparent disregard for adult education at a time of mounting unemployment, has blocked debates about Model E. Rather the problem for higher education is to retain its present level of resources in the face of the argument that there may be spare capacity which should be cut out right away. If the present level of higher education resources can be maintained, then the Model E opportunity may reappear. Fewer traditional students would mean room for other developments, with different categories of students. But that 'if' simply underlines the confusion and uncertainty of the present.

The uncertainty of demand for student places stands out in this catalogue of confusions. Whatever interpretations are put on it, to some extent it must be attributed to assumptions by some young people that what higher education has to offer does not match their requirements as they conceive them. The demand for relevance which was rampant among students during the late 1960s is not now so stridently proclaimed. But whatever was meant then by relevance, as an immediate connection between subjects studied and socially usable knowledge and skills, is likely to be connected with what is now prompting young people to disregard the higher education their immediate predecessors looked for competitively.

There is a paradox here over opportunities and the use made

of them. Some one hundred and fifty institutions are now offering an incredible array of degree courses with innumerable combinations of subjects. The range of opportunities has been extended in an attempt to provide what it was thought larger numbers of students would wish to study. It is an attempt to respond to a changing student population. Yet many young people will say that they can easily feel trapped in the course which they select. They can easily find it difficult – if not impossible – to change the direction of their studies after one or two years, even though the desire and perhaps the need for such a change has grown out of the studies which they have by that time completed. In other words, they do not believe that the higher education system can respond to them as people who may well change over that period of time.

It could be, too, that unresponsiveness is what employers are really complaining about when they claim that newly qualified graduates are not quite what they expect. Ivory towers may no longer exist, but the gap, which some claim separates the world of higher education from the world of work where they earn their living, makes it a convenient scapegoat. In either case it is the perceptions of people outside higher education which is at issue. Part of the problem of the future development in higher education is finding ways of taking these outside perceptions more into account, to prompt questions about what these institutions can most appropriately contribute to the changing world in which they exist.

There is one particular reason why this relative lack of responsiveness to the higher education system is almost cruel. For a relatively long time now successive Education Ministers and their governments have attempted to create a responsive system through an impressive array of White Papers and policy declarations. In 1956, when David Eccles, now Lord Eccles, was Minister of Education the White Paper *Technical Education* was published. It was a quite deliberate boost for the development of further education's contribution to technical education. Through the creation of the Colleges of Advanced Technology (CATs) and the establishment of the National Council for Technological Awards it sought to create a parallel academic provision to that of the universities, with the means of sustaining itself through its system of academic validation. Along with other schemes of development which that White Paper set in train, it was a calculated response to developments in the industrial and commercial world. The Government's acceptance of the main recommendations of the Robbins committee in 1963 led to a different kind of attempt at responsiveness. Nine new universities were created, and eight colleges of advanced technology and Scottish central institutions were given university status. The demand for more places was proven. So the university system was expanded to provide them.

Hard on the heels of this development came another. When Anthony Crosland was Secretary of State for Education, the White Paper on polytechnics was published in 1966, which led to the creation of thirty polytechnics by 1974 with the intention of extending specifically the range of provision offered within the higher education system. Polytechnics were to provide full-time and sandwich course degrees of university standard but more vocationally orientated than those of universities. They were to offer sub-degree courses, and also part-time courses of both degree and sub-degree level. Once again this was a deliberate attempt to use statutory authority to introduce to parts of the higher education system a greater responsiveness to the changing circumstances of the social and economic world. In 1972 the White Paper *Education: a framework for expansion* was Margaret Thatcher's attempt at development through central provision, when she was Secretary of State for Education and Science. In some ways it was the most imaginative of the series. It may have been extremely damaging to teacher education, but the intention was sensible, of creating from the existing polytechnics, the large and established colleges of further education and the one hundred or so colleges of education (which were abolished), a series of institutions throughout the country, at least one for each sizeable urban area, large enough to provide a full range of curriculum and so able (in theory) to respond fairly readily to any changes in demand.

This latest attempt can illustrate the limitations of statutory provision of this kind and perhaps can demonstrate some of the reasons for the failure to achieve a more responsive higher education system. Apart from giving some broad hints about types of course, and some generalisations about what might be considered suitable curricula, in one sense the DES role in the developments it sets in train is completed when the institutions in question are created by the local authorities, which are technically responsible for all the higher education institutions other than universities and the voluntary colleges which mainly originated as religious foundations. The DES has no official part to play in the appointment of academic staff nor in the design of courses. So at this level, central government can do no more than take the initiative in creating institutions with the brief that they should be responsive to the populations they are intended to serve. It has no direct power to require responsive policies to be developed within those institutions which it has been responsible for creating.

In another sense, though, the authority of central government which is used to create institutions seems to prevent these very developments. Every degree course which is taught outside universities has to be approved by the DES through an approval system. Nominally this is run through Regional Advisory Committees composed of representatives of local authorities, industry and commerce, as well as members of the academic institutions, but essentially through the Regional Staff Inspectors who are senior HMIs and, for this purpose, a particularly powerful arm of the DES. There are all kinds of sensible reasons for this procedure such as avoiding undue duplication of courses and waste of resources. However, over the period when the institutions created in the wake of the 1972 White Paper were trying to be responsive in the way which DES policies called for, it seems to have been used primarily as an instrument of financial control which has resulted in an extremely crude form of manipulation of institutional development. Time and again what has happened is that institutions have found their responsive initiatives stymied for the kinds of courses which were intended to extend the range of opportunities in higher education. Their contributions to enable the system to be more responsive to its potential students have often been rejected by the DES which pronounced the policy. Those that have been accepted have mostly been fought through in the face of strong opposition.

Within the existing distribution of powers over the development of higher education outside the universities, it would seem therefore as if the DES has either not enough power, or too much. Having created institutions, it does not have the power positively to promote the academic policies for which they were created. Confronted with plans for institutional and course development which are in line with the policies it has propounded, it has the power to deny institutions those kinds of growth.

This interpretation is not intended to imply that it is all the fault of the DES. Economic factors have overridden the White Paper policies, making their implementation both confused and yet more urgently needed. Like local authorities and the institutions themselves, it is caught up in the special balance between central and local government which characterises the education system of this country. But it is a cautionary tale of the limitations of statutory initiatives which are seeking quite appropriately to make the higher education system more responsive to the surrounding world. The implication is that responsiveness is unlikely to come as a result of institutional reorganisation imposed from the top downwards, as at present. That kind of imposed reorganisation could work, if it were accompanied by considerable devolution of authority to institutions for their own academic and curricular development. But that would require even more radical changes in the national and regional administration of this part of the education service.

There is a more serious implication: it is that the present arrangements for the government of higher education outside the universities appear to be seriously deficient. It was clear that as Secretary of State Shirley Williams was well aware of these problems when she commissioned Gordon Oakes as Minister of State to chair a Committee of Inquiry. But the fate of the Oakes committee recommendations – which tried to produce some solutions to these vexed questions after working at pressure for eighteen months – simply illustrates the difficulty of trying to satisfy everyone concerned.

All these efforts of central government to induce a greater responsiveness on the part of institutions of higher education have been confined to what is called the maintained or public sector. When the universities are included in these considerations, matters become further complicated, for one particular reason. Apart from some research and some highly specialised courses, there is now little significant difference between what a university teaches and what is taught in polytechnics, colleges and institutes of higher education. This leaves on one side the different stories of development of these two sectors with their different systems of financing and government (which will be referred to later in this book), simply to identify this one central point, that what they do now for students is so very similar.

As chartered institutions, financed through the medium of the University Grants Committee (UGC), each university is independent of existing statutory control by the Secretary of State. Its academic departments and courses are, with the exception of certain specialised courses such as medicine, entirely the province of each university Senate. So how a university responds to what it considers to be the demands being made upon it reflects its own perception of its responsibilities as an institution of research and learning. Since there is now almost an entire overlap in provision of courses between universities and polytechnics and colleges/institutes in the public sector, there is little to choose between one group of institutions and another in terms of how they are responding to the needs of individuals in our society. This serves to support the argument offered already: within the present context of administrative and financial arrangements, it is misconceived to seek to change the emphasis of what higher education offers solely by the imposition of institutional reorganisation. Furthermore, to return to an earlier point, there can be little doubt that, whatever may be the intentions of any or all institutions, potential students and perhaps employers and the general public too are not convinced that developments outside the education sphere are exerting sufficient influence on what higher education provides.

Two other factors have their place in an account of a lack of responsiveness by higher education to its actual and potential students: the system of finance, and the role of formal matriculation requirements. The financing of higher education is a complex and even baffling affair. The details are ignored here, save for one salient factor: the manner of financing individuals as students. Once a place has been secured by an individual, subject only to a means test assessment of parent's income, except for students aged 25, or those who have worked full-time for three years, all fees and other academic charges are automatically paid to the institution. On top of that, of course, there is the student's maintenance grant, but that is paid direct in most cases to the student, and only those sums necessary to pay for residence and catering accrue to the institution itself.

Now the issue here is the role of the student in relation to the institution. Once a student takes up the offer of a place he brings an automatic income to the university, polytechnic or college concerned, for three or four years. This means that, although each student represents a considerable sum of money for the Treasurers of institutions who would not be receiving it but for the students choosing to accept a place, the only financial influence a student has on an institution is the negative one of deciding not to study at it.

In some ways this is a powerful influence. The popularity of subjects and disciplines changes. In time institutions tend to respond by introducing new courses or offering more of a kind, provided that academic appointments can be used to facilitate such changes. But it is slow, and the trouble about it is that change in the world around is fast. The two speeds of change should not be the same, but any search for greater responsiveness means that the relationship between the two should be deliberate, not accidental.

Students and potential students living in that fast-changing world would have a considerably greater influence on what institutions of higher education considered they should offer, if the system of payment of tuition fees and other academic charges was arranged so as to make the student more of a customer and less of a captive banker. If at the outset of becoming a registered student each was financed to pay directly for the course he chose to study, a fundamental change would take place in the relationship between the student who wished to study, and the place which would enable him to do so. Emphasis in responsibility would shift. Student choices would make themselves known and felt far more powerfully. Institutions would have to take note of them in relation to enrolments for courses. The questions surrounding the issue of responsiveness would take on a different significance. Structure of courses, facilities for part-time study, recognition of knowledge and skills already acquired, would arise for discussion. Not all would be for the good, perhaps, but a greater responsiveness would undoubtedly result, always with the proviso that it would need to be sought within the traditions of academic standards on which higher education is based.

Some of this alteration in the position of institutions offering courses and those who wish to study them will occur in any case. Fewer potential students of the traditional 18+ category already means that some departments, as well as some institutions, are actively competing for students. But any moves, which come as a result, towards a greater responsiveness would be more by default than deliberate intention. Something more positive is required, and a shift in the basis for payment of academic charges suggests one real opportunity for inducing change.

That is a contentious point – so is the one which follows. It concerns another kind of monopoly related to responsiveness: formal qualification for entry and matriculation. Each university has exceptional admission arrangements to enable candidates to commence degree study without the matriculation requirements of at least two 'A' Levels in appropriate subjects. In most universities this is not significant numerically as an entry route, but the system exists. All degree courses validated by the Council for National Academic Awards (CNAA) also have special admissions arrangements. Usually the ruling is that no one entry shall have more than fifteen per cent of those who are not able to comply with the formal matriculation requirements. For the most part, however, these special admissions procedures involve candidates providing evidence of formal study, often of a kind which has led to some formal qualification which can be taken as equivalent to the matriculation requirements. For mature students some notice may be taken of experience of work in a related field but, with rare exceptions, entry is not allowed on the basis of that kind of experience alone.

This can be taken as indicative of another way in which institutions are not being as responsive as might be expected. The pattern of an 18+ entry predominating, with mature students as the exception rather than the rule, may be changing. With the numbers of 18 year olds deciding against higher education and the numbers increasing of re-trainees, those who have been retired early, and adults interested in continuing education as a way of life, the student population could with ease change its composition significantly. If that happens, and there are signs that it is beginning, many potential students will be at very different stages of development from the typical 18+ entrant. Many will enter their courses likely to know far more about the areas they are going to study. Simply through following their occupations they may well have acquired considerable knowledge and skills, some of which have been the content of formally-taught courses. For those who have acquired such knowledge and skills from their experience of working and living, the question arises whether that kind of attainment level of learning can be accepted as valid in the same way as formally-acquired learning is recognised through the possession of certificates to prove it. If such knowledge and skills are not deemed suitable for consideration on the same terms as formally-acquired learning, it seems that once again higher education will be regarded as somewhat unresponsive to the conditions of life of its potential students.

It is clear that some reliable reasons have to be found to explain why numbers of qualified potential students are deciding against becoming students. One immediate and straightforward reason is that part-time study for degrees is relatively unusual in universities and not all that prevalent in other institutions, apart from the Open University. Were it possible for more to follow more easily their studies on a part-time basis, recruitment figures might be more buoyant.

Without doubt, student recruitment is the most important source of the uncertainty which is the present bane of higher education. If the essential question about student recruitment is the perception of higher education held by potential students – what he or she thinks will be got from it – then the answers may involve deliberate action by institutions that is calculated to alter those perceptions. In other words, universities, polytechnics, and colleges may have to change their ways. If they are to do so they have to look for answers to three fundamental questions. What kinds of students can be recruited? What will encourage them to apply for places? What kinds of changes do these answers suggest are required?

In the future students are going to be less homogeneous. From 18+ onwards, everyone will be a potential higher education student. A smaller proportion of 18 year olds means possibly a larger proportion of older middle-class potential students. That larger proportion of older potential students will all have had periods of employment. Some will be relatively young, those who chose employment rather than higher education and may be seeking a first-degree qualification somewhat later than their predecessors. Some will be in their middle years, in search of forms of retraining, or in early retirement. Others will be students in retirement. Amongst the eighty-six per cent of the population at present making little or no use of the higher education opportunities available to them, there are bound to be many potential students. This becomes more evident when the fourteen per cent who do attend are seen to be composed of approximately twenty per cent of middle-class children and a mere two per cent of working-class children. This bears no relation to the incidence of intellectual ability of either group. Minority ethnic groups are another section of the population from which relatively few young people offer themselves as applicants for higher education courses. Now most unhappily there is another group who need most careful consideration: the increasing numbers of young people who may spend years without employment and who, for a variety of reasons, may at some time want to turn to higher education.

Another way of trying to identify likely sources of students in the future is to consider the kinds of development which are taking place in industry and commerce. Almost every way of working in almost every field of human endeavour is becoming more reliant upon technological equipment of one kind or another. More often than not this requires a fairly demanding level of knowledge and skills from the user and requires an increasingly sophisticated maintenance system, whether of re-placement units produced in a factory or of technical staff on site. Every one of these technical aids can become obsolete rapidly as some improved version comes off the production line somewhere. There are two categories of people here who may well become more valuable to their employers if, at an appropri-ate time, they undertake the kinds of study available through higher education: those whose skill in using technical aids governs the value of the equipment to an employer; and those who keep the aids in full and effective working order.

Developments such as these are often at the core of the problems which now occur so frequently in industrial relation-ships. Trade unions have just as much interest as employers in making sure that the employees who are their members are highly educated and trained in their particular sphere. Knowl-edge is a route to power. The more knowledgeable trade union negotiators can be, the better results they are likely to achieve from negotiations on behalf of their members. Once again there is another constituency of potential students of whom perhaps insufficient notice has been taken in the past.

None of these potential students is going to benefit from all the many things which higher education has to offer unless the higher education institutions attempt to answer the question why their candidates do not take sufficient interest now. Of course there are limits to what institutions can do. For the younger candidates so much depends on what kind of encour-agement is given to them at the CSE or 'O' Level stage in school or college of further education. If young people are not thinking at all of further study at that stage, they are less likely to think seriously about it during later life. For the older ones, much depends on the chancey ways in which everyone assembles opinions. Hearsay, the experience of friends and relatives, prejudices, items in newspapers, and television programmes, they all play their part.

Institutions have two aspects of these perceptions to take into account; what they actually do offer and how it is made known. Advertising their wares is not something most universities take kindly to, at least not publicly. In private there may be quite eager competition between institutions. Polytechnics have always advertised their courses, for the simple reason that they needed to recruit as strongly as possible. They could not rely on any established patterns of careers consultations to do their job for them, as, on the whole, universities have assumed is the case. The newest group of institutions to enter the field of general higher education – the colleges and institutes of higher education – drew on the experience of the polytechnics, and through the professional consultancy of the Careers and Research Advisory Committee (CRAC) they launched a fairly effective campaign to make widely known what they had to offer both collectively and as separate institutions.

Seen from the viewpoint of a careers adviser, of being sufficiently knowledgeable to give accurate information, let alone reliable advice, to young people who may not be too sure exactly what it is they are wanting, then the sheer complexity of understanding the provision of all the 150 institutions, and the effort required to master all that information, is quite overwhelming. For the potential applicant in default of reliable information from careers advisers – unless he or she is very strongly motivated or has a store of general background information about higher education to draw on, or can find reliable assistance – the task of finding the right course seems to many too daunting even to attempt. It would seem that some means needs to be found of making it easier for potential applicants to find their way to what they think they might want. Much has already been done in various institutions and through advice centres of all kinds, but in these days of microprocessors and computerised information systems and the widespread use of telephones there ought to be some way of making information more readily available. At one level this is a technical matter. Improved information sources alone would not be sufficient, however, to meet the needs of those potential students who need the encouragement even to consider higher education as a serious option. It is the context in which the information is given and the support of others which becomes so important. Somehow the information has to be made available in ways which do not require strong self-confidence, the lack of which prevents them applying or seeking information in the first place. Citizens' Advice Centres and Job Centres may be cited as examples here, though not intended to be used as models. Finding out about courses of further study needs to become as ordinary a business as finding out about the weather or food or entertainment.

There is one strange, even remarkable, phenomenon about the discussion of these issues. They take place in a political vacuum. As James Callaghan's intervention at Ruskin College shows, politicians had picked up the message from the public at large that dissatisfaction with education was fairly strong and widespread, and responded by articulating it. He held up a mirror. But apart from a few generalisations and agreeable calls for everyone to talk nicely together about the issues involved, and respecting the proper responsibilities of all concerned, no clear lead was given by a political figure. It is true that the Great Debate followed, instigated by Shirley Williams as Secretary of State for Education and Science as a series of grand discussions throughout the country based on a consultative document prepared by her own Department. This was like an extended seminar which provided valuable discussion opportunities for participants from industry, commerce, and parents as well as professional educators. It did not, however, result in any clear statement of education policy which was integrated with political policies.

It is instructive to place this political vacuum in the context of Party Manifestos. This was what the three main parties had to say about higher education in their 1979 electoral manifestos. Labour led off with its customary commitment: 'The Labour Party believes in equality of opportunity.' These sections followed:

The Needs of Youth. We will provide a universal scheme of education and training for all 16–19 year olds, if necessary backed by statute. We will remove the financial barriers which prevent many young people from low income families from continuing their education after 16.

We will reintroduce legislation for income-related mandatory awards to all 16–18 year olds on all full-time courses.

Further and Higher Education. Further education places have increased by 25,000 under Labour. Labour will substantially increase the opportunities for people from working-class backgrounds – particularly adults – to enter further and higher education. We want to see more workers given time off work for study. To this end, the places at the Open University have increased from 43,000 in 1974 to 80,000 in 1978. We propose to extend the present mandatory grant system. Labour supported the Adult Literacy Scheme, and will ensure its continuation.

The Liberals introduced their section on 'Education and Training' more comprehensively. 'We see education and training as a lifelong process that must be as widely available as possible to people of all ages.' For further and higher education it then went on, 'post-school Education must be integrated with closer links between universities, polytechnics and further education,' and specifically, 'we want to see expansion of adult education and a major expansion of training and retraining facilities in which Britain still lags far behind its industrial competitors', and 'education for retirement from employment'.

The Tory Manifesto's section is headed 'Standards in Education', and its general comments run, 'The Labour Party is still obsessed with the structure of the schools system, paying too little regard to the quality of education.' 'We shall promote higher standards of achievement in basic skills.' Then on higher education it says:

Much of our higher education in Britain has a world-wide reputation for its quality. We shall seek to ensure that this excellence is maintained. We are aware of the special problems associated with the need to increase the number of high-quality entrants to the engineering professions. We shall review the relationship between school, further education and training to see how better use can be made of existing resources.

Political manifestos are not the place to find detailed educational policies, but these comments indicate an awareness that post-school education is part of the educational debate, even though none of them shows how anything can be done. Sketches for action are there. If Labour produced a 'minimal scheme of education and training for all 16–19 year olds', removing 'financial barriers', it could well have the means of substantially increasing 'the opportunities for people from working-class backgrounds – particularly adults – to enter further and higher education.' If the Liberals are really committed to 'education and training as a lifelong process that must be as widely available as possible to people of all ages', they have the means of developing such a service if post-school education was 'integrated with closer links between universities, polytechnics and further education.' The Tories appear to have no such developmental view of higher and further education. Apart from the rather unhappy ring for overseas students in the reference to a 'world-wide reputation' for the quality of higher education provision, standards are again its obsession, save for its proper concern about the proper use of 'existing resources'.

Putting all three together would produce some of the changes in higher education which this book is seeking. Better financial support would encourage some of the new (older) potential students. Collaboration between universities, polytechnics and colleges, which the Liberals rather naughtily omitted, and further education could produce different kinds of encouragement for all those new students. And it is impossible to think of exploiting the present resources without paying increased attention to what is taught, how and to whom. But apart from the implications, nothing in these three general election manifestos seems to be declaring a general interest in measures designed to encourage this higher education system as a whole to take more account of the needs of the population which is paying for most of it through taxes whether it likes what it gets or not.

Since May 1979 nothing constructive has featured in government pronouncements about higher education. They seem to have been restricted to aspects of the reduction of the public expenditure. Neither of the other main political parties has had much to say. The most active and audible comments about higher education affairs being offered at present seem to be coming from the House of Commons Select Committee on Education under the Chairmanship of Christopher Price, the Labour Member of Parliament for Lewisham West. If that Committee can be instrumental in stirring the interest of politicians in the future of higher education, it will be making a vital contribution. A missing dimension to the discussion will be added; the vacuum might even be filled. For if politicians were to discover from their constituents that more of them would be making use of higher education if they believed it had something to offer them, we might hear more about ways in which institutions could respond.

The uncertainty in higher education will only be resolved if government and the general public, and so politicians, are satisfied that universities, polytechnics and colleges are doing their best to answer the following sets of questions which each of the contributors to this book was asked to consider. What are the groups of people from which students are not forthcoming now but might be in the future? What are the factors most likely to encourage them to become students? What changes in the rules and regulations are necessary to enable them to do so? These questions involve considering admissions policies, curriculum course design and teaching methods, attendance, and requirements for graduation – full-time, part-time, periodic and occasional study, as phased programmes of work. A more responsive way of approaching the same issues is to ask: what kinds of changes are necessary for higher education to improve the service it provides to those minority groups on its margins, as well as to trade unions, industry and commerce, those seeking re-training and continuing education, and the present student constituency? And what kinds of changes are most likely to enable higher education to meet the circumstances of those qualified 18+ school leavers who are at present opting for employment rather than any formal post-secondary education?

The contributors were asked to write as they see things and not from any institutional brief. The intention has been not to provide a detailed and exhaustive survey of higher education, or to explore the familiar curriculum controversies of arts versus science and technology, but to ask experienced practitioners to identify the major issues of concern. Each contributor was asked to range freely within the overall remit so that the whole would mirror the tensions of the debate. Where two contributors do treat the same issue, such as Carter and Bragg on administration, the contrast in approach is itself very revealing. They do not all agree with each other, and they give different emphases, but all, except the two employers, have a record of involvement with institutional changes in higher education, and on any assessment the places where they have served show an impressive array of evidence of attempts to achieve the responsiveness which is the theme of this chapter. Two of the contributors are employers looking in at the world of higher education from the outside. David Dennis, in charge of graduate recruitment for Marks and Spencer, writes from the point of view of a recruiter of young graduates for service industry. He is disconcerted, and more than a little impatient at what he takes to be the odd neglect by institutions of their students in so far as the tuition they offer pays scant attention to their personal growth and self knowledge which he claims is crucial in service industry's occupations. Sir Monty Finniston writes as a former Chairman of British Steel who has recently been required to look at higher education both from the outside as well as from inside as Chairman of the Committee of Inquiry into the Engineering Profession, whose best-selling report was published under the title *Engineering our Future*. (Since that report proposes new kinds of engineering degrees, it is underlining the need for responsiveness.) With a lifetime of experience to draw on from the production side of industry he raises some important points about the relation between the professions and higher education. Both contributors make demands upon higher education which are additional and new. They do so believing that a closer connection is required now between place of education and subsequent employment if the individual who moves from one stage to another is to be

adequately served by both. They are looking for greater responsiveness.

Three of the contributors are on the inside of higher education
and write while looking out. Stephen Bragg is Vice-Chancellor
of Brunel University, having brought to that former CAT
twenty years of industrial and commercial experience from
Rolls-Royce. He writes from a background of service on the
UGC before taking up office in Brunel. His call for a wholesale
reordering of the higher education system, standing parts of it
on its head and putting other parts through unwonted exercises,
is therefore based on detailed knowledge of the workings of the
university system as a whole, as well as immediate experience of
administering a university against a background of work in
production industry and as a major employer of university
graduates. Harold Silver has been Principal of Bulmershe College of Higher Education, since 1978 one of the newest groups
of colleges offering first degrees which have evolved from the
reorganisation of teacher education. Bulmershe was one of the
first colleges to offer degrees other than for professional qualifications for teaching, so he writes from the perspective of an
institution which is having to work out its own salvation by
competing for students at a time of diminishing general recruitment. George Tolley, as Principal of Sheffield Polytechnic since
1966, led the development of that institution as it moved from
being a major Technical College to being designated as a
polytechnic when he took office, and took it through the
reorganisation of teacher education when Sheffield Polytechnic
was amalgamated with the City of Sheffield and Totley Colleges
of Education in 1976.

Formerly Vice-Chancellor of one of the nine new universities
created following the Robbins committee's recommendations,
Charles Carter has recently moved from inside the universities
at Lancaster to somewhere in the border zone where the worlds
of universities, government, industry and commerce meet, as
Chairman of the Research and Management Committee of the
Policy Studies Institute. His call for a system of differentiated
institutions is no protectionist polemic. The University of
Lancaster, with a number of further education colleges, has

pioneered what is called the Open College, as referred to by
H. D. Hughes, which seeks to provide for mature students a system
of specially designed courses giving successful candidates matriculation standing, as a way of providing more appropriate study
than can be found in 'A' Level courses written for 16 to 18 year
olds. It also pioneered an Independent Study Option within its
first-degree courses. Through his governorship of a college of
education he was involved twice over with their reorganisation,
as university validating authority and with institutional development of the college itself.

H. D. Hughes is another contributor in the border zone. Until
1979 he was Principal of Ruskin College, Oxford, a college
offering one- and two-year diplomas for mature students,
without formal educational qualifications, who are anxious to
study at a pre-university level. That wealth of experience makes
him a key figure on the Advisory Council for Adult and
Continuing Education and prompts him to write urging, particularly, a more welcoming and open access route to higher
education on the grounds of social equity as well as national self
interest.

As compiler and editor of this book I have spent the last three
years looking in at higher education and looking out from it, as
research into a post experience degree for teachers, the Bachelor
of Education, has taken me into all kinds of institutions. Before
that I was Principal of Bishop Lonsdale College of Education in
Derby, where several years were also spent looking out and in,
as James Report, White Paper and Circular 70/73 brought root
and branch reorganization with them. It was that experience
which is largely responsible for this book. In Derby the reorganization period resulted in the creation of a new charitable
institution, the Derby Lonsdale College of Higher Education
from the College of Education and a College of Art and
Technology. During the complicated negotiations with the
Charity Commission, the Church Commissioners, the DES and
Derbyshire County Council, I was convinced that the only sure
justification for the emergence of a new range of institutions
alongside universities and polytechnics was for them to extend the range of opportunities by introducing new ones to

those already available in higher education. There were quite enough courses in the humanities. Generally speaking, science courses were not practical propositions for the emerging institutions. In the performing arts there were interesting possibilities. But what was missing was the kind of course for which David Dennis calls, provision which broadly speaking could serve as a combination of a general liberal education and career education in what were nevertheless non-vocational courses. Duplication of what was on offer already seemed unnecessary, potentially wasteful, and in the longer run, given the demographic trends which were then emerging, probably self destructive.

The failure to develop such provision is a root cause of much institutional worry at this time. It comes back to student recruitment. It is highly unlikely that a sufficiency of the diminishing numbers of potential applicants of the traditional kind are going to choose to study for their degrees in colleges and institutes of higher education to give all of them adequate numbers of students, when university degree courses are open to the same applicants. The same argument can be posed for the polytechnics. It can even be posed for some universities. If all the present forty-five universities and thirty polytechnics and seventy colleges and institutes are to continue their present provision of first-degree courses, the catchment for student recruitment has to be widened, bringing new kinds of students into the system. Younger 'new' students will only come if they can see likely benefits for them in following a course of hard study instead of earning their living in employment. Older 'new' students will for the most part only arrive if they feel welcomed, wanted and treated as responsible adults, making difficult decisions about themselves. They will want to be sure about what they are undertaking and that their views about what they want to study are taken seriously as an influence on academic matters. The burden of this book is that these developments are unlikely to happen if things just go on as at present. Something is going to change. The only doubt now is how. This is the source of the nagging uncertainty.

Each contributor offers views about means as well as ends. The ends are the ways in which the higher education system in this country adapts itself to the changing economic and social circumstances of the citizens who both finance and use it. The means are any devices which serve to achieve that end. There is one very important point to reiterate about the contributions which follow in regard to the means they may prefer. None writes from within an institutional role. They all write on the basis of their knowledge and experience; they do not argue for any kind of sectional development, whatever their present base. University readers may well be as critical of the arguments put forward by Charles Carter and Stephen Bragg as fellow principals may well be of Harold Silver's plea for relative laissez-faire.

The aim of this book has been to create a collection of ideas from people who know what they are talking about and who are prepared to make practical suggestions for future developments at this crossroads for higher education – without indulging in hypothetical fancies.

1

The issues: from inside the system

CHARLES CARTER

Not enough higher education and too many universities?

The clarity of thinking about higher education suffers from our tendency to treat a sector of it, the taking of degrees, as if it were the whole. Exact definitions can be tiresome, but at least they force us to review all those forms of study which are in some sense 'higher' than the work of the schools. This in turn requires us to consider what we mean by saying that one sort of education is 'higher' than another; for it is not universally true that the lower level is a prerequisite for those who wish to embark on the higher. Higher education in Britain, in fact, is conventionally defined as 'beyond the Advanced Level of the General Certificate of Education' (that is, beyond the highest point of achievement normally attainable in a secondary school). This definition omits adult education at elementary levels which might theoretically be taken at school, and both the Advanced Level examinations and others deemed to be of similar standard or difficulty, which are often taken outside the school system. Evidently the boundary of higher education must be inexact, surrounding those courses which by custom and practice have become regarded as mainly suited to students with 'A' Level or equivalent qualifications.

Among these courses, those for degrees are indeed of major importance: courses for first, or Bachelor's, degrees attainable by three or four years of full-time study, and courses for higher (Master's or Doctor's) degrees requiring one to three or four years of further full-time study, or the part-time equivalent. However, the definition also covers diplomas and certificates, recognising success in courses more limited than those for a first or higher degree, and also a considerable range of professional qualifications whose level of difficulty is regarded as beyond that of 'A' Levels, and the teaching for which is therefore regarded as higher education. Nor is the definition limited to courses for educational qualifications, for the development of 'continuing education' gives rise to many short and non-examined courses which certainly assume a prior education up to 'A' Level or beyond.

We now provide higher education in a great many institutions, most of which also have a stake in education which is less advanced (and which therefore is at a 'level' overlapping that of the school system). Thus, the expected position in England and Wales in 1981 is as follows:

Universities and polytechnics	68
Other colleges with	
more than 90% advanced work (i.e. higher education)	67
30–90% advanced work	57
less than 30% advanced work	264
	——
	456[1]
	——

Within this total, the universities and the freestanding 'colleges of higher education' (developed from former colleges of education) are in general specialised on degree work, though the degrees they offer may in certain cases be used as full or part equivalents of professional qualifications. The polytechnics and some of the remaining colleges divide their effort between degree work, the Higher National Diploma and Certificate, and direct teaching for professional qualifications; while the rest of the colleges (including those with a minority of advanced work) are normally teaching for the HND, HNC and professional qualifications, with little or no involvement in degree work. All

[1] When the Robbins Committee reported, there were 26 universities (including those in process of formation), 146 teacher training colleges, 10 colleges of advanced technology, together with 72 other colleges with some Degree or Diploma in Technology work. A number of other colleges will also have had professional courses beyond 'A' Level.

the institutions may, on occasion, contribute to advanced work in shorter and non-examined courses: in addition, the universities have a major commitment to research, and the polytechnics a commitment which in practice is less and more patchy in its incidence. The remaining colleges (including the former colleges of education) are essentially teaching institutions, with no strong expectation of contributing to research.

The universities and polytechnics are, of course, much larger than the other colleges, and deal with most of the students. Although the polytechnics in principle have a spread of courses, some have shown an increasing concentration on degree work, which is the activity that dominates the whole system. The exact proportion of 'degree-level' work is not easy to derive, because it involves a judgement of the 'level' of some of the professional qualifications; and a substantial element of the lower-level work is for part-time students, thus involving an assessment of how their numbers should be expressed as full-time equivalents. As a rough guide, more than four-fifths of the efforts of the higher education system appear to be devoted to courses at first or higher degree level.

THE PURPOSES OF HIGHER EDUCATION

It would be nice to be able to accept the comfortable conclusion that this rather complex system (with its variants in Scotland and Northern Ireland), having evolved over a considerable period, is in some sort of natural adjustment to the needs of society. But the persistent criticism of its cost and of the relevance of its output suggests that this cannot be true. Let us, then, go back to first principles and ask what the higher education system is there for, and in what ways it needs to change in order to meet the needs of the year AD 2000.

Many people accept a naive economic model of the requirement for higher education. This supposes that, because technology and systems are becoming more advanced, they will require more and more people with high levels of education to operate them. Such an idea was used to support the drive in the 1960s to produce more graduate scientists and technologists, and it lies behind the concern at the unwillingness of young people – until the last year or two – to go in for mechanical and electrical engineering. But the model will not stand serious examination. In order to *devise* advanced products, processes and systems we need creative minds of very high ability with an extensive knowledge of the appropriate subject – or, better still, a knowledge which extends into neighbouring subjects, and can take advantage of the fertile reactions of one discipline on another. The number of inventors, creative designers and constructive and profound thinkers who can be used must, however, be quite small. It is limited partly by the lack of enough human material – and it is uncertain how far the educational system can go in stimulating creativity – and partly by the resistance of economic and social systems to very rapid rates of change. Of course we urgently need people who can design better motor-cars, power-stations, business systems or government policies; but where this argument takes us is that the educational system should be ruthlessly elitist, efficient in identifying exceptional ability and generous in giving it the very finest opportunities for development.

Those who argued for the general expansion of higher education in order to meet economic needs were, however, not at all fond of the elitist, or French, attitude, despite the fact that it is also adopted by the Soviet Union. They believed that high technology and advanced systems, once installed, would need an army of highly educated people to sustain them. It is, of course, true that enough people have to be able to understand the working of a system, in order to be able to control and monitor its operation and to put it right when it goes wrong. But it is easy to think of products and processes which have automatic arrangements for monitoring built into them (such as the latest generation of electronic telephone exchanges), and advanced systems which are easier to repair than simple ones because they report their own faults and can be put right by replacing modular sections. The trend of technology is in fact to displace the simpler functions of control and repair, and this general statement can be extended beyond the hardware of industry to cover many commercial and government activities to which the developments of the computer and the micro-processor are relevant. The belief that the economic system will need increasing numbers of second- and third-rate graduate scientists, technologists, social scientists, administrators and the like was in fact an unexamined assumption. The most that can be said is that it is convenient (bearing in mind the mutability of circumstances) to provide a reasonable surplus over known needs. Apart from a few special cases, most of the complaints of shortages of graduates are complaints about an inadequate supply of first-rate people; and many employers have used those of lower quality to do work which at no time will require the full extent of their education, simply because graduates are more readily found than suitable non-graduates.

There is some offset to be found in the fact that increasing wealth gives rise to a demand for more high-level services. A richer country will in practice use more doctors – though even this development is not very logical, since one might think that the advance of medical science (and particularly of preventive medicine) ought to make us more healthy, and thus in need of fewer doctors. It will have a larger demand for teachers, even though the evidence for an improvement of education by a reduction of class size is equivocal. New services will appear in the public and private sectors (for instance, new areas of social work will be developed); and some services which in the past relied on a lower level of education, combined with practical experience, will be upgraded so as to make demands on higher education. This has, for instance, happened with nursing, which might in time become a degree-level subject for all entrants.

But, when all this is said, it is not possible to deduce from the economic requirements a justification for the present size and shape of British higher education. Outside a few fields (such as medicine and teaching) the quantification of requirements for the present – let alone for the future – is notoriously difficult. Peering through the fog, one can see – in addition to the need for special facilities for the most able – a possible demand for considerable numbers of higher-level technicians with a math-ematical, computing, scientific or technological background. There is no plausible *economic* argument which justifies the production of large numbers of graduates in the arts and in the less vocational parts of the social sciences.

However, most people – even if they begin from the morass of naive economic arguments – will by this point have retreated to firmer ground. Higher education is a form of service to the individual, a means of self-fulfilment. Education is a good thing in its own right, and a means of establishing and extending the general state of civilisation. It is proper that those who are willing and able to benefit by it should be given the chance to do so, even if the actual knowledge they acquire has no evident economic value. They will thus be enabled to be better citizens and to live fuller lives, with benefits to all of us and especially to the next generation of children.

A small degree of cynicism is appropriate in examining these arguments. There is (for instance) no evidence known to me that higher education in general makes people happier, or better able to deal with some of the problems and dilemmas of personal relations. (This may be a criticism of the content of higher education as it at present exists.) However, it seems reasonable to suppose that a developed and well-stocked mind, like a vigorous and healthy body, is a good thing: that the value of education, which is accepted as real and significant through the school years, cannot be negligible when it becomes higher education. The principle enshrined in the Robbins report, that courses should be available for 'all those who are qualified by ability and attainment to pursue them and who wish to do so', looks as if it should command our continued assent.

The trouble is, however, that this celebrated principle has no precise meaning. What is the test of 'qualification by ability and attainment'? Granted that Education is a Good Thing, how much of it is good? How do we avoid an open-ended commitment, and decide the point at which the marginal increment of education is not worth its cost? No significant part of *higher* education in Britain is sold at its cost on a free market,[2] so we

[2] The exceptions are certain correspondence courses and private language schools: and, apart from its subventions from donors, the Independent University, which has been a valuable source of new thinking (e.g. by experimenting with more concentrated courses).

have no test that the value placed on it by its recipients justifies its cost. Those who enter may sometimes have a pure desire for self-improvement, but more often they seem to be motivated by a belief that a course of higher education (even if non-vocational) will help to get a better job, or they are proceeding down tram-lines of custom laid down by their school or family.

However, something can be deduced, and it is not consistent with the higher education system which now exists. If the purpose of higher education is to offer something more to those who have successfully completed a secondary school course (or its equivalent) and who are capable of further development, then it would be expected that the number capable of benefiting by an additional year of education would exceed the number capable of benefiting by two years, which in turn would exceed the number capable of benefiting by three years, and so on. We take it as perfectly natural that eighty per cent or more of first-degree graduates ought not to be encouraged to go on to a year, or to several years, of post-graduate study. In the common phrase, they have 'reached their ceiling': which does not necessarily mean that they would gain *nothing* from postgraduate work, but implies a judgement that they could more usefully be doing something else. But the higher education system makes only a minor provision for courses lasting less than three years. Implicitly, it assumes that far more students will benefit by three years' study than can be expected to reach their ceiling after two years. This is contrary to any reasonable expectation about the distribution of ability.[3]

---

[3] Higher education is provided (according to the classification used in the DES memorandum to the House of Commons Select Committee on Education, Science and Arts) in nearly four hundred establishments in Great Britain, and most of the effort (on my estimate, over eighty per cent) is given to courses at first or higher degree level – including courses for degree-equivalent professional qualifications. It is not credible that, of those who complete a secondary school course or its equivalent, the number capable of profiting by a further three years of full-time study or its part-time equivalent should greatly exceed the number capable of profiting by two years; the opposite would be expected. It would be possible to argue that periods of higher education of less than three years are in some way too short to be effective: but I know of no evidence to support this, and some doubt is cast on the argument by the large and successful development of junior and community colleges in the United States. (Two-year colleges accounted for 27·6 per cent of total enrolments in 1970 and for 35·6 per cent in 1976: Carnegie Council, Final Report, *Three Thousand Futures*, 1980.) (*Editor's note:* this footnote is from a memorandum by the author to the Select Committee on Education, Science and Arts.)

One can readily see why things have happened in this way: a degree is an ancient and prestigious qualification, and the various diplomas and certificates below degree level carry no equivalent prestige; some are, indeed, liable to be interpreted as evidence of failure in a degree. The Government's attempt, following the James report (*Teacher Education and Training*, 1972), to stimulate the appearance of a two-year Diploma of Higher Education, failed because the grant regulations effectively limited entrance to those who could also aspire to a degree. The great majority of Dip HEs which appeared in the regulations of colleges and universities are in fact consolation prizes for degree aspirants who leave early. But, if one starts from the justification of higher education as personal development, the only conceivable defence of the concentration on degrees is that, for some reason, a course of less than three years is inherently unsatisfactory. There is a proper argument for a minimum period in any sector of education, because benefits do not flow immediately; time is taken to get accustomed to a mode of work and to particular surroundings. On these grounds it would be perfectly proper to make provision for one-year rather than six-month courses, and perhaps plausible to give two-year courses preference over one-year. But can it really be argued that the wastes involved in shorter courses are so great that most students should be offered the choice of three years or nothing? It seems more likely that the concentration on three-year courses arises from the weight of past tradition, and has nothing to do with a genuine educational assessment.

The effect of concentration on degree courses is that the entry to most of higher education has to be restricted to those who can evidently go considerably beyond the limits of the secondary school courses; and, even so, many are admitted who know themselves, and who are known to their teachers, as gaining little extra benefit from the grind of an undistinguished third year at a university or college. Of course it is sometimes good for people to attempt things which are too difficult for them, for, even if no success is achieved, consistency of effort can be good for the character. But others who attempt to go 'beyond their ceiling' simply lose confidence in themselves, and they may take long to recover from the experience of failure. My personal view is that at least twenty per cent of those at present taking degree courses would gain more benefit, in terms of personal development, and contribute more to the community, if they could leave after two years without the stigma of failure or of leaving work half-done.

Let us conceive it as possible, therefore, that a rational higher education system would have much more provision for two-year courses than for first degrees; and, in doing so, would provide for some of those who at present take degrees, and for a much larger number who are at present judged 'not degree material'. There is some indication that such a pattern might emerge, if we could make free choices unhampered by old habits and institutional structures. The United States system of higher education, which because of its variety of type and method of provision reacts more like a 'free market' under the influence of consumer demand, is growing most quickly in the community and junior colleges, which provide both a terminal training and an entry into the later years of degree courses. And – referring back to the discussion of economic needs – it seems very likely that it would be advantageous to have a system which backed every highly-trained graduate by several well-trained 'technicians' or other workers capable of adapting themselves to a wide range of practical tasks.

The implication of my argument so far is that we do not have enough higher education – because we have no sufficient provision for developing the abilities of those who reach the 'A' Level standard but ought not to attempt to tackle a full degree course: and what we have is wrongly distributed, with much too much emphasis on degree studies. What does this imply for the institutional structure which we ought to create?

THE INSTITUTIONAL STRUCTURE

What we desire is a higher education system which is effective in achieving its aims and which uses resources wisely. But what we have is far from ideal, even before making the changes suggested in the preceding paragraph. In order to understand some of the faults, it is necessary to look back a little.

Higher education in the 1950s had three elements which were largely distinct. The universities provided degree-level studies, and were in effect the only bodies authorised to grant degrees. The teacher training colleges concentrated on a lower-level teaching qualification, the certificate; strictly speaking, they were only counted as higher education by courtesy, for the minimum entrance requirement was below 'A' Level. A wide range of local technical and business colleges provided certificate and diploma courses and professional training. The only important blurring of the distinction between these elements was produced by the external degrees of the University of London, which were available to students in a number of the better technical colleges.

There were two evident faults in this system. Teacher training was at too low a level to meet the needs of the profession: the process of lengthening the certificate course, and then upgrading it to become a degree, has taken a long time, being delayed by pressure in the 1960s to produce more teachers quickly. The advanced work in technical colleges, generally a minor part of the activity in any one college, was distributed so widely that its quality was in doubt. Gradually, therefore, the Education Departments proceeded to built up particular institutions on which advanced work could be concentrated.

But in the early 1960s the prestige of university education stood high, and many people saw the way forward in terms of multiplying university places. New universities were founded as centres of experiment, and (encouraged by the report of the Robbins committee) a great expansion of the older universities was set in motion. Decisions following the Robbins report swept into the university system the first efforts at providing new centres for concentrating advanced work, the Colleges of Advanced Technology. The same report, however, introduced a new blurring of the distinctions between parts of the system, by proposing to relieve the University of London of the increasingly insupportable burden of its external degrees. From this derives the Council for National Academic Awards, a means by which degree studies have become available in many colleges: though it is interesting to note that some other universities have also in recent years rediscovered the external degree.

The next effort at concentrating advanced work came with the designation of the polytechnics, which were intended to have a wide range of studies and to be responsive to local needs in the great cities in which most of them are situated. But this did not have quite the effect intended. Some of the polytechnics moved with surprising speed to lessen their commitment to work below degree level, so that they began to be seen as copies of the universities. The process of concentration went slowly, and strong further education colleges (as they were now called), with a long experience of advanced work, tended to find good reason for hanging on to it. The spread of advanced studies across many institutions therefore continued.

In the 1970s the picture was further complicated by the belated adjustment to the discovery that teacher education was grossly over-expanded in relation to the needs of a school system, now adjusting itself to a declining birth-rate. Some colleges of education (teacher training colleges) were closed, and others were combined with polytechnics or universities, or other further education colleges. Some, however, were left 'freestanding' as 'colleges of higher education' within the further education system, the idea being that their activity of providing degrees for intending teachers (which would, at a reduced scale, no longer be viable) would now be supported by other types of advanced work. But these other types very often turned out to be other degrees in the arts and social sciences validated by the CNAA or a university: so the result was to strengthen degree studies (relative to work at a lower level) still further, and to multiply the number of institutions providing them.

The system so created is unstable. Because of the fall in the birth rate, the numbers suitable for higher education at degree level in the 1990s are certain to fall. Those who believe otherwise have to make heroic assumptions about the ineffectiveness of the present school system in fostering talent. (The total numbers in higher education could nevertheless increase, by opening up opportunities for courses below degree level, as I have suggested.) The colleges of higher education often provide non-vocational degrees directly competitive with those in the universities, and they cannot possibly expect to survive in this competition at a time of falling numbers. The polytechnics also have a heavy commitment to courses, especially in the social sciences, for which the future demand is uncertain: contrary to popular belief, their commitment to science and technology is commonly not as great as that of the universities, for as late-comers they have been unable to attract students in the less popular areas.

The spread of first-degree studies over so many institutions has consequential disadvantages. All the universities and poly-technics, and some at least of the colleges of higher education, think it proper and desirable to provide also for higher degrees. Indeed, there has come to be an expectation among those who teach first degrees that they should also have the prestige of higher-degree teaching. The result is a ridiculous multiplication of small courses, costly to provide and sometimes of poor quality. The number of 'graduate schools' in which research for a PhD can be done is also far too great, and many students do not have access to the range of facilities and advice necessary for a proper training. I find it difficult to conceive that in any one subject a country of the size of the UK ought to attempt to provide more than fifteen centres of research training.

The ill effects carry over also into research itself. The belief in universities that research is a necessary stimulant to teaching, and should take about half of the effort of the teacher, spills over into the polytechnics. The quantity of research is not determined by the need to perform it or by its pure intellectual interest, but as a by-product of the number of students (and therefore of teachers) in the subject. In my view the stress laid on research should properly belong to 'scholarship', that is, to the activity of becoming 'learned' about a subject (which does not necessarily involve new discovery): and true research within the higher education system should, to a much greater degree, be the consequence of an informed decision that its subject shows 'timeliness and promise' – a decision which might appropriately be made through Research Councils. But the consequence of this ought certainly to be that research in a subject would be concentrated at a few centres, in order to get advantages of cross-fertilisation of minds within a strong team.

However, the concentration of research and graduate teaching in a subject in (say) ten institutions does not imply that only ten institutions would have a stake in research, for natural evolution from what exists now would cause a particular centre to carry (say) chemistry but not physics, and philosophy but not theology, as subjects for full development at research level. I would be surprised, however, if an impartial attempt to identify 'centres of excellence' at research and higher-degree level caused a spread over more than thirty-five institutions; all or nearly all of these would be universities, and they would be fewer than the present number of universities.

But it would not only be better (and also, probably, cheaper) to concentrate on fewer places as centres for serious research and graduate teaching; it is also desirable to reduce considerably the number of centres for first-degree work and courses at equivalent level. This is in part a consequence of the fall in the birth rate, though too much should not be made of this argument, since around the year 2000 a partial recovery of numbers may occur. But it is also related to the virtual certainty that some who now attempt degree courses would, with a proper provision for courses at a lower level, be better served by taking them. Furthermore, even if the system of incentives for teachers in higher education is changed so as to reduce the attraction of doing first- and higher-degree work, it will be a long time before the habit of mind which gives undue attention to degrees is changed. While that habit persists, institutions which offer degrees at all will tend to give them undue preference; so a condition for changing the balance of the system is to reduce the number of places empowered to teach for degrees.

The reduction must, however, take account of the desirability of enabling a reasonably high proportion of students who live at home – including part-time students – to take degrees. It is true that a nationwide system of local 'community colleges' would lessen the problem, by making it possible in some cases to take the first part of a degree (or of a degree-equivalent professional qualification) at a nearby college. The Open University also exists as a major facility for part-time students. The residue of the home student problem can be adequately dealt with by substantially fewer centres for degree work than exist now, for it should nowadays be possible to assume mobility over a twenty-five mile radius (with State assistance for the cost, where necessary). More than a century ago, the studies which decided the siting of the University of Manchester assumed that students would come by train from towns fifteen miles around.

The picture which begins to emerge, therefore, requires:

Up to 35 institutions which offer first degrees, and each of which is, for some subjects, a centre for research and/or for higher-degree work.

Perhaps 50 more institutions which offer first degrees (though in some cases only in a small range of subjects) but which are not expected to be major contributors to research or providers of higher degrees. As many as possible should also provide, on a significant scale, two-year courses of higher education.

Perhaps 200 institutions which (apart from any remaining degree work in the transitional period) would offer two-year courses and short courses only.

Because of the relatively large size of the universities, such a plan would require many years of development before the places available for non-degree courses in higher education became more numerous than those available for degrees. Nevertheless, it implies:

Limiting several existing universities to first-degree work only: they might appropriately be given the name 'university colleges'.

Removing degree work altogether from some polytechnics, and using them as part of the community college system. (The 50 first-degree institutions will have to include some non-polytechnic colleges which provide teacher education: otherwise the geographical spread of good facilities for in-service education would be inadequate.)

Encouraging other polytechnics to develop non-degree work as their *major* activity.

Building up a number of further education colleges so that they become substantial community colleges for higher education (though they might also keep their lower-level work).

SOME CONSEQUENTIAL PROBLEMS

Such a list has only to be written down to provoke thoughts of the enormous weight of opposition to be expected. The universities established by Royal Charter or Act regard themselves as having a right in perpetuity to develop whatever teaching or research they may wish – subject only to financial limitations. The polytechnics have increasingly been claiming a similar freedom. Only the colleges of education have recent experience of government policy tough enough to cause closures and redirections of effort.

Nevertheless, the problem has to be tackled. If the degree-giving part of the system is left in its present form, and adequate provision for non-degree studies is made in addition, the public and social cost of higher education will become unreasonably great. As the fall in the birth rate takes effect, an attempt might be made to fill up degree places by lowering entrance standards; but this would be a recipe for inefficiency and bad education. Even apart from demographic changes, it would not be satisfactory to leave the degree-giving system as it is, for (as we have seen) it spreads its effort too widely in units which are sometimes too small. Furthermore, it is overweighted with places which are by custom used for students living away from home, a fact which puts substantial extra cost on the State. It is not legitimate to deduce from the fact that *some* students benefit greatly by leaving home a belief that this is an essential element for the education of *most* students. The larger proportion of home-based students in Scotland is not taken as proof of the inferiority of Scottish higher education. A significant advantage of the development of community colleges would be that some students could have two years of higher education while based at home, and then (if their ability justifies this) could move away to complete a degree course.

There are two necessary conditions for success in developing two-year courses. One is that the student entering such a course should be no worse off than if he enters for a degree: this implies that awards must be mandatory, and at the same level of maintenance as for a degree course. I would favour a mixed system of grants and loans, by which a minimum subsistence level is available as a grant, but extra costs (including the cost of pursuing studies away from home) can be met without difficulty by loans on reasonable terms.[4] The other condition of success is that those who enter two-year courses, and who later obtain transfer to a degree course, should not be seriously worse off than those who enter degree courses direct. This is a more difficult condition, since the structure of courses rightly varies from one institution to another. It is certainly not possible for a student who is successful in *any* two-year course in (say) physics to enter *any* degree course in physics at the third year. It is necessary, therefore, for agreements about the conformity of courses to be made between limited groups of institutions, perhaps on a regional basis. The difficulties of achieving this have, I think, been exaggerated; there is at present no incentive for the degree-giving institutions to co-operate with colleges which they see as of lower 'status'.[5]

[4] Such loans could be from a State fund, or from private sources encouraged by a State guarantee. It might be possible to devise an 'equity' system, by which the lender would be recompensed by a proportion of future earnings.

[5] But these are changes which, however sensible as a national policy, would be bitterly and effectively opposed: 'effectively' because there is at present no satisfactory means of securing the observance of the national interest. I therefore propose that a single Higher Education Grants Committee should be responsible for the funding of all higher education (including the contribution to be made to the cost of the higher-education element in colleges which also undertake lower-level work); that, to avoid complexity, as much as possible of the administration of the committee should be delegated to a regional level; and that the grants to be made should be tied explicitly to the provision of higher education at stated levels, an institution desiring to undertake work at a higher level being required to provide to the Committee convincing evidence for reclassification. While all institutions would be expected to provide satisfactory facilities for the development of the scholarship of their staff, supplementary funds for the support of centres of excellence in research would be confined to

It will be objected that the change I have proposed involves an undue State interference in higher education. But State 'interference' is an essential consequence of the fact that the State meets nearly all the cost; and that cost is so high that questions about the appropriateness and efficiency of the system must necessarily be asked. Those who want a 'free' system should argue for one in which higher education is purchased by its students at a market price: the place of the State in such a system might be to loan money for the purchase. I suspect that a 'private enterprise' system of this kind would rapidly redistribute places between degrees and shorter courses, in the manner which I have recommended.[6]

those institutions selected as appropriate for significant research and higher degree work. The Higher Education Grants Committee would be a body similar to the University Grants Committee, and would take over its functions. The Committee might think it wise to ensure that a significant part of the income of each institution continues to come from fees, so that the system can be encouraged to change and adapt in response to changes in student demand. (*Editor's note:* this footnote is from a memorandum by the author to the Select Committee.)

[6] This chapter is reproduced by kind permission of the *Three Banks Review*, where it first appeared.

HAROLD SILVER

Enforced conformity
or hierarchical diversity

In 1963 Lord James predicted that, so far as the universities and
their standards were concerned, 'no expansion that we are likely
to achieve in the next 20 years will raise any really profound
questions of principle'. Expansion would simply bring into the
universities – as the expansion of higher education in the United
States had shown – that additional proportion of our population
'capable of following courses that satisfy the ambiguous criterion of being appropriate to universities'. As James realised,
there were immediate implications for non-university institutions of higher education, and he perceptively suggested a
rationale for development that was in fact covertly to govern
development and diversification from the mid-1960s:

> We must realise that we shall actually safeguard the standards
> of the universities themselves by raising the standards of other
> institutions and providing new kinds of higher education. By
> so doing we shall diminish the pressure from those who
> cannot really benefit from the rigours of our present courses
> but who quite properly desire a higher education (*Observer*, 15
> September 1963).

This was a time when the Robbins committee was redrawing
the contours of an expanded higher education, and when
Kingsley Amis was forecasting a 'more means worse' disaster.
James was right. Expansion did provide for those who 'properly
desire a higher education', without raising 'profound questions
of principle' – or even of the meaning of the terms. The binary
system and the creation of the polytechnics at the end of the
1960s caused ripples of opposition (including from Lord Rob-

bins himself). The closures, amalgamations and new institutions – the colleges and institutes of higher education – which resulted from the cuts in teacher education from the mid-1970s, produced anguish and controversy, but not any serious, sustained concern about the fundamentals of the system as a whole. Again, James proved to be right: 'profound questions of principle' had been avoided. The history of two decades of British higher education is in fact contained in James's forecast, but it is a history that is still unwritten and unexplored. There is a respectable literature of 1960s and 1970s discussion in the United States about the fundamentals of higher education. There is virtually none in Britain. (The small number of exceptions would include W. R. Niblett (ed.), *The Expanding University* (1962), and Peter Marris, *The Experience of Higher Education* (1964).)

If the majority of commentators and policy-makers in the 1960s were in favour of expansion, so were they also in favour of diversity. What few realised was how completely commitment to the former obscured any understanding of the latter. The ambiguities, contradictory interpretations, absence of any declared values – all inherent in James's formulations and most formulations of support for expanded and enhanced 'other institutions' – were not revealed until the camouflage of expansion was stripped way. When conservative (and Conservative) policies began to be implemented from the end of the 1970s, the ambiguities involved in the concept of diversity became more visible, in a situation of retrenchment and competition for resources, for students – and for survival. At the point at which understanding became more difficult it also became more necessary.

A measure of the difficulties we bequeathed to ourselves in the 1960s and 1970s can be obtained by taking another example from that memorable year for higher education, 1963. Tyrrell Burgess, taking part in the main national exercise of that year – the discussion of expansion – commented on what had been happening to technological education. The colleges of advanced technology, created in the 1950s out of a small group of elite technical institutions, had – Burgess suggested – taken or been

directed along the wrong path: 'there has been . . . an insidious
tendency for them to sidle up to the universities'. The CATs
were being treated 'as if they were universities'. The essential
problem for the technical colleges, as he saw it, was 'to meet the
demands on them for higher education without sacrificing their
unique function of maintaining an alternative and more open
way through all levels of education' (*New Society*, 7 March
1963). Here is support for expansion, similarity and separateness, even uniqueness. But the 'profound questions of principle'
that remain unanswered lie in the words 'alternative' and 'more
open'. Why was an alternative way necessary, and what were
the characteristics of its 'alternativeness'? And why should the
alternative way be more open than that of the universities? Why
should the universities themselves not be made more open – in a
single, expanded, democratised system? Such questions were
not confronted in the 1960s because the notion of separateness
stood in the way – implying separate functions, different
management and control, alternative methods, other kinds of
student, teacher and teaching methods, an 'otherness' which left
unchallenged the sacrosanct nature of what was 'appropriate to
universities'. Somehow, it was expected, new and promoted
institutions would fill gaps, solve the problem of numbers,
satisfy emergent needs, and leave the universities essentially to
get on with the job which they knew best and were best fitted to
perform. Although, again, the job of the universities was not
very clear (James drew attention to the 'ambiguous criterion' by
which their courses were judged), many people felt that too
extensive an expansion of universities would disturb their
traditional patterns, to the detriment of 'scholarship', 'research'
and 'standards'. It was generally assumed that different categories of institution had different 'functions'.

A paradox of British higher education, therefore, has been
that in this century it has consisted on the one hand of what
Boris Ford in 1966 called an 'extraordinary jumble of institutions . . . 31 universities plus 10 new technological universities
. . . 50 or so colleges of education . . . 25 regional and about 160
area colleges of technology and the six national colleges of
specialised technology . . . the many colleges of commerce and

the 165 art schools . . . its distribution and rationale are only intelligible to a very powerful historical eye' (*New Statesman*, 21 January 1964). On the other hand, the component parts of this 'system' have had assumed but ill-understood different functions. The central assumption about the functions of the university has been its 'autonomous' pursuit of scholarship and the transmission of knowledge. This function was underlined most emphatically in Britain and the United States in the years after the Second World War as a defence of academic freedom against outside political and other pressures and interference. Sir Walter Moberly comprehensively summarised the nature of this defence against threat to the Sixth Congress of Universities of the British Commonwealth in 1948:

> Anything which threatens the autonomy of Universities must be resisted, whatever form it takes. It may be political interference . . . It may be just tidy-minded administration, the passion for standardization. It may be an unrestricted popular outcry for some quick and tangible returns . . . It may be only a flattering but quite crushing demand made for services of all kinds. In all these ways demands may be made upon Universities which are inconsistent with the carrying out of their function as they understand it . . . (*Report of Proceedings*, 1951).

'Their function as they understand it' is another form of what Martin Trow called the 'elite function' of the universities – that which they determine for themselves, as distinct from the 'popular function' – that which is pressed upon them from outside (in W. R. Niblett (ed.), *Higher Education: demand and response*). The universities' definition of their own scholarly autonomy, as underlined by Moberly, was seen to be most directly threatened by the expansion of the 1960s, and most of all by the Robbins committee's strong advocacy of expansion.

However strong the pressures for university expansion had become by 1963, the ditches of academic defence were being dug deep, before and after publication of the Robbins report. The Robbins report was preceded in 1963 by the report of a Labour Party enquiry under Lord Taylor. It advocated massive expansion of higher education by the creation of some 45 new universities, some based on existing institutions, some new, one a 'university of the air' (what in fact became the Open University), and some by fission (London University was to become four or five separate universities). While the *Guardian* received the proposals with caution, and even implied support, *The Times* waxed hysterical, under a leader entitled 'Paper Universities'. This was, it proclaimed, 'fairy-tale pamphleteering'. It was 'doctrinaire absurdity' to ignore the conditions a degree-granting institution should be able to satisfy. It expected the Robbins committee to provide 'a stronger foundation for a policy than does the over-heated enthusiasm of this pamphlet' (6 March 1963).

In the event, using different arithmetic and tactics, the Robbins committee made not dissimilar suggestions, and looked for an expansion of the university sector. It coupled proposals for an expansion in the size of universities and a widening of their curricula with proposals for new entrants to the sector by the promotion of the colleges of advanced technology to university status: 'the needs of the future should be met by developing present types of institution . . . in doing so we shall not be attempting to perpetuate the irrational distinction and the rigid barriers between institutions [criticised earlier in the report] . . . the giving of university status to the Colleges of Advanced Technology and other institutions will provide a means of ensuring that other educational experiments . . . can be preserved and developed in a university setting' (*Higher Education*, 1963). The Robbins ethos was resisted by many academics. The universities in general feared expansion as the implementation of the kind of threats of which Moberly had warned. What Robbins sought to do, however, was to protect the university by bringing rival 'experiments' into its territory. His personal reaction to the binary policy introduced by the Labour Government from 1966 made that clear. Although the Robbins report contained the often-quoted section on the 'aims of higher education', and detailed analyses of the various categories of institution, the landscape it painted was still far from clear. Robbins told an American audience in 1964 that the British government had accepted various of the committee's recommendations, including the upgrading of the CATs to university status and for 'accessibility to degree courses of qualified students not in institutions of university standing' (*The University in the Modern World*, 1966). The 'jumble' was not entirely removed by such categorisation, and it would be difficult to couple it with clear portrayals of what was meant by the functions of a university. In a sense the binary policy of the Labour government rescued the universities' self-definitions from confusion and dilution.

If the universities were intent on continuing to define their function as they understood it, the polytechnics were created in the late 1960s within definitions strongly urged from outside. Any attempt to define an alternative category implied, of course, a definition of the universities themselves, but discussion of the nature of the university went by default. The attempt at strong categorisation of the polytechnics carried the assumptions underlying the various parts of the existing higher education system further from ambiguity into fantasy.

The apparent and declared intention of the binary policy and the creation of the polytechnics was to establish a more publicly accountable second sector of higher education, parallel with the universities, different from them, more related to the nation's economic needs, to industry, to the planned production of manpower (although the Robbins report had included this category of purpose amongst its aims for the universities also). The new sector was indeed differently, but it is not clear that it was more, accountable. To what extent it was more directly related to the nation's economic needs is also debatable. John Vaizey's view in 1970 was that 'Anthony Crosland's so-called "binary policy" for developing polytechnics separately from universities was not a policy but a piece of rhetoric designed to make the university/non-university split sound acceptable to socialists' (*New Society*, 21 May 1970). In 1966, before the 'policy' had begun to be implemented, the Vice-Chancellor designate of Bradford University Institute of Technology expressed the view that Crosland's claim that the demand for vocational courses 'requires a separate sector, with a separate tradition and outlook . . . presupposes a distinction between the vocational and the fundamental in technological education which belongs to the 19th century' (Dr Edwards, quoted by Boris Ford, op. cit.). The binary plan, commented Boris Ford, was not as neat as it was supposed to be, since the colleges of education had remained linked with the universities, and in any case the real need was to break the universities' isolationism, 'to bring them into the national pattern, into the Precinct, into association with other traditions and institutions' (ibid.). Lord Robbins regretted the binary plan, as he and his committee had opted for the elevation of university-level institutions *into* the university sector, or, as he put it in an interview in 1977:

> We preferred to think of higher education as a spectrum in which advanced further education colleges could be fattened up and moved into the autonomous university sector as their performance indicated and the need arose (*Times Higher Education Supplement*, 4 November).

The creation of the polytechnics neither tidied up the jumble in higher education, nor clarified the categories and confusions, nor convinced large numbers of people that this was the way to serve national industrial and economic needs. Ambiguities remained, and new ones appeared. With the universities moving into more general courses of study, extending their commitment to engineering and other professional training, feeling the need to respond to the pressures of a changing society which brought them increasingly under scrutiny, what was the real justification for two parallel systems? Were there really two different categories of students, responding to the blandishments of two different types of institution? When a polytechnic had settled down with its degrees awarded by the Council for National Academic Awards, how did it differ – except in terms of management and resources – from a university? Was Bradford University not more like some polytechnics than like some other universities?

Ambiguities were not, of course, purely a question of defined function or of status. They also related to questions of level of work, range of curriculum, type of degree structure, academic structure and institutional management, and the definition of 'vocational' and 'professional' education. Teacher education in particular has in this century been increasingly engaged with these ambiguities – with the status of its institutions, its curriculum and its awards (not to mention the teaching profession itself). Was teacher education vocational in some way that was different from the training of doctors or architects – or of social workers or radiographers? The crisis of demography, school rolls, teacher numbers and teacher education that brought about the reshaping of higher education again in the second half of the 1970s, was different from the binary changes of the late 1960s in being less deliberate and accompanied by less rhetoric. The differences, however, can be exaggerated. The argument that the new colleges and institutes of higher education had been cobbled together out of old colleges of education and quasi-polytechnics, without any serious, underlying policy, in some ways matched the arguments used by the critics of the binary system. If the new colleges and institutes could not easily be defined by function, neither – at the end of the argument – could the universities and polytechnics. The categories, the definitions, the frontiers remained difficult, if not impossible, to locate.

Britain has not been alone in possessing such complexity in its higher education. Some American commentators have in fact gloried in what Burton R. Clark calls 'an ever growing complexity that boggles the minds of those who want to understand what goes on in all parts of the American system'. The American complexity, he points out, contains fifty state components, each of which in turn contains five major types of colleges and universities, and each of these again contains great diversity. The whole brings what Clark entitles 'The benefits of disorder' (*Change*, October 1976). Other American commentators emphasise less the diversity than the uniformity of the system, its failure to encourage or to sustain innovation, its slavish imitation of what David Riesman called 'national models', a tendency which had led to the loss of 'innovatory elan' (*Constraint and Variety in American Education*, 1956). The first point to make about complexity, therefore, is that it may be

superficial, and may not be seen by everyone as complex. The
second point is the confusing picture it presents of its responsiveness to outside pressures – a point we have already noted
over the difficulty of differentiating the functions of the British
university and polytechnic. An American example helps to
strengthen the point.

At the end of the 1960s, in changing and sometimes dramatic
campus conditions, a whole American literature appeared which
attempted to analyse the new tensions and militancies, and
which included a great deal of discussion of the mission, the
relevance, the purpose of the American university and college.
Nathan E. Cohen, for example, reflected that the university
traditionally produces 'researchers' or 'pursuers of truth'. What,
then, he reflected, is a 'relevant' university? A university advanced organised knowledge, transmitted it from generation to
generation, but also extended 'these central functions beyond
the campus into the community'. The issue of relevance now
pointed to the need for the university's functions to be applied in
a rapidly changing society. One aspect of this situation was as
follows:

> It is the social problems of poverty, welfare, education,
> health, race relations, housing, social control, and political
> capacity for which the university is being turned to more and
> more for leadership in a problem-solving role. If the univer-
> sity is to meet this challenge it will have to find new structural
> patterns which permit greater involvement in policy-oriented
> problems and action-oriented programs (National Confer-
> ence on Social Welfare, *The Social Welfare Forum*, 1969).

In the late 1960s this was the problem of the university the world
over, but nowhere was it felt more acutely than in the United
States. American cities, underlined a former Secretary of the
Department of Health, Education and Welfare, were 'plagued
with every conceivable ill: apathy, crime, poverty, racial conflict, slum housing, air and water pollution, inadequate schools
and hospitals, and a breakdown in transportation'. He forecast
that coping with those problems would be top of the national
agenda in the 1970s, and expressed the view that 'there are no

institutions better equipped to serve as a base for that struggle than the colleges and universities, but they have played a negligible role so far' (John W. Gardner in A. C. Eurich (ed.), *Campus 1980*, 1968). These were not new pressures, but the demand for a response, and even leadership, was being made with a new vigour. The British university was being turned to for responses in similar ways, and was struggling in similar ways to marry traditional and new roles, amidst controversy about its allegiances, its purposes, its standards, and its relationship to what Boris Ford termed 'other traditions and institutions'.

In both countries, however, the question had to be asked: does relevance apply differently to the university than to other institutions of higher education? In British terms, have the polytechnic, the college and institute of higher education, not had responses and 'leadership' roles to share with universities? In what way is any of them, and the institutions of further education, not engaged with policy and action, with responding and initiating? Have universities been any more or less able to meet the 'challenge' of a changing society than other institutions of further and higher education? Have they been more willing and more able to find 'new structural patterns' and achieve new balances? What Cohen points to, in fact, is the ambiguity inherent in the term 'university' – with both its American and British connotations – as only *apparently* distinct from the terms 'college' or 'polytechnic', or whatever other parallel or different component of higher education that might be discussed in relation to the problems he raises.

Attempted definitions of institutions by criteria other than relevance or leadership have also revealed other ambiguities. It is in continuing attempts to define the different categories of higher education, and to produce tidy patterns based on them, that the main dangers are emerging at the beginning of the 1980s. It is important to confront the implications of these attempts to explain institutional diversity. Let us take a number of the criteria that are often applied in distinguishing between different categories of institution – most frequently the universities on the one hand, and the rest on the other.

First, research. The assumption that universities are sanctuaries for conducting and promoting research raises two related questions. Do other institutions not conduct research? Even where they do not, should they or might they not? The research roles of the polytechnics have never been clearly defined and were filled with uncertainties from the beginning. But the polytechnics have developed research. CNAA pronouncements on polytechnic and college course developments have often assumed that a research presence in the institution or the subject is desirable, that teaching is strengthened by research, and that the research thrust enhances the quality of all aspects of the institution. The reality and the criteria of the university/polytechnic distinction as based on research of various kinds have been seen to be illusory, and the same has become true of many of the colleges and institutes of higher education. In the latter case the firm need for experimentation in teacher education, and the colleges' firm base in a number of aspects of educational research, have made their research and development roles doubly desirable and inevitable. It is not only universities that produce 'researchers' and 'pursuers of truth'.

Second, the cluster of criteria related to part-time and full-time, mature (and presumably the converse – 'immature') students, and the general area of student recruitment. Again, it has been assumed that the traditions of university and 'other' recruitment have been different, should remain so, and point to different institutional identities. It is true that the technical education tradition involves a high level of commitment to part-time and 'sandwich' courses, a 'second chance' route for older students, and a more 'open' approach to recruitment. There is here an obvious, continuing, partial criterion by which to distinguish amongst institutions, but it is not easy to do so. Many of the colleges of higher education have a commitment to part-time courses only or mainly at the in-service level – and in this they are no different from university education and extra-mural departments. Some universities, especially those which were converted from colleges of advanced technology, have continued the tradition of sandwich courses. Some universities and university institutions (Birkbeck College, London, is the most notable example) have strong part-time traditions. The distinctions are not neat across the binary line, and there are substantial differences on either side of it. It is also clear that even such distinctions as do exist are capable of being jettisoned for quite expedient reasons, and this is in fact happening. The moment at which, for example, competition for resources and students became intensified from the late 1970s, and the prospects for recruitment beyond the mid-1980s began to look bleak, the universities proved not unwilling to relax their traditional self-definitions and criteria for recruitment. The lowering of entry qualifications by universities began to be voiced as a serious possibility. The recruitment of more adult, 'unqualified' students began to be proposed by some universities, which began to think of and describe themselves as 'second chance' institutions. Under financial pressures the universities began to respond, chameleon-like, in ways which not merely brought them into competition with other institutions and traditions, but led them to take on or to intensify characteristics which they shared with other institutions. It was no longer in the interests of many universities to be defined rigidly by their traditional, 'exclusive' functions, for which they recruited predominantly post-school, well-qualified students, for three-year, clearly demarcated programmes.

Third, therefore, is differentiation by curriculum, and in this respect the differentiation has never been tenable. The Robbins committee argued strongly for broader-based university courses, and although the results up to the early 1960s had been what it called 'meagre', the committee recognised that 'in many universities the need to offer a more general education has already begun to influence policy'. The committee analysed a series of ways in which this had already begun to happen. Yet it was assumed from the late 1960s by many commentators that there was a basic curricular difference between the universities and the others based on notions of university specialisation and higher 'honours' standards, as against more general degree structures elsewhere. Again, under competitive and other pressures, the universities were willing in the 1970s, however, to move into more open, modular and combined-subject degrees, and to

accept new forms of assessment and examination. Some, like
Sussex and East Anglia, had experimented with such broadly-
based degree structures from their beginnings in the 1960s.
Others moved in that direction as they saw the polytechnics
successfully recruiting for new kinds of degrees in the 1970s. Yet
others found themselves in the late 1970s validating courses of
this nature in the former colleges of education for which they
accepted responsibility. At the same time, of course, many of the
polytechnics and then the colleges and institutes, developed
curriculum areas and degree (including master's degree) structures more close to those assumed to be the prerogatives of the
universities. Single-honours subjects, high-level social science
degrees, master's degrees in education in some of the colleges of
higher education, all matched 'university' offerings. Differentiation by criteria of this kind was not, and could not be, sustained.

Fourth, distinguishing characteristics were sought in a variety
of areas such as size, style, and student choice. Under strong
pressures for expansion in the early and mid-1960s the universities resisted the idea that they could expand more than in marginal
ways. They contrasted themselves with the large, mainly urban
technical-college type of institution, with its thousands of full-
and part-time students, and resisted that expansion of university
numbers that would reduce university quality. They contrasted
themselves, until the second half of the 1960s with the teacher
training colleges and their certificates and diplomas, and then
with the colleges of education and their B Ed degrees, which they
publicly or secretly saw as second-rank, vocational awards. In the
post-Robbins period, however, they began to find reasons for
being able to share in the general expansionist developments, and
discovered that it was not too painful to do so. There was also
tempting experience across the Atlantic (despite the smirk with
which British academics normally referred to American higher
education) to indicate that increased scale need not mean reduced
'excellence'. The *Times Educational Supplement* pointed to this
experience in 1964 (13 March), in a discussion of California's
master plan for the development of higher education:

To an Englishman the notion of a university campus with

27,000 students almost defeats the imagination. Certainly doubts arise as to whether any institution of such size can fulfil the functions traditionally associated with a university. Some of the developments taking place in California . . . indicate that such doubts may be unfounded . . . In the University of California research does not seem to have suffered as a consequence of expansion. Berkeley, the largest campus, has also produced the finest research . . .

Images of differences by scale receded as British universities expanded rapidly. So did categorisation by differences of residence, care or welfare. If the polytechnics were largely urban and non-residential, most of the colleges and institutes of higher education were not. Many of these colleges had traditions of residence, counselling and welfare greatly different from those of the polytechnics, but either similar or superior to those of even the smaller universities.

Research in the late 1970s indicated that students did not, on these or other scales, see some kind of clear tripartite hierarchy, with the universities as the traditional, high-quality institution, the polytechnics as the second-rank alternative, and the colleges and institutes as the third-best late-comers and last resort choice. A study of students at three colleges of higher education reported that just under two-thirds of those entering in 1978 'placed entry to a college of higher education above entry to a university or polytechnic'. Although forty-five per cent of BA students in the colleges would have preferred a university place, an insignificant number of BA and B Ed students would have preferred a polytechnic. These college students 'do not form, in their preferences, part of an overlapping sector with those entering polytechnics' (C. Adelman and I. Gibbs, *A Study of Student Choice in the Context of Institutional Change*, 1979). It is equally clear that there is no easy distinction between university and polytechnic students, whose preferences are based not just on status but also on curricular, regional, institutional and a range of other characteristics. As John Vaizey pointed out in 1970, even if there were then three sectors of higher education – universities, colleges of education and technical institutions –

The very large number of students now arriving in higher education from school or from the local tech every year want many differing things of the higher education system. But they do *not* divide into three types – intending teachers, university students and technical college students. Their wants and needs (not necessarily the same) overlap in a most complex fashion (op. cit.).

If all of these kinds of distinction are difficult to sustain, the final attempted differentiation has to be seen as more over-arching, and more insidious. This is the assumption that universities are historically concerned with a liberal education, with a range of values which include an open, critical approach to knowledge and the furtherance of understanding. This, it is assumed, gives the universities pride of place in any educational hierarchy. Presumably behind the Robbins view of 'fattening up' other institutions to enter the university sector lay questions not just of standards of achievement and resources, but also of their ability to represent the same sort of values and critical approaches as the universities. This discussion was muddied in the 1950s and 1960s, however, by the peculiarly British discussion about the 'two cultures' and the nature of science and technology. There was some feeling that institutions concerned primarily with these 'illiberal' territories would inevitably be narrower, but would need to be admitted to the higher reaches of the educational system – though on special terms. In the American context the problem and the confusion lay in a tension defined by Kenneth Keniston as being between 'the critical university' and 'the service station'. In a discussion entitled 'The University as Critic' Keniston talked of higher education (by which he meant the American university) 'as a countervailing center to the dominant pressures of society':

> While I disagree with the charge of some radicals that universities are nothing but 'service stations' for the *status quo*, neither do I believe that it is accurate to describe the 'critical university' as the real university in America. In fact, American higher education is partly service station and partly critical university. The implication of my argument here is that it

should become less of the former and more of the latter (*Youth and Dissent: the rise of a new opposition*, 1971).

The assumption in Britain was that the university represented the 'critical' end of this spectrum, and the polytechnic-technical college represented the 'service station' end. Some promotion of the latter was a necessary tactic to enable the former to retain the purity of its scholarly-critical commitment. Parallelism, it was hoped by many, would enable the two functions to be firmly separated, and would enable society to make increasing demands on the service station without thereby contaminating the university tradition. As pressure for university responsiveness to social change, increasingly expressed in the language of accountability, increased in the 1970s, and as the university service station functions (or in Martin Trow's expression, 'popular' functions) became more demanded and inevitable, so did worries about the autonomy of the universities, their traditions of academic freedom and self-definition. The strategy was, as James pointed out, to 'diminish the pressures' on the universities by raising the standards of other institutions, at the same time as defending the concept of university autonomy along Moberly lines. A third, post-Robbins ingredient was to join the race for expansion, and to face and to contain at least some of the risks. A fourth, under threat from competition in the late 1970s, was to loosen the grip on as many principles as necessary in order to survive.

The central issue, however, is that of an assumed hierarchy, based not on curriculum or size or recruitment or anything other than a 'tradition' – though as the *Guardian* pointed out in its leader on the Taylor report in 1963 (6 March), 'the gulf between universities and CATs is an accidental one . . . for a number of largely irrelevant historical reasons the name "university" happens to enjoy greater prestige'. In this sense, diversity normally implies hierarchy. Any attempt to tidy up the British higher education jumble on an apparent basis of the rational distribution of resources or manpower training, or above all of neat distinctions of vocational and non-vocational and so on, raises direct questions about the preservation of the hierarchy of institutions and of values. The vocabulary of rational diversity conceals the intention to produce sharper hierarchy.

It is here that the main danger of 'rationalising' the system lies. The attempt in both the United States and Britain from the end of the 1970s is to tighten up the definitions of the different parts of the system. It is the view of American sociologists like Burton R. Clark and Martin Trow that these functional definitions are becoming and should become more precise, so that the different parts of the system (two-year community colleges, four-year state colleges, universities) can most easily and rationally fulfil their proper 'functions' and obligations (see, for example, B. R. Clark in *Comparative Education Review*, June 1978; M. Trow in H. Gans (ed.), *Essays in Honor of David Riesman*, 1979). The attempt in this case is to identify the research, service, teaching, vocational and other roles of the constituent parts of the system, and enable them to do what they do best – whether that be high-level research, the teaching of the average student, catering for the student from a minority ethnic background, training for the professions or producing critical thinkers. In Britain there are pointers in the same direction. The Conservative Government of 1979, in imposing financial pressures on the educational system as a whole, explicitly raised questions of increasing efficiency through a rational diversification of roles. Government ministers criticised the polytechnics for having strayed from their originally intended roles as centres of vocational and professional training. They implied an endorsement of the binary divide between the 'academic', 'research-oriented' universities, and the more applied, publicly responsive maintained sector of higher education. They turned assumed and questionable definitions into instruments of policy. It is not unlikely that the previous Labour Government, had it stayed in power, would have done the same.

A second indication of the direction of thinking about higher education is in Charles Carter's analysis in the previous chapter of the overlapping, competitive, over-ambitious nature of the higher education system, within which, for example, diversified colleges of higher education cannot expect to survive in competition with universities at a time of falling numbers. He argues for greater institutional specialisation, including the restriction of research training in any one subject to fifteen centres, and identifying thirty-five or so 'centres of excellence' at research and higher degree level.

The difficulty with these kinds of argument is that they pursue the same unilinear paths as all those which begin with tidy but untenable definitions. The colleges of higher education are not simply in curricular competition with the universities: in their diversification, their search for interstices in which to operate, their exploitation of their traditional strengths, they have indicated that they may survive and prosper for reasons other than their curriculum. Polytechnics may have a range of choices to offer students that are different and acceptable for reasons other than simple popularity scales. The identification of research not only with universities, but with selected universities, is a stress not on rational distribution – as is suggested – but on inevitable status differences based on unexamined assumptions about the categories involved. Such a view of research propels the whole system of higher education towards a tighter pattern based on a stronger confidence than ever that we understand the meaning and implications of long-mismanaged terms. This is very much the case with Conservative policy, and its 'commonsense' view of the jobs that everyone has to do.

Sharp and imposed definitions by imagined functions therefore indicate a price to be paid. The price for this kind of safeguarding of a critical, research–oriented university is permanently uncritical, docile, unimaginative, non-innovatory, instrumental, permanently low-grade and conformist non-university higher and further eduation. That, in the final analysis, is what Moberly wanted in 1948, James in 1963, and a variety of British and American commentators and policy-makers at the beginning of the 1980s. That, and not economics, finance, retrenchment, rationalisation and common sense, is what the future of higher education in Britain is essentially about, and where the main debates should focus. It is utterly impossible to discuss seriously the nature and roles of the colleges, institutes and polytechnics, or technical, further, adult and continuing education, without abandoning an anachronistic and irrelevant terminology, including and above all the crude assumptions about 'university'. Peter Scott has described 'the hegemony of the universities over higher education', which remained undisturbed by the binary policy. As we have seen, it is more than that. New policies have concealed an intention to ensure that the university as we have known it in the past remains the exclusive heir of the higher education tradition. Scott rightly suggests that the most fundamental flaw in the binary policy was its attempt 'to impose change from above by manipulating institutions, without making a parallel attempt to influence the values that underlie them' (*What Future for Higher Education?*, 1979). The failure to confront questions of value stems in the main not just from a general neglect of higher education policy (not only by the Labour Party, which is the focus of Scott's discussion), but also from a misplaced confidence that the questions of values were being taken care of. Expansion itself would look after such questions as the nature and purpose of diversity, and the provision and meaning of greater equality of opportunity. Too late we discovered that it did nothing of the sort.

The immediate danger is that economic constraints and retrenchment will lead to forms of control or manipulation which prevent even further any attempt to escape from easy assumptions, and further reinforce existing statuses and hegemonies. The disembodied discussion of polytechnic autonomy or of regional co-ordination in higher education or of rationalisation amongst *sectors* of education again ignores the ambiguities and leaves aside the central question of the meaning of frontiers between the universities and the 'others', and amongst the 'others'. The danger of definitions now is that they inevitably allow universities maximum room for academic, or scholarly, or autonomous, or critical, manoeuvre, and imprison the rest in various forms of enforced conformity. They also strengthen hierarchies of conformity in the maintained sector of further and higher education.

What is required for the 1980s, therefore, is a more profound and sustained debate about the nature of diversity, not in terms of sectors but in terms of the capacities, will and responsiveness of individual institutions. The real question is not whether there should be diversity – because for over a quarter of a century there has been ritualistic, but superficial, agreement that there should. The central issue is now less the ways in which the various categories in further and higher education differ, than in the values which they do or should share, and can explore and implement in their own ways. The liberal, research tradition cannot remain exclusive to a group of institutions which for largely irrelevant historical reasons enjoy a prestigious title. The remainder of higher and further education cannot allow itself to be so organised as to safeguard the traditional values of the university, without being allowed to share in them. Those institutions, polytechnics, colleges and institutes of higher education, which have the capacity and the spirit to compete with the universities on a number of possible, different levels, should not be prevented from doing so, and should not be denied the encouragement to do so. We cannot continue to talk in abstract terms about sectors of higher education – *the* universities, *the* polytechnics, *the* colleges and institutes of higher education, *the* colleges of technology. The emergent pattern of higher education must not be based on fortuitous similarities within groups of institutions, rather than on the strengths of individual institutions and their ability to respond in a range of ways to the perceived needs of local, regional and national constituencies of students of all kinds. A college of technology, or a college of higher education, cannot be expected to plan all or part of its range of curricula and levels of work on the assumption that it does not share the same Precinct as the university, that it inhabits instead some kind of subterranean or shadow world. The discussion of higher education can no longer start with old and outmoded categories and assumptions. It cannot begin with definitions and systems and economics, rather than with the likely needs of students, of populations – knowing as we do that the traditional categories of students are themselves unlikely to persist.

The universities, like other institutions, must not be exempt from facing up to the implications of such questions. The same constraints, or lack of them, should apply to all institutions. The same requirements of responsiveness or leadership or critical attitudes to the transmission of knowledge and values should apply to all. The same capacity to explore and innovate should be expected of all. The need is not for set formulae and permanent exclusions. It is not just for a token 'flexibility', but for what Maurice Peston, in a discussion of centralisation and decentralisation, described as policy measures which 'must be susceptible of rapid reversal' (*Oxford Review of Education*, 1979).

The categories and definitions that have been discussed contain, of course, readily visible hierarchies – including of institutions, of knowledge, and of qualifications and awards. The discussion here has been concerned with hierarchies of sectors rather than with these, but many of the 'commonsense' formulae for neat and rigid reorganisations disguise ways of intensifying these old hierarchies and smuggling in new ones. In an age of restriction and competition the definition that surrounds a sector may be seen as protection for individual institutions within it which feel themselves challenged or threatened by newcomers. If there are differences between sectors based on functions or the absence of them, then the same criteria strengthen hierarchical differences within sectors. Without adequate discussion, therefore, the old and the established retain positions, and the pecking order that was of little importance in an age of expansion becomes an explicit system of congealed power and prestige. The concentration of research, the focus on applied studies, the involvement with minority groups, the concern for community development, become rationalised features not just of different institutions, but of institutions in strict hierarchies. Intentional or not, that is the logic.

The need is not for drummed-up definitions and neat categorisations, but for an abandonment of past confident assumptions that we all know what our common definitions and categorisations mean. The penalty for using strong and unquestioned definitions on which to base 'rational' diversity at this stage will, in fact, be increased hierarchy and stronger pressures for more widespread conformity.

GEORGE TOLLEY

Access, community and curriculum

It may be doubted whether the United Kingdom has ever come to terms with the twentieth century. The British Empire bestrode the nineteenth century like a Colossus, built upon foundations of an insatiable desire for trade, brilliant administration and indestructible superiority, and energised by the morality of the British Navy and evangelical piety. But at the fag end of the twentieth century the nation is economically fragile, gripped in an industrial decline it has been unable to stop for fifty years or more, and uncertain how to capitalise its newly found oil wealth or its other resources. The story is one not so much of lack of effort, but of misdirected effort, of mistaken priorities, or rather of a refusal to consider carefully the consequences of choosing priorities. So we are at something of a crossroads, with no obvious political consensus, with no overriding national objective other than that of survival, and with a machinery of government that creaks woefully, not so much from lack of oil as from lack of policy or from repeated changes of policy so that meshing parts do not get bedded in. Higher education, too, for all its apparent smugness and self-satisfaction, is in disarray and must accept its share of responsibility for the decline and the missed and unrealised opportunities of the century.

Between 1968 and 1978, the proportion of the age group in higher education in the UK increased from 11·8 per cent to 13·5 per cent. It has been one of the fastest growing businesses in the country. No faster, of course, than the expansion of higher education in many other countries. But it is interesting to ask why the proportion of the gross domestic product spent on higher education in the USA provides for a substantially greater age participation rate than in the UK. That question is not an idle one; to pursue it would take us into the territory of much heated argument. It is one we should not forget, for it underlies many of the issues to be referred to in this chapter. These issues relate to the need radically to reassess the purposes, objectives and structures of higher education in a time of change. For the era of rapid growth in higher education is over and we are faced, not merely with no growth, but with contraction and at a time when two pressures must make themselves felt. First is the relative economic decline of the country, which means closer scrutiny, at least, of all public expenditure. That is to say, resource margins will be tight. Any fat that there might have been (and there was a good deal in certain quarters of higher education) will have to be cut out; where there is no fat, it will mean cutting into the bone. Second is the growing public and political disillusion with education generally, and higher education in particular, for not delivering the goods. It was, perhaps, never quite clear what goods were expected, but there were certain general expectations that more higher education would guarantee the better and easier life. That higher education of itself could do no such thing is neither here nor there. Vast sums of public money were committed in the belief that there was some sort of equation linking this expenditure with a return that would be visible in a sounder economy and a more stable and rewarding social fabric. So higher education has to change at a time when doing less or more of the same is not possible within the financial constraints and not acceptable within the social and political constraints.

The pressures for contraction of higher education arise not so much from demography, but from two other factors. One, inevitably, is money – reduced public expenditure and a sluggish economy combine to cut into institutional budgets. Whether this pressure will be reflected in greater incentives and rewards for institutional effectiveness remains to be seen. The other arises from evident doubts about the value, relevance and necessity of higher education. Take-up of places in higher education by qualified school-leavers continues to decline, for whatever reason. Buf if school-leavers prefer the job in hand now to the degree in the bush in three or four years time, this reflects their own and their parents' and contemporaries' assessment of value.

The pressures for change arise essentially from these same two factors also, and especially from the second, which should force a reassessment of values and purpose in terms of personal and social priorities and needs. It is much more difficult to plan for and to achieve significant and necessary change in a time of contraction or constraint than during expansion. Whether there is to be contraction in higher education over the next decade continues to be a matter of argument; about constraint there can be no difference of opinion. Neither contraction nor constraint (as now being experienced) are well known or well understood in the British higher education system. The expectations and the practices of the 1960s and 1970s will die hard and painfully in the cold and critical austerity now upon us. These boom years gave us a greatly expanded university system, generously encouraged by the State to live beyond its means, a system dependent upon variable quality, yet strenuously maintaining that everything is of the highest quality. The colleges of education, until they were massacred in the mid-1970s, were expanded over-rapidly and well endowed with land and bricks and mortar, but were not well provided for either in teaching resources, or in quality of teaching staff or students. The polytechnics, under-resourced by comparison with the universities, have exceeded all that was required of them when they were established and are suffering now because of their very success. The binary system clearly had its advantages during a period of growth, when a variety of responses was possible and when it could be argued that it was a good thing to have some slack in the system to be taken up at the appropriate time. It has yet to face the conflicts and the tensions of severe constraint and of possible contraction, which are now upon us.

It is the intention in this chapter to explore three themes which, it is held, are central to the concerns of higher education, and which take on enhanced relevance when priorities and policies need to be resolved against a background of constraint and of the need for significant change. The themes could be approached from the structural aspects of the system, that is

with a view to identifying those changes which require government action, legislative or otherwise. That will not be the
approach here, where the emphasis will be more concerned with
institutional responsibility and response. The three themes will
be called Access, Community and Curriculum.

ACCESS

Higher Education into the 1990s proposed a number of models in
response to the demographic analysis contained in that document. Model E seems to be the one to have found favour in
educational circles, largely one suspects because it is the model
which allows some dreams still of growth. The Document does
not seem to have made any great impact upon thinking in
education because it was not apparent in the first place how
discussion was supposed to affect policy, and also because policy
is now seen to reside much more in public expenditure White
Papers than in DES Discussion Documents. However, given the
brave attempt of the DES to encourage discussion, what is it
that we ought to be discussing? One matter, undoubtedly, must
be that of the accessibility of higher education. Why is it that so
much of education is a closed cycle? Why is it that in the
polytechnics twenty-one per cent of their full-time students are
over the age of twenty-one, whereas in the universities the
corresponding figure is six per cent? What do we mean by
continuing education – continuing what? Why does the term
'adult' education live on, even though the age of legal majority
was lowered to eighteen many years ago and, hence, all students
in higher education are adult? What would happen in higher
education if access were made much easier or more flexible?

Discussion of access to higher education quickly leads to a
parade of hobby horses, of vested interests and of prejudices.
Better (easier?) access to higher education is sought, ostensibly
for a number of reasons:

to encourage greater participation by working-class students
   (the social or equity argument)
to make higher education (as something that is 'good') available

to more people (the numbers, or 'everyone profits from it', argument)

to provide for those who currently are effectively denied access, e.g. housewives, retired people (the deprivation argument)

to change what is taught and how it is taught (the Trojan Horse argument).

In discussing access we need to differentiate clearly between those changes which could allow greater access to what is currently available and changes in what is currently available which would, of themselves, encourage greater demand for the products of higher education. The two to some extent overlap, but the first is largely a matter of regulating entry, whereas the second is more a matter of marketing and adapting the product to satisfy and to develop a market. Current interest in questions of access seems to concentrate much more upon the first than the second and then largely with a view to preserving or increasing the total size of the present system (and therefore preserving the jobs and promotion prospects of present staff of higher education institutions).

The case for more flexible and adaptable access turns essentially upon two things: a belief that many who could profit from higher education (and, in turn, profit the community) are denied access; and the claims of social justice recognising, for whatever reason, the class bias of higher education and the ways in which it is geared to such a large extent to the needs of the qualified school-leaver. It is not reassuring to see that more and more of those young people who are qualified to enter higher education are turning away and choosing other things. It is disappointing in some ways to see so many places in Open University courses taken up by those who have already had some experience of higher education. But two observations strengthen the view that more adaptable access is justified. The first takes account of the success which accompanies almost any scheme introduced by any institution to widen access, and has regard also to the impressive performance of so many of those who are admitted into degree courses under 'exceptional entry' conditions. The fact is that there is little evidence of dilution of academic standards when students are admitted who do not conform to 'normal' entry requirements. The second observation has to do with international comparisons which admittedly often raise more questions than they answer. But can we effectively compete with other developed industrial nations if our man-power lacks a comparably broad base of higher education? In thinking of more adaptable access we should not fail to question the effectiveness of selection and assessment of the present clientele. It is a worrying question why, for example, wastage rates in polytechnics should be double those in universities. In addition to making access more adaptable and more flexible, we need also to do something to ease transfer between courses after entry into higher education.

Pressures to bring about significant changes in access to higher education will come from four major causes:

1. The perceived need amongst staff in higher education institu-tions to maintain numbers. This may be an expression of self-preservation but is not motivated wholly by self-interest.
2. The growth of new client groups: the unemployed; the early retired; those for whom a change of career is essential in order to maintain employment; or those for whom changing technology means, in effect, a new beginning.
3. Changing patterns of post-compulsory schooling and further education. Staying on in full-time education will increasingly not equate to a traditional preparation for entry into higher education.
4. Social pressures for lower priorities on public spending and resources for the 18 to 21 year olds.

If this is so, then the pressures are not likely to be wholly or even largely relieved by merely tinkering with entry conditions. Undoubtedly the grant system needs attention but that, of itself, may not bring about significant changes in accessibility unless there are accompanying changes in attitudes within higher education.

Three massive barriers have to be surmounted if accessibility is to be improved, and there is little sign at present to indicate that serious and sustained attempts are being made on behalf of more open access. The first barrier is the general satisfaction that teaching staff in higher education have with what they are doing and the conditions under which they work. More open access is perceived by many as a potential threat to existing relationships, to generous staffing ratios, to research and scholarship and to the mystique of the lecturer. The threat is rationalised, often enough, as a potential undermining of standards and quality. This is not so much a 'more means worse' syndrome, as a 'different, and therefore unknown, means unpredictable' syndrome. Associated with an unwillingness to consider significant change in the processes and structures of teaching is a lack of understanding of the need to market higher education. The universities have created a largely captive market tied to the rigidities of UCCA, which does not market anything. Apart from that, the universities, polytechnics and other colleges indulge in a few low-key promotional exercises such as not very informative prospectuses, rather more informative open days and dependence upon an old boy network that is probably highly effective in transmitting out of date information. Now let us be clear. Teaching staff put a great deal of time and effort into selecting and advising students and in recruiting up to the target numbers set for their courses. They will consider opening up access provided that it is to those courses, and involves exceptional entry confined to a small and readily identifiable proportion of the total entry. But that is not making access more open; it is merely applying existing criteria of selection for existing courses. More open access will come only if selection criteria and the nature of teaching are changed to take account of the needs of the market for different products.

The second barrier arises from the conviction, or the affirmation, that all resources in higher education are under pressure, and therefore there is no possibility of doing more, or even anything much different, without extra resources. This of course, masks the presupposition that no significant changes ought to be made either to release resources or to allow them to be used differently. The conviction is strongest of all when the major resource, teaching staff, is under consideration, but it is also very strong in maintaining that library and other prime learning resources are overstretched and could not cope with increased demands or with a multiplicity of widely differing demands. The argument from resources was developed into a fine tool and used to great purpose in the boom years when the incremental annexation of resources was so successful and no opportunity was presented for an overall review of how resources were being used. It takes its stand now as a prime defence against the erosion of standards and stands foursquare against any radical change, however carefully thought out and however justifiable.

The third barrier is the devotion to sharply identifiable entry criteria, expressed preferably in terms of subjects and grades at 'A' Level. It is held that these criteria do much to guarantee the standard of teaching in courses and therefore the final standards of award. In fact, they do much to assure the homogeneity of the groups selected for courses. Exceptions to the entry norms must therefore be translated back into the entry norms and access to higher education is therefore built upon the schools' examination system.

If there is to be more open access to higher education it will come only if there is a willingness on the part of teaching staff in higher education to recognise and to act upon four things:

1. To change courses and teaching methods.
2. To market the higher education product.
3. To achieve a much more effective use of resources.
4. To accept that minor changes in entry regulations are cosmetic only.

But why should teaching staff set about making significant changes, some of which would undoubtedly be both demanding and painful? After all, conditions of work and the general environment are congenial. Why change? That is a question which underlines a good deal of the debate in higher education, a question which is often made to turn upon deeply-held views and prejudices about what is claimed as the maintenance of standards. The reasons for change fall into three categories. First is the instinct and careful regard for self-preservation. The most obvious way of preserving jobs is to keep up numbers in higher education and, if possible, to increase them. One thing is certain: if the numbers are not there, then jobs will have to go – and numbers will only be retained by doing something different to what goes on at the moment. Secondly, there has been growing discontent and growing pressures for change, even during the boom years of expansion, from consumers of the product of higher education and from those who control the purse strings. It is being said, with measured insistence, that what is currently provided is not appropriate. Attitudes of graduates; isolation and remoteness of staff; mismatch of demand and supply; under-utilisation of resources: all these things and more have come under sharp and consistent criticism. Thirdly, there is the area of issues of incentives relating to job satisfaction. The age profile of teaching staff shows a marked bunching in the mid-thirties age group. If this large group of people is to avoid the severe tensions and conflicts arising from lack of promotion prospects in a non-expanding system, it must not be expected merely to accept the status quo. If job mobility is reduced (as it undoubtedly is), then the job itself must change in some degree if personal satisfaction is to be assured. Underlying these pressures and causes of change there remains the professional responsibility of the teacher for education for a changing world. The teacher is there to meet certain needs and expectations of the student.

But what is it that students selected for higher education gain access to? These perceptions vary widely and this is not the place to attempt a summary or a judgement. The reality of the higher education experience will be shaped to a considerable degree by those perceptions and the motivation that underlies them. The reality will also be shaped by whatever it is that constitutes the community of the institution to which they are admitted and by the curriculum. It is to these we will now turn.

COMMUNITY

During their time at a university, polytechnic or college, students will identify with a course (more usually with one year of that course), a department, a hall of residence or smaller residential unit, a 'college', some student activity be it football or Union politics, and perhaps with the town or city in which the institution is placed. The phrase 'I am at X University' or 'at Y Polytechnic' signifies study for some particular qualification; it also signifies belonging to an elite of a kind which, however much it may belong to the world, is also withdrawn into its own community. The myths of that community are strong, witness the post-Robbins 'hundred acre syndrome' for new universities and the strenuous insistence upon collegiality or upon residence as forming necessary constituents of community. The myths may have been weakened by increasing participation in higher education, by the sillier and more strident excesses of student disruption and by the moves from discipline by regulation to government by consent – yet they still live on. No doubt it is the myths of community that have ensured priorities for students which might be considered remarkable when put against provision from public money for other sections of society: residential accommodation; refectories; student union buildings providing, mostly, facilities for social activities; health and counselling facilities; physical recreation provision. These things are considered necessary, not merely as an adjunct to learning (for manifestly, they are not essential to learning), but as a required part of that total experience which those entering higher education (or at least certain parts of it) have the right to expect. Now, I am not saying that none of these things should be provided as part of higher education, neither am I saying that the spending of public money on such provision is not justifiable. I am asking two questions:

What sort of experience of community is being sought by students in higher education?

To what extent are the expectations of students realised in and through extra-curricular provision?

Comprehensive answers to these questions will not be attempted here, but relevant comments will be made which relate to the setting in which answers have to be found. If the higher education system contracts, then for every institution, even one in which there may be only slight or no contraction, there will be significant issues of cost effectiveness, value for money, and spending priorities. For the first time in many institutions of higher education there will be direct competition between spending upon teaching activities and spending upon extra-curricular activities. For some institutions, contraction would raise serious doubts about the balance of resources between teaching and other activities. So, in a time of contraction, the issues of community, insofar as these relate to physical and other resources (as they undoubtedly do) will be brought sharply into a focus of decisions about spending. If, however, institutions seek to avoid contraction by changing the age profile or mode of attendance of students, or if they seek greater cost effectiveness with much the same student mix as now but with more of them, then the issues of community remain and may be more difficult to resolve if the nature of the student body changes.

There are two issues here, are there not? Firstly, what is necessary for effective learning and for that maturing and rounding of the personality which makes possible the effective application of learning? Secondly, if there are significant reductions in expenditure, where should the remaining money be spent? In relation to the first question it is fair to ask to what extent effective learning and maturing are dependent upon halls of residence, medical and counselling services and student union facilities and activities. In relation to the second it would be surprising if reassessment of priorities did not bring into question some of the myths of the academic community. This is not to belittle those myths, but it is only fair that they should be probed, since they can be very expensive.

Apart from extra-curricular provision, of variable quantity and quality, there remains a firm commitment to the 'abrasion' theory of education and its significance for community. That is to say a belief that, by bringing together staff and students from a variety of backgrounds, experience and disciplines, something of value will rub off from one to the other. Now there are many arguments in favour of a multi-disciplinary institution (notably those arguments that relate to the necessity of having an adequate resource base) but it is doubtful whether the abrasion theory can be maintained, given the difficulties in communica-

tion evident in a large multi-disciplinary institution. Neither
does the abrasion theory appear relevant for a diversified college
of education in which there may be a notable absence of
technological disciplines and a rather restricted range of vocational courses. Indeed, the one mark of the higher education
community which is consistent is not that of internal coherence
or even that of evident shared values, but rather a significant
measure of isolation from external and surrounding communities. True, a university, polytechnic or college impinges upon
society in many ways but, as an institution, it does not engage in
a direct fashion with other communities, preferring to internal-
ise many of its concerns and responsibilities.

Some important changes are on the way (indeed, some have
already arrived) which will affect the style and character of our
institutions. For many polytechnics, and for some other colleges, mergers following the run-down of the former colleges of
education have resulted in multi-site operation on a considerable
and complex scale. Financial constraints are beginning to force a
reconsideration of spending on student union and extra-
curricular activities. Here and there the needs of mature students
are beginning to be met in ways that challenge accepted norms
of procedure for selection and assessment. Vocational courses
are showing an upsurge of popularity, and areas of study that for
years have been able to turn away students with ease are having
to get out into the market to recruit. Part-time courses are
beginning to figure prominently in the prospectuses of many
institutions which in the recent past regarded part-time students
as of little concern.

Each one of these changes must affect in some way the
concept and the experience of community within the institution.
Yet little is known of such effects. Higher education institutions
are clearly adaptable communities but whether they show
sufficient adaptation as learning communities is to be questioned. The commonly found formal structures of Senate and
Faculty Boards or of students' unions are probably supportive of
a rather different concept of community to that which will be
required during a period of constraint and change. The emphasis
upon internal autonomy which is so evident in that formal

structure may well be misplaced and could well be questioned since it does so much to make a foreign and isolated territory of higher education to many potential students.

CURRICULUM

The one thing which sets apart the educational community from all others is its responsibility and concern for the curriculum. Who then controls the curriculum in higher education? Certainly not the higher education institution itself which, whilst being responsible for the curriculum, must respond to a wide range of outside influences, pressures and requirements. In designing and structuring the curriculum a delicate balance has to be sought and maintained between three responsibilities which may conflict. These are: upholding the integrity of the subject discipline; fulfilling the requirements of professional competence and understanding; providing for the needs of students, both in an orderly and logical development of learning and in opportunities for justifiable transfer to other areas of study. The point of balance will differ from one course to another. For a 'pure' single-subject honours degree the emphasis will undoubtedly lie largely with the subject discipline. For a vocational course directly related to one of the professions, such as accountancy, librarianship, medicine or social work, professional requirements will predominate. In some modular or foundation courses a major objective may be that of allowing a range of possibilities for transfer. But irrespective of where the point of balance is seen to lie, consideration of the curriculum must involve attention to the three responsibilities and especially to that responsibility for the structuring of learning.

Many students entering higher education will have little appreciation of the demands of the curriculum in terms of these three responsibilities or, indeed, in terms of the work load or methods required. Some will see the curriculum as an extension of the academic work they have done to gain entry; some will perceive it as related to acquiring professional standing; others as an opportunity to delay decisions about future careers. But irrespective of the views they assume, it is likely that their knowledge of the curriculum that faces them will be limited. One of the reasons for relatively high non-completion rates in polytechnics may well be that students are not made sufficiently aware of the vocational requirements of the courses or of the academic demands when a number of disciplines are involved. Irrespective therefore of the processes whereby the curriculum is agreed and implemented, it is incumbent upon higher education institutions to present to prospective students information about the curriculum which will better inform them about demands likely to be placed upon them.

Apart from these general observations about the nature of understanding of the curriculum, four issues call for comment. They are: the concept of vocational study; skills in the curriculum; research and teaching; and choice in the curriculum. The first issue is both perennial and topical. Vocational courses are lauded and they are derided. If the vocation under discussion is one of the 'superior' professions of medicine or law, then the vocational course is claimed as virtuous (even though the relationships between the content of a degree course in law and practice as a solicitor or barrister may be somewhat tenuous). But the idea of a liberal education still exerts its influence and disparaging remarks about the narrowness or lack of intellectual content of the 'lesser' vocational courses are not unknown. (By 'lesser' we are meant to include such professions as engineering, accountancy, metallurgy, pharmacy and other apparently misunderstood activities.)

It would remove a good deal of snobbery from higher education, and not a little downright bad advice in schools, if only those of us in education would remove ourselves from the empty battlefields of the nineteenth century. In an age when it is entirely normal to change careers two or three times during a working lifetime, when new technology can and does change the nature of professional responsibilities and when inter-professional dependence and flexibility are vitally necessary, it would be helpful (not to say realistic) to eschew an over-simple categorisation of courses into vocational and non-vocational. For whether a course is vocational or not will be determined more by context than by content; that is, the process of the curriculum is significant. True, one is fully entitled to ask of any course what saleable skills it offers, for, after all, there are very few students in higher education who are there only to imbibe intellectual pursuits. But an engineer with a poorly developed intellect will be no more saleable than a brilliantly intellectual historian who lacks the equipment to make judgements in a modern technological society. These observations are stimulated by the evident conflicts between those who seek to relate vocational training to manpower planning in higher education and those who go to inordinate lengths to maintain the intrinsic value of courses in the humanities. Whether a course in the humanities is of value or not will depend not upon the intrinsic merit of the subject discipline involved nor upon the creative accomplishments of the human soul, but upon the quality of the teachers and the balance and incisiveness of the curriculum. Mediocre courses in the humanities are as much an affront to academic and human dignity as are out of date or intellectually unsatisfying courses in engineering. But at least the products of the latter are likely to be found out more quickly.

We should ask ourselves and others more often what skills are being sought in the curriculum, both by those who construct it and those who are taught it. There are some curricula (especially in the humanities) where it is considered indecorous if not indecent to ask questions about skills. By asking such a question one is in danger of being accused of demeaning an intellectual activity or turning it into instruction suitable for technicians. Yet the question has its value, not only in ascertaining saleable skills but also in uncovering perhaps just how much obsolescence is built into many curricula. The most skills–laden curricula often have an alarmingly high content of obsolescent skills and redundant material. Such content is more likely to be critically appraised by the student as client or by experienced professionals from outside the institution than it is by those who have a proprietorial interest in the curriculum. In academic courses the teaching of skills must take place within a framework of concepts, but if the latter are dealt with without recognition of the objectives of the former, then the curriculum is unbalanced and the student will be sold short.

Research in higher education institutions is justified essentially on two counts. It is held that research maintains the freshness, the competence, the creativity and hence the quality of teaching staff. It is also held that research activity and findings inform the curriculum, not merely keeping it up to date but ensuring that it is lively and demanding. If these claims are not justifiable then research should be consigned to research institutes and should not occupy such a large proportion of the resources of universities. Yet whatever may be claimed for the ambience resulting from research, it must be said that there is no known direct correlation between research performance and teaching ability; furthermore, a great deal of research going on in higher education is no more than mediocre, repetitive, unremarkable and intellectually unstimulating. Quality and liveliness in the curriculum is just as likely (more likely?) to be achieved by giving some real thought to what is taught and how it is taught, as it is by expecting some fertile symbiosis between research and teaching interests.

Whatever the quality and content of the curriculum (whether dependent upon excellence in research or not) there will be demands for choice. Firstly from teaching staff anxious to display and maintain their specialist expertise; and the students too will want to choose and to reject optional areas of study. No student likes to feel constrained within a fixed curriculum. Secondly from students who are uncertain about making a fixed commitment at the beginning of a course. They will wish to delay final choice and perhaps make substantial changes in direction, having once had the opportunity to explore other avenues. It is this latter demand for choice which appears to be growing and it has led, in some institutions, to a broadening of the curriculum, to modular courses, to changes in course structures and in relationships between courses, and to a search for more effective ways of using teaching staff. Financial pressures are likely to force a reduction in the number of options offered in courses, whatever the desires of teaching staff to preserve their own speciality – or, at least, these will only be preserved if there are some consequent and significant changes in organisation and teaching in other parts of courses. Financial constraints could therefore, if applied insensitively or rigidly, lead to a loss of choice at a time of growing demand for greater choice. The likelihood is that, faced with changing student demand and with the need at least to maintain student numbers, institutions will have to provide opportunities for wider choice and will have to make transfer less difficult whilst improving overall effectiveness in the use of all resources.

Now it is probable that the combination of financial constraint, lower social priority for higher education and less homogeneity in the student clientele (in terms of age, mode of attendance and expectations) will have their effect upon the curriculum in the four areas of interest referred to above. Some clearer vocational definition of courses will undoubtedly be sought by many students and over-simple categorisation into specific career opportunities will not be enough. Sharper definition of the skills taught in courses is going to be required to satisfy the requirements of students who wish to know just what skills are being developed, over against interesting and stimulating but perhaps largely abstract intellectual explorations. The latter, it has to be recognised, are an essential part of higher education, but if they are provided at the expense of, or without any regard to, the necessary skills element of the curriculum, then higher education is in danger of becoming a mere pastime.

It is evident that many teachers are of the view (when they think about these things) that skills belong to technician courses or to those courses that are narrowly vocational. Higher education for them is concerned with the higher reaches of the mind. Even in many avowedly practically-biased courses such as art and design, engineering or some of the sciences, there is often no coherent thinking-through of the development of necessary skills. Learning skills themselves are not approached systematically. Communication skills tend to get lost in the formalities (or informalities) of teaching and writing. Inter-personal skills and the requirements of teamwork may have no place in the curriculum. The skill of designing an experiment may never be tested at all adequately in a degree course. The place of research is going to come under closer scrutiny as budgets tighten, as demands for economic relevance increase, and as students assert more strongly the need for the primacy of learning. And greater opportunities for choice will certainly be sought by students who see the dangers of rigidity in the curriculum and in course structures. Greater choice in no way lessens the seriousness and importance of the decisions that have to be made by students and with greater choice (however provided) must come a need for more effective counselling.

Looking at the curriculum as it now is in higher education one sees an incredibly complex picture. The range of interests, influences and pressures that may have to be taken account of in devising and maintaining curricula is legion: professional bodies; validating bodies; claims of subject disciplines; vested interests of teachers; fads and fashions. Keeping some sort of balance between these interests is often very difficult; worthwhile innovation may be resisted in some vital quarter; the inertia in outdated curricula can be almost impossible to move. The best defence is a lively teaching staff and a lively and discriminating student body. Better to focus attention on achieving those things than upon seeking to devise some interventionist curriculum machinery. Better still to seek a substantial shift of emphasis to learning and so lessen the grip which content has upon the energies and interests of staff. The objectives, the structures and the context of courses are made to relate far too much to content and not nearly enough to learning processes and learning achievements. It is, all too often, a matter of 'what do you know?', rather than 'how [or why] do you know?'. Improved effectiveness in courses, required by financial constraint, will not be achieved by concentrating upon the content of the curriculum. Improved effectiveness required both by more discriminating students and by their not fitting into a conventional mould, will only be achieved by having much greater regard to learning, which is, after all, what the curriculum is all about.

Let us return to where we started. The past twenty years have seen a massive growth in higher education. Whether 'more means worse' is now hardly worth debating. It is a non-question; more has meant, essentially, more of the same. That there has been change in higher education is not in question, but we have, at the beginning of the 1980s, a system which is poorly articulated to respond to or to bring about significant change in demand or need. A substantial part of the system (or non-system) will expend its energies in preserving institutions as they now are and, in particular, in defending claimed autonomy – another name for limited engagement with society only on their own terms. Some institutions, not having that autonomy, will seek it in the belief that, in so doing, they are strengthening academic values, however these are defined. Meanwhile, the overall objectives of, or the national priorities for, the system remain unclear. Furthermore, the purpose and function of institutions, or of groups of institutions, in the system are inadequately defined or expressed, and the machinery for bringing about change in the system is of doubtful effectiveness for the tasks to be undertaken. Overhaul of the machinery is badly needed, but that is not the concern of this essay. Rather it is its purpose to state that, irrespective of changes in machinery or in the structure of the system, there is need to address thinking to those issues which demand changes in attitudes and definition of the tasks most likely to be facing higher education in the next decade.

There is great danger in thinking that the system will change for the better or in some desired way in response to pressures that are imposed from outside. The demographic pressure of declining numbers of 18 to 21 year olds as we move into the 1990s is thought by some to be a likely enforcer of change. Manpower planning, bringing about rigidities in recruitment and a direct relationship to the labour market, is sought by some as a regulatory mechanism. Yet such imposition of external pressures without changes in attitudes within the system would create intolerable tensions and would cause only greater confusion and result in a dissipation of energy in seeking remedies for the wrong or wrongly diagnosed symptoms. Financial constraints, unless they are outrageously savage, could be contained by tinkering with the system, by adjustments at the margin, within institutions (even though some of these may be sensitive or painful), and by a strenuous refusal of staff to admit the possibility of or necessity for significant change. But financial constraints as we now have them and as they are likely to continue, coupled with doubts in the political and public mind about the value and direction of higher education and with stirrings towards a new or changing clientele for higher education cannot and will not be contained by tinkering at the margin. Some institutions are likely to go to the wall; others are likely to change so appreciably as to be unrecognisable within a decade; yet others are likely to be seen clinging grimly to what they perceive to be distinctiveness or status. These changes will not take place and cannot even be envisaged, without some radical assessment of what we are currently doing and what it is we ought to be doing. Higher education is still conditioned by values which relate to a very different world to the one in which we now live – one in which admittance to higher education was a reward for academic achievement at school by a very small proportion of the total population and that reward was the opportunity to proceed to still more academic achievement in a sheltered and artificial environment. It is because this is no longer the setting for higher education that we must be more open to changes in access, in community and in curriculum.

H. D. HUGHES

Continuing education in higher education

There is at the present time a widespread feeling in the country that the time is ripe for a radical review of the role of higher education. The expansion of the universities following the Robbins report has turned out largely to produce only 'more of the same'. The socio-economic composition of the student body has scarcely changed; the proportion of part-time courses in higher education as a whole has actually fallen in the last decade. Now that demographic factors indicate a fall in the 18-year-old qualified entry in the years ahead, quite apart from the current reduction in the age-participation rate, there are calls in high places for a decrease in the proportion of national resources devoted to higher education, reversing the trend that has prevailed since 1945. The Robbins principle is under attack. It is not surprising that the first subject chosen for review by the new House of Commons Select Committee on Education, Science and Arts in 1979/80 was the 'Funding and Organisation of Courses in Higher Education'.

The growing body of opinion that has accepted the need for a transfer from initial to continuing (lifelong, recurrent, perman-ent) education bases its arguments for the reform of higher education not on transitory demographic factors but on fun-damental grounds of educational and social principle. Interpreta-tions vary. As Kenneth Lawson has pointed out (*A Critique of Recurrent Education*, ARE), there are radical and moderate schools of thought, the former seeing recurrent education 'as a real force for changing the concrete situations people have to face at work as well as in other social institutions . . . and within the whole society'. The moderates advocate continuing education on the grounds of 'social equity, educational, economic and technological efficiency as a means of improving society as it already exists'. There is agreement about the inadequacy of the front-end pattern of initial education – the radicals would seek to make sweeping changes here, whilst the moderates are content in the first instance to seek to build a comprehensive system of post-initial education to complement it and compensate for its deficiencies. The 'middle way' 'is not about building conceptual castles in the sky but about adapting the details of academic organisations to make post-school education more accessible to the people' (*Times Higher Education Supplement* leader, 2 May 1980). My own basic premises are that:

1. It is desirable both on ethical grounds of justice to individual needs, and on social and economic grounds of community and national benefit, that resources for further and higher education should be provided to cater for an increasing proportion of the population.
2. It is desirable on both grounds to readjust the present imbalance of social and educational opportunity by taking steps to increase substantially the proportion of working-class entry to higher education.
3. It is desirable to increase substantially the provision of open access to higher education for mature students on the basis of motivation, experience and ability, irrespective of formal qualifications.
4. There should be a radical re-examination of the pattern of provision of full-time and part-time courses of varying duration, with the aim of providing a comprehensive and flexible system of continuing (recurrent) education geared to the needs of society in the light of social, economic and technological change.

The economic case for recurrent education has been well argued by Professor Maurice Peston, in the *World Yearbook of Education 1979*, and elsewhere (*Recurrent Education and Lifelong Learning*, ed. T. Schuller). He assumes the economic background to be one of technological change, leading to a decline of some ten per cent in work input, in the form of under-

mployment and/or a reduction of the working life, year or
week. This will demand an increased need for specific training in
he new technology, for general training to increase flexibility
nd mobility of labour, and for services complementary to
ncreased leisure time, including education. All these should be
egarded as 'economic activities' of benefit to the community.
ome would argue that too high a proportion of national
esources are devoted to education – given that the new tech-
ology will provide increased time and productive capacity,
there is no financial problem in the sense of the country being
nable to afford education . . . the issues are whether we should,
ow we set about doing it, how we determine the financial
rrangements in detail'. If the alternative to recurrent education
s unemployment and social security payments, the net cost is
small.

By comparative standards, the United Kingdom is lagging far
behind other Western countries in the proportion of the popula-
ion benefiting from higher education.

Proportionate Increase in Student Numbers

A = the number of students in full-time higher education
B = A as a proportion of the total national population

	Percentage increase 1964–70		Percentage increase 1970–76	
	A	B	A	B
Great Britain	66	62	16	15
France	79	71	27	21
Italy	89	81	41	36
West Germany	55	49	107	104
USA	60	50	39	34

Source: article by E. G. Edwards, former Vice-Chancellor, University of
Bradford, *Times Higher Education Supplement*, 11 January 1980

The social and educational inequalities of opportunity, and the
consequent waste of talent, previously described by J. W. B.
Douglas and others (*All Our Future*, 1968), have now been even
more fully documented in subsequent studies, notably *Origins &*

Destinations: Family Class and Education in Modern Britain, by A
H. Halsey, A. F. Heath and J. M. Ridge (1980):

> Our evidence holds no comfort for those who believe tha
> class differences in educational attainment reflect a fair distri
> bution of opportunities to those with the intellectual ability o
> cultural capacity to profit therefrom . . . Wastage of talen
> continues and was massive over most of the period witl
> which we are concerned (birth cohorts 1913–52).
>
> By the seventies at least 7000 boys each year could have
> obtained A level passes but were not in fact remaining a
> school long enough to do so. Further back in time, the
> wastage was much greater. In the early sixties it was running
> at an annual rate of around 30,000, and in the early fifties i
> would have been well over 40,000.

The authors conclude that the proportion of working-class boy
qualifying for university entrance 'could comfortably be
doubled without any necessary lowering of standards'. A simila
analysis for girls might well be even more striking.

The tables in *Origins & Destinations* show that in 1972 on
fifth of the children of the 'service classes' (13·7 per cent of the
population; professionals, administrators, managers, etc.) got to
university, as compared with 1·8 per cent of the children o
'workers' (54·9 per cent of the population; skilled, semi-skille
and unskilled manual workers in industry and agriculture). On
half of the university population came from the service classes
19·7 per cent from the working-class sector of the population
The 'IQ threshold' for service-class entry to university wa
120·8; for the working class 127·4, a handicap of 6·6. (Th
handicap for staying on at school at 17 was 10·3; 'the distance a
university entrance is largely a consequence of earlier decision
in the educational process'.) Taking the birth cohorts of the fou
decades, the proportion of service-class children reaching uni
versity has risen from 7·2 per cent for the 1913–22 cohort to 26·
per cent for the 1943–52 cohort, and the proportion of working
class children from 0·9 per cent to 3·1 per cent. Though th
working-class entry records the highest rate of growth, th

largest absolute gains have gone to the service class. The disparities are to some extent modified by entry to part-time further education, but it is only in the last decade (1943–52) that the proportion of working-class entry to this sector (50·8 per cent) exceeds that from the service class (45·1 per cent), and it is still below the entry from the intermediate classes (57·2 per cent; clerical workers, small proprietors and self-employed, lower grade technicians and foremen, comprising 31·4 per cent of the population).

Achieving equality of opportunity and full scope for talent thus requires further radical change in the school system and in the financial support (maintenance allowances, for example) offered for the post–compulsory stages.

> A concern for equality will require a broadening of alternative routes to post-secondary education and in particular the provision of truly open recurrent education . . . Plans for recurrent education have, in any case, to be drawn to a vastly greater scale. Building a structure of recurrent education should certainly not be made to await completion of its pre-school foundations (ibid.).

So, even for the present school generation, we cannot afford to postpone reform, let alone remedying the needs of the adult population.

In February 1978, some twenty years after the Robbins report, the DES opened a new phase of discussion with its document *Higher Education into the 1990s*. It was a pity that the problem was posed primarily in demographic terms, and that the calculations were based on planning assumptions that were soon overtaken by events and rendered obsolete. Already by March 1979 a follow-up report, *Future Trends in Higher Education*, had postponed the target figure of 560,000 full-time and sandwich students in Great Britain from 1981/82 to the following year, and indicated a likely fall in the Age Participation Rate (APR) of 18- to 21-year-old qualified applicants for admission. Later projections fell from the more expansionist assumptions in the documents of 18 per cent APR to as low as 12·6 per cent in 1982/83 (bringing the target figure of student numbers down to

531,000). There would still, however, be a 'hump' in the likely 18+ intake to higher education in the 1980s, followed by a slump in the 1990s. What to do?

Most of the analysis in the two DES reports was based on the assumption that the pattern of higher education would continue broadly on the existing lines, catering mainly for the 18+ school-leavers with two 'A' Levels or equivalent qualifications. There was, however, one innovation. Model E envisaged that social and economic requirements might bring about significant changes in the pattern and composition of the student body. 'There is also the possibility of taking positive steps as a matter of social policy to encourage participation by children of manual workers to approach more closely the level of participation by children of non-manual workers.' (The respective rates in 1974 were 5 per cent manual workers' children and 13 per cent professional workers' – if the manual workers' rate could be raised to 13 per cent by the 1980s some 48,000 extra places would be required.) Another possibility envisaged in the document was 'a systematic scheme for continuing education at an advanced level, or indeed at a non-advanced level'; more educational resources might also be devoted to those already in employment and more systematic opportunities be provided for recurrent education for mature students. (If the expansion rate of mature students realised in the decade to 1975/76 could be maintained, the number of entrants would rise by some 55,000 by 1985/86 (17,600 in universities, the rest in advanced further education courses).) A major lead from Government would be needed, with new financial incentives in the form of paid educational leave or an adequate grant system. 'This prospect needs to be viewed in the perspective of continuous social, economic and technological change, which may demand more emphasis on continued education, and may be accompanied by changes in the patterns of employment or unemployment' (*Higher Education into the 1990s*). There were gremlins at the bottom of the Department!

Not surprisingly, Model E was given strong Ministerial support in public speeches by Shirley Williams and by Gordon Oakes, the Minister of State. It attracted wide attention, and the responses to the document indicated a surprisingly favourable reception in the most unlikely quarters, including many universities. (Cynics were inclined to attribute this to growing fears of academic redundancy if radical steps were not taken to plug the demographic gap, rather than to any very genuine conversion to change on the merit of the case.)

Even so, *Future Trends in Higher Education* relegated the issues involved in Model E to its final three paragraphs, as suitable for long-term research and enquiry into funding arrangements, fee policy, student support and academic implications. Utopia was not just round the corner! Following the change of Government it receded rapidly. The emphasis switched to economy cuts and attempts to limit the prospective bulge in the traditional intake of 18 year olds. The momentum for social change was dissipated.

In its initial response to the DES documents, the Advisory Council for Adult and Continuing Education (a quango surprisingly allowed to continue for a further three years) based its support for the substantial changes of far-reaching social importance involved in Model E on principles of educational philosophy rather than on the use of fortuitous demographic factors related to the existing system. It stressed the urgent need for a transition from the front-end model based on full-time initial higher education for selected adolescents straight from school to 'an open-access model based upon the continuing or recurrent provision of full-time and part-time further and higher education for all who by virtue of ability, experience and motivation are able to benefit by it regardless of age'. This was a conscious and radical restatement of the Robbins principle, linked as that appeared to be to formal qualifications for entry through the existing system.

The main arguments for change advanced by the Council were the social and educational inequalities of opportunity resulting from the existing system, and the consequent waste of untapped talent among the children of manual workers; in the older generations it was magnified by the even greater inequalities of opportunity from which they had suffered in childhood and youth. We were far from being a meritocracy. 'It has long

been the experience of adult education, from the long-term
residential colleges and the WEA to the university extra-mural
departments and the Open University, that there are substantial
numbers of adult students lacking formal educational qualifications who have the capacity to benefit from higher education.'

Furthermore, it was argued, 'a significant proportion of
school leavers would positively benefit from a period of voluntary deferment of entry to higher education, to enable them to
mature, to acquire some experience of life, and to reflect on their
real motivation and academic interests.' Though the number of
mature entrants to universities has doubled in the last decade (to
8800 in 1975/76), and the mature entry to advanced further
education has trebled (to 12,500), the total remains pitiably small
as compared with that in other advanced countries such as
Sweden. 'At present we have no strategy or articulated policy of
recurrent education. But we accepted the principle at the
European Ministers of Education Conference at Stockholm in
1975' (Shirley Williams, Secretary of State for Education and
Science, Foundation Oration, Birkbeck College, 30 November
1977).

Acceptance of the principle of continuing education obviously
involves radical changes in the educational system as a whole,
including the schools and provision for non-advanced further
education. A full treatment of the necessary reforms in this
sector is beyond the scope of this chapter, which is primarily
concerned with the future of higher education. Increasing the
proportion of working-class children proceeding to higher
education does, however, imply the elimination at all stages of
systems of selection which preclude children of ability at any age
from proceeding with their education. It involves a system of
financial support which encourages young people to continue
their schooling beyond the compulsory school-leaving age,
namely a system of maintenance allowances at least comparable
with social security benefits and juvenile rates of pay for the 16
to 19 age range. We must put an end to the system whereby
youngsters benefit financially by leaving school for unemployment or dead-end jobs. *Origins & Destinations* shows that the
major fall-out of working-class boys occurs at the minimum

school-leaving age: 23·7 per cent of their sample proceeded to selective secondary schools, only 11·8 per cent to 'O' Levels and 2·8 per cent to 'A's, as compared with 71·9 per cent, 58·1 per cent and 26·9 per cent respectively for the service-class sample, resulting in 1·8 per cent reaching university as against 20·1 per cent. The key factor in diminishing this rate of drop-out would be an adequate and universal scheme of maintenance allowances for those staying on in full-time education after the statutory leaving age.

Following the Great Debate it is now recognised that changes are needed in the curriculum, and in the teaching and assessment methods of schools, to make them more relevant to the needs of society and the interests of the majority of the age-group concerned. There is need for 'a system of financial and academic credits which would relieve or remove the pressure to conform to any fixed pattern of immediate post-school education'. For those starting work, there should be 'a universal scheme of education and training opportunities for 16 to 18 year olds as envisaged in the consultative papers published by the Secretaries of State for Education and Science, and Employment and Industry in 1979' (see the ACACE responses to *Education & Training for 16–18 year-olds* and *A Better Start in Working Life*).

Both the Fisher Act at the end of the First World War, and the 1944 Act at the end of the Second, had provided for compulsory day release for the education of young people in the first years of their working lives, though these provisions were not implemented. If we are no longer prepared to envisage compulsion, we should at least insist on the mandatory right to day-release for all youngsters willing to proceed with either vocational courses or general education. This should be backed up by a well-developed advisory service capable of guiding the school-leaver through the bewildering variety of options on offer through further education, industrial training schemes, MSC programmes, and so on. The various agencies concerned also need to review their provision for the reinforcement of study skills and basic education designed to meet the learning needs of those who have parted company with school, often dissatisfied, disillusioned and discouraged by their experience.

In 1977/78 only 27·6 per cent of 16 to 18 year olds were in full-time education, and a further 13 per cent in non-advanced part-time courses, leaving 60 per cent out of contact with the education system at a vital period of their adolescence. Many of these will never return. What is required is an 'entitlement' to take up deferred educational rights at a later stage in life, for all those willing and able to benefit at any stage. At present, 40 per cent of the 16 to 18 age group, predominantly from the service and intermediate classes, receive free full-time education at the public expense, and over 20 per cent of the service class proceed to university with mandatory grants covering tuition and maintenance (admittedly with a parental income test) for at least a further three years. Is there any reason, in logic or justice, why those who do not benefit at the 'normal' age, but who are subsequently accepted for equivalent courses, should not be equally entitled to financial support? (The principle has in fact been accepted for degree and other 'designated' courses.) The cost of a universal five-year entitlement for all beyond the age of 16 might at first sight appear intimidating. However, it is much reduced if set against the alternative for many of receiving unemployment or other social security benefits, if an appropriate income test is applied, and if one makes a realistic assessment of the likely participation rate.

So far, I have been considering in broad outline some of the main changes required in the system prior to entry to higher education, if continuing education is to become a reality. I turn now to the equally radical reforms required in higher education itself, if (without lowering standards) it is to meet its share of such a system catering for the needs of 15 to 20 per cent of people at some stage or other of their lives. The major reforms required would involve changes in selection methods, in the system of fees and financial support, in the pattern of courses and teaching, in accommodation and equipment, and probably in administrative structures and control.

Selection methods

The present system of university selection and, to a large extent that of the polytechnics, colleges and institutions of higher education, is geared to the needs of 18+ school-leavers with the appropriate 'A' Levels as the main entry criterion. Whilst most institutions state that they have some provision for exceptional cases, the proportion of entry by those without the normal qualifications is small. (The figures often quoted for mature students in universities and polytechnics, totalling some 21,300 in 1975/76, include a majority possessing formal entry qualifications.) If there is to be a real attempt to recruit those with incomplete secondary education, far more will have to be done to develop appropriate preparatory courses and to give adequate recognition to other forms of credit, including recognition of relevant experience outside the academic walls. In 1979, an Educational Credit Transfer Feasibility Study (the Toyne report) estimated that about 15 per cent of applications and 11 per cent of admissions to university first-degree courses, and approximately 20 per cent of polytechnic admissions, were of students offering alternative qualifications. Only 6 per cent of university and polytechnic admissions in 1977/78 were granted advanced standing in respect of other qualifications – apart from the Open University which granted entry with advanced standing to over half its students (including those with other university qualifications). Apart from a need for greater flexibility in the recognition of credits, the Toyne report concluded that a national information service on credit possibilities, independent of any existing institutions, was urgently needed and would be technically feasible to set up.

The experience of established adult education bodies proves beyond doubt that there are substantial numbers of people without formal qualifications who are fully capable of benefiting from higher education, given the opportunity of taking appropriate preparatory courses. The long-term adult residential colleges (such as Ruskin and Coleg Harlech) have long experience in recruiting early school-leavers of mature years without formal qualifications of any kind, selecting them on the basis of essay work, curricula vitae, personal references and oral interview. Given appropriate tutorial help in 'tool subjects' (use of English, maths, statistics, and so on) the majority so selected prove themselves well capable of proceeding to university honours degrees at the end of four, or five years' full-time study. The colleges' problem has been to secure adequate credit for their courses from universities. Oxford University was the pioneer in giving 'advanced standing' (senior status, with exemption from the first year of a degree course) to Ruskin students with two-year diplomas, and a limited number of other universities have now followed suit. The majority, however, still insist on mature students retreading ground they have already covered, with consequent staleness and frustration, in the first year of a university course designed for immature school-leavers.

The performance of mature students in higher education compares very favourably with that of the school-leaver intake (see *Adult Students and Higher Education*, by H. A. Jones and K. E. Williams, ACACE, for a full study). A Warwick University survey in 1965/71 showed that mature students gained 5·1 per cent firsts, 40 per cent seconds and only 9·7 per cent thirds as compared with 5·3 per cent, 29 per cent, and 12·8 per cent for other students. In 1975 the Lancaster figures were 12 per cent firsts and 45 per cent upper seconds for mature students; 4 per cent firsts and 30 per cent II i's for other students. Ruskin students who have been admitted direct to post-graduate study have acquitted themselves with credit. Motivation, and relevant practical experience of life and work, often more than compensates for the lack of 'A' Level studies, which are notably uncertain predictors of subsequent academic performance.

NEW ROUTES TO HIGHER EDUCATION

In recent years, a number of new types of preparatory courses and alternative and more flexible routes to higher education have begun to develop, with promising results. Although the original intentions of the DES was to confine the two-year Dip HE to entrants with two 'A' Levels, and only reluctant recognition was given to courses like that at the North East London Polytechnic with a high percentage of admissions given to those without formal qualifications, light is now dawning. A recent survey shows an increasing proportion of candidates (78 per cent of the 1979 entry) over 21, and that 61 per cent of the entry did not possess the conventional two 'A's. 'This in itself could be taken as ample justification for the Dip HE movement if such opening of access [to degree courses] could not have been brought about in any other way' (John Davidson, Secretary of ACID – Association of Colleges Implementing Dip HE Programmes). The Dip HE might well have won wider recognition and made a greater impact if it had not, mistakenly in my view, sought and been accorded full equivalence with degree-level work. Most mature students and unqualified students in the 16 to 19 range need at least a year's foundation study before achieving effective higher education standards. The 'Ruskin model' of a two-year diploma course with open access without formal qualifications, claiming only the equivalence of one year's degree level study, provides a valuable and legitimate bridging course for those without sixth-form training. Parallel types of course, if they could be made available throughout the country, either full-time or part-time, with day or block release for those in employment, and an adequate system of student financial support, would meet a real need. Only a minority of mature students are in a position to give up their jobs and leave their families for the length of time involved in a full-time residential course.

The need is evident from the success of a number of experiments. Some five years ago Lancaster University and Preston Polytechnic agreed to co-operate with Nelson and Colne and other local institutions of further education in pioneering an 'Open College' in East Lancashire. It employed modular course units, informal teaching methods and continuous assessment, and was designed to cater for mature students without formal qualifications, a number of whom go on to higher education. The model is now being imitated elsewhere. The Liverpool University Institute of Extension Studies and the Workers' Educational Association provide a 'Second Chance to Learn' in the form of a twenty-week social studies course for working-class adults, which can lead on to a degree course. In 1971 Hatfield Polytechnic developed a 'New Opportunities for Women' course which has led to preparatory and degree courses on a part-time day basis. Jones and Williams quote other examples, which are proliferating. They all intensify the need for a proper system of credit transfer.

Preparatory and bridging courses of this type might well provide an exciting innovatory role for some of the colleges and institutions of higher education which have yet to find a satisfying role. As it stands, the Dip HE is in danger of being regarded as a soft option without adequate recognition, and the colleges catering for it may well remain the poor relations of the higher education system and find themselves increasingly vulnerable in an era of retrenchment and falling demand.

Fees and financial support

The fortunate favoured 14 per cent who secure places in designated courses of higher education benefit from mandatory grants covering their fees and maintenance during full-time degree and other courses. In the case of mature students, their grants include provision for dependants, a 'two homes' allowance, and some recognition of their previous level of earnings in a supplementary grant. Austere though the scales may be, they provide probably the most adequate system of student support according to need in the world. Visitors from Scandinavia, or from the 'socialist countries' of Eastern Europe, blink with amazement when they learn the facts. Gerry Fowler, in his brief sojourn as Minister of State at the DES, managed to extend the same system to students at long-term adult residential colleges. Once accepted, a determined student is not precluded from taking up a place on financial grounds, and if he can secure vacation employment will not suffer serious loss of annual income as compared with average full-time manual earnings. There are anomalies which need rectifying, but the basic provision is adequate. What needs to be done is to extend the mandatory system as rapidly as is practicable to part-time courses of higher education, and to sub-degree courses of further education, including preparatory courses like those described above. The system of discretionary grants applied to these proved seriously inadequate even before it was exposed to the economy cuts introduced in 1979, which induced some

LEAs to suspend it. What logic or justice can there be in granting 18-year-old school-leavers proceeding to degree courses in any subject – say, classics – more favourable treatment than their contemporaries or seniors taking further education courses which may be far more relevant to the needs of society, and more cost-effective? In socio-economic terms, the distinction between mandatory and discretionary awards accentuates the privilege of the service classes whose children absorb the majority of designated places, privilege which would be further magnified if the pressure from the National Union of Students succeeded in reducing or abolishing the parental income test.

The grant system, as well as the inadequate weighting given in funding and staffing arrangements, inhibits the development of part-time courses for which students do not qualify for mandatory awards. The development of part-time courses on an adequate scale also depends, for those in employment, on introducing a comprehensive system of educational leave. The British Government has ratified ILO Convention 140 on Paid Educational Leave, providing for a policy designed to promote the granting of PEL for 'training at any level', for general, social and civic education, and for trade union education. The Committee of Experts who paved the way for this Convention regarded PEL as a new social right. So far, the only statutory provision for PEL in this country is for short courses of training for trade union representatives under the Employment Protection Act. At degree level (undergraduate and post-graduate) it is estimated that some 2500 students, one-third of them part-time, were recipients of PEL in 1976/77. It is a delicate matter for political decision as to how far and for what type of courses employers should be expected to pay. Paid educational leave needs to be supplemented by provisions for unpaid leave with resinstatement and superannuation rights and so on, and a grants system giving the necessary financial assistance and support to the students, subject to an appropriate income scale for those in part-time employment.

To what extent should the individual student (or his family) be expected to contribute towards the cost of his or her higher education? I have argued above that those leaving school at 16 should be entitled to the equivalent of the education benefits received by the fortunate 14 per cent who stay on to 18 and proceed to an institution of higher education for the normal three-year first degree. (A minority, such as medical or law students, live even longer at the public expense, but no doubt make part restitution subsequently through taxation on their resulting incomes!) Once this entitlement is exhausted, people might earn further educational rights by periods in employment, as in France and Italy and some other countries. It would be a matter for political decision as to what extent the public educational system should subsidise the cost of courses, whether students should be expected to pay full tuition costs or full economic costs, and what concessions should be made according to need. These arguments are only too familiar in the current controversy on the appropriate level of fees for adult education being conducted in the blizzard of cuts in public expenditure, which began in 1979 under the malign influence of Milton Friedman and his acolytes in government circles.

If, however, we are serious in seeking to develop continuing education, we must seek to introduce a comprehensive system of financial support according to need, for all those willing and selected to participate, at all levels, irrespective of age. In such a system, paid and unpaid educational leave and a mandatory grant structure both have a part to play. Positive discrimination for the educationally underprivileged, and income scales applied to the economically overprivileged in relation to student contributions, are both legitimate and practical.

CHANGES IN COURSE PATTERNS

There has been much discussion in recent years about the relevance of the school curriculum, and of the pattern of courses in further and higher education, to the needs of industry and society in an age of rapidly increasing technological change. This ranges from fundamental philosophical and sociological questions down to detailed problems affecting the syllabus and structure of available courses. Should the aim of education be egalitarian or meritocratic? Is its role the transmission of a common accepted culture, or a form of class or generation control? Is part of the reason for working-class fall-out due not to the inequalities of opportunity but rather to resistance to the prevailing cultural ethos in academic institutions? How far can, or should, education seek to generate mobility in an unequal society? At another level of discussion, is the assumption that full-time initial education – without a break – through the years of adolescence, without experience of life or work, is the ideal model, justified in terms of psychology or learning theory? If it is so for music or mathematics, does the same apply to social studies or applied technology or science? In some subjects at least, might not better results have been achieved by the extension of universal part-time day release than by the raising of the compulsory school-leaving age? Might not a gap between school and higher education offset the break in rhythm by an increase in motivation, greater maturity of judgement and analysis, a capacity to relate theory to practical experience? There is at least sufficient validity in these questions to cause us to challenge and regret the prevailing emphasis on initial full-time education and the failure to expand part-time higher education.

The number of university part-time students taking under-graduate courses declined from about 5000 in 1970/71 to 4000 in 1978/79, whilst full-timers rose from 228,000 to over 288,000. In advanced further education, part-timers increased from 110,000 to 148,000 (34 per cent) whilst full-timers increased from 84,800 to 148,000 (74 per cent; full-time and sandwich students, not including teacher training; DES figures). We need more Birkbeck and Goldsmiths Colleges, and more out-reach facilities for mature men and women students, spread over the whole range of higher education courses. Day-release, block release, module courses, all have their advocates. The interesting experiments in independent study and individual learning at Lancaster University, the North East London Polytechnic and elsewhere surely have a wider application (K. Percy and P. Ramsden, *Independent Study*). The Open University, in combi-nation with a number of other bodies, has demonstrated the possibilities of individual 'study at a distance', combining television and radio with correspondence courses and limited face-to-face instruction in summer schools and meetings with counsellors and tutors. Recent developments in communications offer extended possibilities for access to teaching materials at steadily reducing costs.

The three-year degree course will no doubt remain the basic pattern for undergraduate work in higher education, but it needs complementing by other and more flexible structures. The Dip HE and other diploma courses, post-experience courses of varying lengths, the associate student programme of the Open University, are examples of responses to and awareness of the different needs for higher education facilities. Dr Parkes, Chairman of the UGC, made this point forcibly in evidence to the Select Committee:

> We are going to have an increasing demand for the through-life education of people, particularly in the specialist disciplines. It will no longer be true that the general education given at the age of twenty-one is going to see a person in a particular profession or industry . . . to retiring age. They are already coming back . . . already in terms of actual bodies, more people walk over the doorsteps of universities to receive some form of education – it may be a three-month short course or it may be part-time over a number of years – than there are in the undergraduate and postgraduate full-time student group, and this number is growing. We think that it is about ten per cent of the universities' total effort at the moment, but if the 18–21 year old age group declines, and demand for this increases, it will become an increasing proportion of the work at universities. (Funding and Organisation of Higher Education; Minutes of Evidence 23 January 1980.)

The pace of change in technology has profound implications for general as well as vocational education, in a period in which the professional and the average man may well be faced with demands for changing skills, with periods of unemployment, with increased leisure time, on a scale not previously anticipated. Some of the professional bodies are well aware of this – the Royal Institute of British Architects, for example, has set up a Professional Development Working Group which is highly critical of the slow response of higher education to the needs of continuing education.

Most universities and polytechnics have yet to realise their potential in the field of continuing education. There are several reasons for this. First, their priorities still lie with their undergraduate and post-graduate courses. Second, demand from the professions tends to be ephemeral, focused on the immediate problems of the industry concerned. Third, the financial mechanisms in both sectors do not make allowance for the special difficulties, both academic and administrative, inherent in offering 'advanced' educational services to practitioners. Finally, the present cutback in education is seen by most institutions to militate still further against starting up new initiatives.

There are notable exceptions, largely due to personal enthusiasm or connections, but:

Our conclusion must be that polytechnics and universities could and would do more, even under the present difficult circumstances, if demand was more certain and directorates and heads of departments could be convinced of the advantages to them. At the same time both the UGC and the DES must be persuaded to modify some of their blanket constraints. ('Continuing Professional Development', October 1979.)

Similarly, the Finniston report on the 'Continuing Formation' of engineers recommends statutory paid study leave for registered engineers and the establishment of regional engineering centres with the participation of universities and polytechnics for this purpose. As ACACE said in its response to Finniston, paid study leave should be implemented widely throughout large sections of the country's workforce, and in this context the report's argument should be seen as relevant to most of the employees and employers in Britain's manufacturing and service industries.

In France, for example, employers are obliged to spend the equivalent of two per cent of their annual payroll on continuing formation provision and all employees have a statutory right to paid leave for the purpose of study; some German Länder have adopted similar 'right of release' laws, and we understand that the European Commission is considering an EEC Directive to the same effect (*Engineering Our Future*).

Physical and teaching resources

Continuing education demands a very different approach from that which led to the remote and cloistered campuses of the new universities designed in the post-Robbins era. Part-time courses and out-reach work related to industry and the community involve localised centres within reach of busy people and in close contact with the centres of industrial and social life. Most mature students have families, who do not adapt easily to the monastic life of residential institutions. Traditional adult education has long recognised the importance of extra-mural work, and this now needs to be extended through higher education as a whole. This is recognised in the changing role of many university extra-mural departments, now being increasingly regarded as agencies of liaison between the university as a whole and the outside world, with increased emphasis on the provision of post-experience courses for a wide range of professional groups.

A further role for university adult education lies in the expansion of provision for training tutors. Continuing education demands teaching techniques very different from the formal lecture method so beloved by many university dons. It implies a two-way process of interaction between academics and mature and experienced students who have much to contribute, and who expect to participate both in the development of their courses and in the discussion of their subjects.

A STRUCTURE FOR CONTINUING EDUCATION?

What we need, then, is the development of a comprehensive

system of higher education, linked with schools and further and adult education, responding to the needs of the community and catering for all those requiring 'advanced' education at whatever stage of their life and careers. The student population should be recruited on the basis of motivation, experience and potential, from all sections of society, irrespective of age.

Is there any prospect of our present system of higher education – consisting as it does of largely self-governing universities financed through the UGC, and polytechnics and institutions of higher education subject to local authority control – being able to adjust itself in time to meet the challenge of continuing education? Or do we need a national plan establishing priorities and co-ordinating the response to them of higher education as a whole, as argued forcibly by Peter Scott, the editor of the *Times Higher Education Supplement*, in a recent Fabian tract (*What Future for Higher Education?*). He advocates a simplified two-tier system, the extension of the university sector to include most of the polytechnics, and the creation of a network of feeder institutions in the form of local colleges which would be the main vehicles of continuing education 'bringing higher education closer to the community and offering courses in less formal and perhaps less intense forms', with a national system of academic credit transfer between the tiers. These 'open colleges' would be student-centred and widely dispersed. Their nucleus would be in the existing institutions of further and higher education. Richard Hoggart, chairman of ACACE, has likewise called for a chain of local community colleges and for 'closer links between universities and other parts of the education system as a seamless fabric of education provision for all ages (*After Expansion: A Time for Diversity*, ACACE, 1979). NATFHE advocates a National Council for Further and Higher Education for post-school education as a whole including the university sector (*Higher Education: A Policy Statement*, NATFHE, 1978).

No doubt the House of Commons Select Committee, with Christopher Price in the chair, will come up with an interesting answer to these questions, having heard the views of all the interested parties, from the DES and the UGC to ACACE and the NUS. A number of witnesses appearing before them have shown a refreshing interest in and awareness of the need for continuing education.

Whatever the structure of higher education, binary or unitary, that emerges, the essential point is that the component institutions should understand and operate the basic principles of continuing education, and should provide access to those capable of benefiting from their courses irrespective of age and formal qualifications, and that there should be an adequate system of student financial support covering both full-time and part-time courses at all levels, according to need. The basis for this already exists in the principle that all those accepted for full-time degree courses should be eligible for mandatory grants, and this needs extending to part-time degrees and to other types of course.

The publication of *Higher Education into the 1990s*, the subsequent discussion, and the current controversies over the education cuts, have revealed the lack of any national consensus on the role of higher education in society or any coherent national policy for its development. The post-Robbins expansion, and the development of the binary system, has done little to open the doors to a wider section of society. The academic drift of a hierarchic system has done little to produce a more comprehensive and flexible approach to the changing needs. At government level, though lip-service is paid to the principles of continuing education and wider access there is no coherent strategy for the development of either. Model E, which attracted wide interest and support, seems likely to be pigeonholed. What is needed is a positive lead from the top, a challenge to entrenched academic attitudes, and a plan embracing institutional reform combined with a comprehensive system of student financial support designed to meet the needs of the many and not simply of the few. 'Educationally we are still two nations' (Russell), and we are likely to remain so until schools and further and higher education are integrated to provide for the needs of the whole population in a comprehensive system of continuing education.

2

A new approach

STEPHEN BRAGG

Inverting the system

INTRODUCTION

Despite the tremendous growth of higher education in the last forty years we have still retained, for the great majority of students, the standard British three-year honours degree. The course is normally started immediately after leaving school, and most students expect to leave home to follow it. Teaching methods are labour-intensive. The institution and the student are heavily subsidised by the State. Apart from the Cambridge suggestion of a system providing two years for all students plus two more years for a few, and the proposal in the 1972 White Paper for the two-year Dip HE for some students, there seem to have been few suggestions that this nine-term course for the school leaver should be changed. For example, the paper *Higher Education into the 1990s*, published in 1978 by the Department of Education and Science, was almost entirely taken up by a discussion on how many school-leavers were likely to qualify for such courses and what arrangements should be made to accommodate them. No attempt was there made to discuss whether this scheme of studies was still suited to the needs of today, or indeed whether there were other uses to which the country's resource of scholarship should be put.

Yet expansion is threatening to burst the system at its seams. Staff:student ratios weaken as costs per student are reduced. Some courses are duplicated because of lack of co-ordination: others are not started because of lack of funds. New capital expenditure is severely restricted and un-replaced equipment becomes obsolete. It is not realistic to imagine that we will ever have the resources to provide for twenty per cent of the population the very expensive kind of education we once provided for one per cent. This is especially true when we consider the very poor provision currently made for the education and training of young people who do not go on to higher education. Nor is it evident that the type of education provided for one per cent of the population when Britain ruled a large Empire is necessarily appropriate for one fifth of the population of an independent island. Small changes, therefore, will not be enough. A complete reappraisal is needed.

An attempt is made here to tackle the problem, not by extrapolating the trends of today but by starting at what one would like to happen and then working back. A system of higher education, and of universities in particular, is postulated which might be appropriate to the 1990s and which might also avoid some of the difficulties and uncertainties of present arrangements.

In the system proposed, institutions of higher education – that is their staff, equipment and buildings – are considered as a national Resource of scholarship. Stability is essential for the well-being of this Resource, but its size is limited by the availability of people and materials. Consideration of the Resource itself may be separated from consideration of the use to which it is put; and alternatives to the three-year honours degree are suggested. A more logical method of financing the system and of determining tuition fees is then recommended. The internal government and external co-ordination of institutions is discussed as is the role of an enlarged Higher Education Grants Committee. Finally, some changes in the conditions of service of academics are suggested.

Some of the proposals are more radical than others. Some could be adopted with little change to current arrangements. Some may be condemned out of hand as *dirigiste*: that is, they do not accept that university staff and students should have unlimited freedom and funds to do what they like. Those who read more carefully, however, will find an attempt to protect scholarship while simultaneously satisfying basic social accountability. Academics must be free to publish or teach in their own way and to follow the truth where it leads, but universities can hardly ask for nearly a pound a week from every wage earner in the country without expecting some strings to be attached. Most of the proposals stand by themselves, so perhaps some could be agreed quickly while others were debated and modified. Publication of the arguments will have served its main purpose if such debate is stimulated.

Although I must take personal responsibility for all the views expressed, many of them have been formed after discussion with helpful colleagues. I am particularly grateful to Professor Lord Vaizey for some trenchant comments on the original text.

THE HIGHER EDUCATION SYSTEM AS A RESOURCE

The objectives of the higher education system may be put simply as:

A. The preservation and enhancement of scholarship and critical standards.
B. Education, mostly but not entirely of the young, by exposure to scholarship.
C. Transmission and dissemination of knowledge and techniques, including vocational training in certain professions.

These are the aims of some fifty universities, thirty polytechnics and sixty-five colleges and institutes of higher education. One way of looking at this array of institutions and the ways of using them is to make a clear distinction between two separate elements of the system.

The first, which one might call the basic *Resource*, is the fixed element. It consists of the human resources, represented by the academic and support staff, and the physical resources, represented by equipment and buildings. Although a capital resource in the sense of being fixed assets, both buildings and staff involve continuing costs. Buildings and equipment need maintenance and replacement or major modification when they become obsolete. Staff need, at the very least, their basic salaries and wages to be paid. In fact most of the total recurrent expenditure in an institution comes from the provision of the basic resource, before its use is ever considered. This expenditure is stable, too, in the sense that (inflation apart) it can be quite accurately predicted for some time ahead.

One might call the second element the actual *Use*. It represents the work of education, training, and research which the institutions are actually called on to perform. The associated running costs include all supplies and consumables, for example oil, electricity, water, paper, test-tubes, chemicals, films, travel, hospitality, telephones. The list includes nearly all the items that have to be ordered or could theoretically not be ordered. Indeed the distinction might be that the recurrent costs of the basic Resource are those that would be incurred if the whole institution was put on stand-by, with the staff sent home on full pay and the buildings fully maintained. All other costs are those of actual use. Even then the lines are a bit difficult to draw exactly: the first copy of a book in the library may be part of the resource cost, but the cost of duplicates might be attributed to use.

In nearly all discussions about the British higher education system it is presumed that the size of the Resource should be proportional to a particular Use, which is the education of those school leavers with two 'A' Levels who want to take a traditional degree course based on three years full-time study at a staff:student ratio of about 1:10. The arguments of the 1972 White Paper followed these lines, and so did the extrapolations in *Higher Education into the 1990s*. It is, however, possible to look at the position from the opposite side. The question is then, 'given a total Resource, how should we use it?' rather than, 'given a Use, what resources should be provided?'. I believe that in higher education there are sound reasons for preferring to ask the question in the first way.

One reason is found in the inertia of the system, using this noun in a realistic, not a pejorative sense. A Resource of a given size exists in the form of the present institutions and their staff, and is currently employed on activities such as undergraduate courses and research programmes which have a life cycle of at least three or four years. It simply is not possible to make rapid changes efficiently. Certainly the Government may make long-term estimates of likely Use as one of several factors which determine how big the Resource should be. But the resulting changes ought to be slow, deliberate and long-term.

A second reason is that the quality of the Resource is inevitably linked with its size. By definition, higher education requires a relatively high intellectual standard and the supply of staff of the highest calibre is limited. It has been said, for example, that only one person in a million has the capacity to be a physicist of the front rank. So the possible size of the Resource is limited by the quality required.

A third reason is that by fixing the size of the Resource first, attention may be concentrated on finding the best way of using it. If the Resource is assumed limitless, those responsible spend their time justifying expansion rather than eliminating functions that have become unimportant. Cash limits were introduced in government departments with the same objective of concentrating attention on priorities.

Finally, the Government has to consider the need for highly intelligent people in other sectors. If too many work full-time in institutes of higher education then industry, commerce and the services may be starved. Conversely a certain proportion of a country's intellect must always be reserved for the preservation, refinement and transmission of knowledge.

Now the preservation of scholarship and standards requires stability. The continuous study needed to reach the boundaries of a subject and to make a significant contribution to their extension requires concentrated effort for at least three years and perhaps as much as twenty. Such concentration is impossible if there is doubt about the short-term future.

Up until 1972 this stability was provided for universities by the quinquennial plan. Almost alone among government-funded institutions, the universities were given a guaranteed allocation of money for five years at a time. The system had certain disadvantages: the planning exercise took a lot of effort; the plan might not be agreed by the time the quinquennium started so that little could be achieved in the first year; and the final year tended to be one of consolidation rather than progress. But during a period when the rate of inflation was much lower than that of expansion the system made possible an orderly development in response to national needs.

Since 1973 the combination of high rates of inflation and a very much smaller increase in real resources has made the system unworkable. Even the return in 1978 to a three-year rolling forecast contained uncertainties that were much larger than the changes proposed between one year and the next. In 1979 the forecast was abandoned and the final recurrent grant for 1979/80 was not determined until most of the year had already passed. In fact it seems clear that long-term planning in the financial sense is no longer possible. It is meaningless for the DES to announce the money that will be available to universities five years in advance if no one knows what that money will buy. It is equally meaningless for the Government to make a plan for five years ahead and then make another one the following year: those are *not* plans. In fact the length of time for which a credible plan can be made is no longer than the time for which it is expected that the plan will be held to. Experience over the last five years has shown that the chance of any government declaring five years in advance the money to be allocated to universities, promising that the sums will be completely compensated for inflation, and then keeping to their promises, is so small as to be discounted. Once it is accepted that there may be deviations of one or two per cent then, since these amounts are significant compared with the total disposable resources of the university, the whole plan is in ruins. So a completely new approach is necessary.

It would be possible to provide this approach by quinquennial planning of the size of the Resource primarily in terms of staff, not money, with a due allowance for buildings and equipment which will be discussed later. That is, the Government, acting on the advice of the University Grants Committee (UGC), could decide the total complement of staff (academic plus support) that it was prepared to finance over the quinquennium. Since it is the Government itself which negotiates the salary levels on an annual basis at present, it would still control the total bill. Indeed the outcome for the universities themselves would be little different from the present system, which has produced a virtual standstill in academic staff numbers over the last three years. But all the effort wasted in abortive planning

could have been avoided, and the stability required for scholarly
pursuits achieved, if the universities had been told at the outset
that their establishments were fixed for the next five years.
Similarly the traumas of university finance committees battling
with budgets in which the imposed cash limits did not cover
commitments to staff whose rates of pay were outside their
control, and who could not be dismissed but must be paid
nationally agreed rates, might become a thing of the past.

What might happen is this: at the beginning of the quinquennium universities would put in their bids, based on current
activities and possible developments, for certain complements of
academic and support staff, and for certain levels of expenditure
on the maintenance and replacement of equipment and buildings. The UGC would no doubt establish norms on matters
such as the support:academic staff ratios and equipment costs in
different disciplines, the minimum number of staff needed for a
department or group, and the maintenance and replacement cost
of buildings. After the usual consultation the Committee would
advise the Government on the appropriate size of the total basic
university Resource for the coming quinquennium. The Government would balance the various national needs, and decide
on the total allocation. Each university would be informed of its
proposed complement for the quinquennium. This basic complement could always be increased for customer–contractor
work, or by government action if additions were needed for
specific programmes. National salary negotiations would continue as they do at the moment and full supplements for any
salary changes would be automatic.

The quinquennial plan could, of course, envisage a run-down
in staff if it was part of the Government's plan that the
redeployment of some highly intelligent people into other
sectors of the economy should be encouraged. This would not
be the casual result of inability to make sound financial plans but
a calculated arrangement, accepting that redundancy in one
sector was necessary to provide expansion in another. It is not
satisfactory to use normal retirements as a method of adjustment
of staff numbers, since this method skews the age distribution,
preventing normal recruitment of young staff, and leading to

stagnation. Early retirement, which means in effect the enforced unemployment of experienced members of the population, is hardly a sensible arrangement either.

The quinquennium could roll, in the sense that the Government could guarantee a particular minimum complement five years ahead and perhaps increase it nearer the time. But institutions would not be asked to prepare long-term plans more often than once in five years.

The actual basic grant would be based on the average salaries of academic and support staff. Universities would be free to allocate actual posts within the total according to local circumstances; and of course they would be allowed to deploy any savings as they thought fit. It is always superficially attractive to civil servants to apply the principle of Morton's fork (if you were able to save you obviously had too large an allocation and can be cut; if you did not save you were obviously extravagant and can be squeezed), but it is a sure recipe for waste. If people know that any savings they make are going to be clawed back, they make certain that they spend their full allocation, whether they need it or not. But if people know that savings can be kept and deployed towards improvements in quality or new developments they will have every incentive to spend wisely.

The present practice of allocating capital grants to particular institutions for particular buildings does not seem to work any longer in the real interests of the universities or the Government. Considerable central direction may have been necessary during a period of expansion. The establishment of norms meant that provision for different universities could be kept roughly equivalent. But if we are now reaching a period of comparative stability in size of institution, maintenance and replacement are far more important than new construction. If the universities were run on normal business principles, depreciation would be accepted as a proper charge. It has been one of the major faults of the present system that the tremendous emphasis on reducing the first cost has produced buildings that are expensive to maintain. The system has also tended to provide purpose-built and inflexible buildings at the same time that money for modifications and other minor works was severely restricted.

There is a strong argument that in a stable system there should be *no* separate capital grants. The recurrent government grant should include an element for depreciation which universities would be free to use for non-salary purposes. Any capital buildings they required would be paid for out of accumulated savings. This would be really cost-effective in the long run, since modifications for which the costs must be found internally are tightly controlled by those who really understand the local situation: the art of economy is a more useful one than the art of pleading a good cause, and ought to be preferentially encouraged. Such arrangements would of course cut across present methods of government finance. It would therefore be necessary to accept them as part of a special and perhaps anomalous scheme until they could be proved in practice.

Nevertheless, a system in which the Government controls overall manpower totals, and buildings are treated as part of the recurrent expense, is really in tune with the facts of life. The staff of an institution are its most expensive asset and it is reasonable for the Government to be interested in how they are deployed. Buildings are more easily modified and represent a much smaller fraction of the total university Resource. Surely it is an anachronism that buildings and plant are treated as if they should control the whole development of the university system.

To take a practical example, the total historic cost of buildings in Brunel University is about 1·5 times the present annual turnover. Since building costs have been inflated by a factor of nearly 2 since the buildings were erected the true ratio is about 3·0. So if the buildings last sixty years on average it would not be unreasonable to assume a depreciation of about five per cent of total income. Minor works, modifications and basic maintenance should account for a similar figure. The present allowance of only two and a half per cent for minor works is certainly inadequate in practice to pay for all the changes that need to be made to accommodate developments within a constant size during a steady-state period. The capital allowance for the whole university system of about one per cent of the recurrent grant is of course ludicrous and can only be excused as a panic measure to preserve recurrent income at a time of severe cuts in total expenditure. A total allowance of the order of ten per cent of the budget for buildings would therefore seem reasonable.

Similar figures can be derived for equipment. The total purchase cost of equipment in use at Brunel is comparable to about one year's income. If we assume an average life of little over ten years the cost of maintenance and replacement would again be ten per cent of turnover. So we conclude that in a technological university about twenty per cent of the cost of the basic Resource should be buildings and equipment, the other eighty per cent covering salaries and wages.

The argument has been based on the fact that the size of the Resource is controlled by the people and equipment made available, or which could and should eventually be made available. It is proper that the Government should control this size as part of an overall plan and not as they do at present through continual financial adjustments. But the uses to which the Resource can be put – how many students educated, how many trained or what research conducted – is a discussion which can be carried on quite separately when the size of the Resource has been determined: they may not directly control the size of the Resource itself, which is affected by so many other factors.

Once the size of the basic Resource has been determined the actual Use to which it is put determines its additional running costs. The immediate costs of running a three-year undergraduate course or a short course for industrialists or conducting research may be quite different even if they use the same basic Resource of staff, buildings and plant. It is therefore logical that these marginal costs should be paid by or for the users in the form of tuition fees, research grants or contracts. How they can be decided and by whom paid are questions covered in later sections. But first it is necessary to consider how the quality of the Resource is to be maintained.

PRESERVATION OF THE RESOURCE

Nothing was said in the preceding section about student numbers. This is because we started by regarding the universities as a national Resource of scholarship, whose size was determined partly by historical development, partly by the number of people possessed of the high intellectual talent required of academics, and partly by the overall balance of society's needs or desires for research, scholarship, education and training as compared with immediate material development, social services or other benefits. Having found this balance and provided a Resource from central funds, how should it be used?

There are four principal ways in which the Resource is used. The first is in providing students with a general education, by which is meant helping the general intellectual development of individuals by exposing them to scholarship and teaching them to learn and criticise. The second is the provision to students of training for particular vocations or professions which require intellectual effort: medicine and law being the classic examples. The third is the development of knowledge and understanding by research and scholarship of a fundamental nature, often without an immediate application in view. Finally, the Resource may be used by government or industry to assist with specific investigations of an ad hoc nature either by giving advice or by conducting tactical research.

In this section the steps that must be taken to preserve scholarship are first discussed and it is suggested that certain resources must be reserved for this, even though the element may be less in proportion to the total than was the case when the total Resource was smaller. It will then be argued that, once this element has been secured, the Government, which provides the funds, may quite legitimately ask the universities to take more students, at lower unit costs, than they have in the past, while accepting that their experience as students may as a result be different. The universities could respond to this by accepting all students for two years and only allowing a small number to proceed further on a full-length honours course. As an alternative, particularly suitable to well-motivated students, they could consciously redesign courses for weaker staff:student ratios, as has been done by the Open University. Both possibilities are explored and suggestions are made as to how they might co-exist.

The preservation of standards requires stability, as we have already discussed. The acquisition and refinement of knowledge requires that academics have sufficient time to pursue their own research work and scholarship, whether this is funded through the institution itself, by research council grants or by contracts from government departments or from industry. It also requires that some of the institution's resources be used to train the next generation of scholars. The universities themselves must be satisfied that standards are preserved: under the present arrangements, where they are being asked to accept more and more students at steadily weakening staff:student ratios, it is at least arguable that the quality is falling below what might be achieved, even though each generation of students seems to have gone further than its predecessors. This may account in part for the largely defensive attitude adopted so frequently by university spokesmen.

When the Vice-Chancellors' Committee sponsored an examination of how academics used their time, nearly ten years ago, it was found that about twenty-five per cent was spent on research or what one might loosely term 'external professional activities'. Since then the universities have expanded considerably and it seems likely that the proportion has fallen. For if 240,000 students are taught at a student:staff ratio of 8:1, and staff spend twenty-five per cent of their time on research and allied activities, the total effort on research is 7500 man years per year. When the student total has expanded to 297,000 students at a student:staff ratio of 9:1, and there has been no change in basic teaching methods, the time required for teaching has risen to 28,000 man years per year leaving only 5000 for research. That is, the proportion of their time available to individuals for their research has gone down to only fifteen per cent.

In deciding what the proportion ought to be there are a number of points to consider. The first is, of course, that there is a basic minimum of fundamental research which should be done irrespective of the total size of the universities. The disinterested pursuit of truth for its own sake is an essential activity in any civilisation. A limited amount of such work must be done in any country to preserve its own stock of knowledge and to alert its members to developments abroad. There are, however, two upper limits on the amount of research. The first is that the number of people competent to conduct worthwhile fundamental research may not be large. If it really requires the highest intellect, then that capacity may only be possessed by a few. Others may not have the conceptual capacity required, just as the majority of the population are incapable of running a mile in four minutes, however hard they train. No stigma should attach to such limitations: it is just that every individual has different abilities and different talents.

The second point is that there must be a proper balance between the intellectual power dedicated to research and that dedicated to practical application. If the whole population were to spend all its time quarrying for new knowledge and understanding, no one would be left to support them. Research has been likened to seed corn, which must be preserved for future generations. But those generations will never come into being unless most of the available corn is used for bread – a society which kept all its corn for seed would starve before the next harvest.

Research in universities has also been justified by its effect on teachers, in keeping them fresh and masters of their subject. Indeed as universities have expanded it has been generally claimed that it was essential to preserve the same opportunities for each individual academic to follow his own line of research or scholarship as there were when the universities were much smaller. Similar claims are now being made for other sectors of education. However, as will be discussed in a later section, there are other possible ways of maintaining intellectual freshness, such as exposing oneself to a new discipline, or working on consultancies or contracts. It is an observed fact that many excellent and successful teachers make their contribution by finding new methods of presenting known truths. The second law of thermodynamics, for example, is not new, nor is the concept of entropy; yet real understanding is needed to help the uninitiated comprehend these difficult ideas, which are absolutely fundamental to science. Even those teachers who can conduct research may go through cycles, at some times being productive, at others becoming stale and needing to learn a new discipline before again starting a fresh line of investigation.

One suspects then that a nationally-agreed average figure for effort deployed on pure scholarship would be of the order of fifteen to twenty per cent of the total Resource, if that total were of its present size. But whatever it was, it would be essential in any new arrangement that there was a definite indication of the proportion of the Use that should be dedicated to basic research and scholarship. This would be independent of other uses, such as the teaching of a given number of undergraduate students, and it would be recognised that if the latter were increased the research capacity could not be surreptitiously raided to provide extra teaching capacity.

We might find when this indication has been made that it does not provide for every academic to spend as much time on basic, undirected research as he would have done when universities were one-fifth their present size. We might even find that the average time available was less than an individual could sensibly be allocated if his research was to be effective. But as was argued above, and will be argued again later, not every academic may need the opportunity for research every year. It might be considered a reduction in academic privilege to reduce the time available to an individual academic for research. But it must be recognised that we simply are not rich enough to continue to allow the same degree of privilege automatically to an ever-increasing proportion of the population. By the same token a permanent appointment to a Research Fellowship is likely to become rarer. The total resources available for research are limited and it is unlikely that a high proportion of those available would be offered to certain individuals, leaving much less for others. An arrangement in which holders of ten teaching posts spent an average twenty per cent of their time on research would seem preferable to one in which there was one permanent research post and nine teachers who could only spend an average eleven per cent of their time on their research, though the total teaching and research man hours are the same in both arrangements.

Finally, we should consider the research activity in so far as it affects students directly. Champions of the PhD degree have always argued that it has educational value and that, even when the universities expanded, every good student should be encouraged to proceed immediately to further study. It may be that if resources were infinite, and everyone had unlimited time to spend before embarking on a career, an extra three or four years could usefully be spent in this way. But resources are limited and there is little evidence to suggest that providing that particular experience for that particular period at that particular time is helpful for those destined for careers other than research. Indeed, as employers outside academe have said over and over again (consider for instance the evidence to the Doxey and Swann committees in the 1960s), PhD study can be a narrowing experience which is a positive disadvantage to a student who intends to follow a general career in industry. The academics' riposte that industry should be re-organised to absorb what universities produce is no more justified than the suggestion that university curricula should be controlled by employers. Surely education and training must be carried out on a co-operative basis with sympathy on each side for the other's viewpoint and needs.

The primary justification for the traditional PhD is as a training for research and for research-like careers such as industrial chemistry or pharmacology to which it leads fairly directly. The number of graduates whose careers will be in this field is relatively small. In any organisation there are at least ten times (perhaps even twenty times) as many graduates involved in applying what is already known as there are involved in generating new information. Each academic currently produces about one hundred graduates in a lifetime, only one of whom is needed to provide for the succession in a stable situation. Even when allowance is made for research outside academe and for wastage of all sorts, it does not seem necessary to give this type f research training to more than five per cent of the student intake. But this does not of course preclude the development of additional co-operative awards with industry such as have recently been initiated by the SRC.

It has, incidentally, been suggested that, quite apart from any education element, the PhD student provides a useful pair of hands to assist an academic's own research. Granted the hands are inexperienced, but their owner is intelligent and may have more initiative than an experimental officer or technician. This really amounts to a suggestion that the doctoral degree may be used as a bribe to obtain services more cheaply than the normal market would allow. There would be no harm in this provided that the cost of the exercise was included in the cost of maintaining scholarship and not in that of providing training.

Although the number of permanent staff or students working on research projects may be limited by the funds available, the basic Resource must be organised so as to offer facilities for guest researchers from other organisations. It is an essential element of the continuous refreshment of academics by interaction with new ideas that there should always be room to accommodate visitors in a department as well as the established staff. A university department should be a sort of academic hotel, where individuals can come to work out an idea in stimulating surroundings: it is not a private house or ivory tower where a few chosen hermits live in undisturbed and academically debilitating isolation.

USE OF THE RESOURCE

Having made allowance for the essential maintenance of the quality of the university Resource, I think it must be accepted that central government, as representatives of the populace which through its taxes has provided the Resource, has some right to determine to what use it is put. Of course there must be the fullest consultation with all interested parties. Of course we must avoid any direct intervention in the way courses are taught, or in the subject matter that is or is not included, or in the choice of individual students. But a university which depends on the state for its funds cannot make demands such as, for example, that it only teach graduate courses: or even that it will take more or less than the number of students the Government, having been fully apprised of the possible effects of numbers on quality, wishes to support.

This introduces a most difficult point, that of standards. How do we resolve a conflict between a Government which provides a certain resource in the expectation that it is sufficient to cope with a student population of a certain size, and a university system which insists that the quality of its output would fall if more than nine-tenths of that number of students were admitted – or, conceivably, which takes even more students than expected in the hope that its resources will be increased as a result? The Government may believe quite genuinely that the needs of the country are better served by educating the number of students it chooses to a particular level. The universities may believe, equally genuinely, that education is all about standards and that they should be the arbiter of these themselves.

It will no doubt be argued that the difficulty can be resolved by improving the efficiency of the university, or that extra students can be taken in at the margin at a reduced cost. Technically this is true, but taken in its widest sense quality must suffer unless there is actual waste in the system. One would hope that most of this has been eliminated in the cuts and squeezes of the last few years and if it has not it is unlikely to be corrected by central direction.

One might here consider the analogy of a typical airline, which is known to run with an average of one-third of its seats unfilled. Surely, says the thoughtless onlooker, it could take fifty per cent more passengers without adding to its cost and then the fares would come down. In theory that is true. But in practice some aeroplanes are already full while others, pioneering new services or on less popular routes, are nearly empty. A uniform load factor of one hundred per cent can only be achieved by cutting out all services for which there is not always a queue of standby passengers. Although the fares would be lower the quality of the resulting service would be abysmal. In the same way any university could take on more students in certain faculties comparatively inexpensively; or it could cut out certain options which happen to be unpopular at the time; or it could stop all innovations, since they are always relatively expensive until developed. But the inevitable result in the longer term would be a decline in quality and a stifling of innovation.

Given that each generation of students needs as much help as the last, progressive weakening of the staff:student ratio must have an effect somewhere. If the students get the same amount of individual attention the academic has less time for research and scholarship. If he maintains his effort there he must work longer hours, at a time when the official working week for others is becoming shorter, and so his domestic life suffers. It may be that the system started with considerable spare fat; but insidious impoverishment cannot continue indefinitely without major effects.

The standard attainable by students in continuing subjects – that is, those not started fresh at university – may also be affected by changes in the school syllabus. Attempts to broaden this and indeed to make it a better preparation for those who do not go on immediately to further study may worsen the preparation for those who do. This could mean that some higher education courses themselves will have to start at a different level (as in the Scottish system) or will have to make allowance for a larger variation in entry standards (as in the foundation courses of the Open University). There may also be an increase in the numbers entering higher education who have not come straight from school and who need to be reintroduced to academic work.

Any discussion of standards is vitiated by the absence of any absolute criteria. If the standard of a degree were loosely defined as that which can be achieved in nine terms by a student who started with three 'A' Levels and had the attention of one-eighth of a member of staff then any change in course length, staff:student ratio or school leaving attainment must have some effect. Furthermore the requirements of employers and the needs of life in a resource-depleted and increasingly belligerent society show no sign of decreasing. These factors will all increase the demands on and for the basic Resource without making it easy to increase its size. The desire of the Government to increase the number of university entrants but not to increase the size of the basic Resource *pro rata* is a proper one. So is the universities' insistence that standards must be kept high in spite of the increased access. How is this impasse to be resolved?

There seem to be two possible solutions to the problem of increasing access to higher education without increasing the basic Resource. One solution is to argue that the highest standards must be maintained, and to accept that if entry numbers are to increase, and resources are insufficient to provide education of that quality for everyone, then there must be a natural break point in the course at which many students move out: only a few will then remain to take the second part of the course, so the total numbers in the institutions are not increased and quality is assured. The other solution is to argue that the different quality implied by a staff:student ratio of 1:15 or 1:20 must be accepted as the consequence of introducing more students to higher education and consciously to design courses on that basis.

The first solution has extensive implications, but it is not new. Some time ago Professor Pippard and others suggested that the single honours degree course was not appropriate for a wide variety of students and that a course designed in two two-year parts, with many students leaving after the first two years, would be academically advantageous. It has long been accepted at Cambridge that in certain cases, at least, a student might transfer from Part I of the Tripos in one subject to Part II of another. So it would be hard to argue that it was not possible to design a first-degree course in such a way that the first two years led to a satisfying change point. For some students it was followed by vocational studies either immediately before or after work experience; but it was only an intermediate point for the most gifted academically who were to continue academic study for a further two years. The Dip HE, incidentally, which was another attempt to produce a two-year qualification, has had limited appeal because it was regarded as an *alternative* to a three-year degree, not a first step which would be universal.

The present full-time specialist honours degree course in a subject chosen by a student while still at school is *not* a qualification that is actually necessary for most of the jobs currently available. The fact that many employers specify graduates when they advertise vacancies may only reflect the fact that they require intelligent people capable of thinking for themselves and learning by themselves and that the university system has sorted such people out for them. Nearly half the vacancy advertisements circulated by the Central Services Unit of the University and Polytechnics Appointments Services do not specify the subject in which the candidate should have graduated.

This merely emphasises the fact that for many, in fact for the majority, the degree course is regarded as general education that does not lead to a particular career. Most of those who leave university with a degree require some vocational training or experience when they have decided what career to follow. But of course school leavers also require vocational training. In fact the preparation for any career may be divided roughly into a period of education, when a person is developing a general behaviour pattern and learning universal truths; a transition period of vocational training when he is developing the specific skills and learning the particular facts required for his trade or profession; and retraining and updating during the actual following of that trade or profession.

Looked at this way it is rather surprising that in Britain at the present time it is only considered normal to leave the educational system and start vocational training at the particular ages of 16, 17 or 18 (as a school leaver), or 21 (as Bachelor), 22 (as Master) or 24 (as Doctor). It seems more logical to imagine a system in which education continues to the ages of 16, 18, 20, or 22, according to the student's capacity, and in which there is a possibility of branching into specialist training at each of these points. In postulating such a system I am not suggesting that capacity is uniquely related to age. The ages quoted represent a typical standard, just as the normal degree represents the standard that can be achieved by a typical student who started with two 'A' Levels three years before.

There is, incidentally, no evidence of a general shortage of graduates on the employment market. There appears to be an almost insatiable demand at the moment for certain specialists such as electronic engineers or computer specialists, and there are chronic shortages of schoolteachers of mathematical, scientific and craft subjects. But demand for some specialisms, such as town planning, quickly became saturated and an advertisement for a university teacher in most subjects would receive many qualified applicants. Complaints are voiced more about the quality of graduates than their quantity (see, for example the evidence of the Confederation of British Industries to the Finniston Committee on Engineering). The Finniston committee itself, in proposing B Eng and M Eng courses, clearly thought in terms of an intermediate break point after which the two types of course, long and short, would diverge. These arguments, taken together, provide a strong case for the proposition that university degree courses should be so structured as to provide a break point after the first two years. Only a small proportion of students, those who had demonstrated particularly high academic capacity, would continue immediately for the second two years of a traditional non-vocational honours degree. These students would include those destined for academic careers and other careers where such study was essential. The implication is that within a given Resource more students could be admitted for the first two years since fewer would proceed to the second two years.

The students who left a general honours course after two years would branch out into other vocational training courses. Some of these, such as medicine and veterinary science, have traditionally been taken in universities (though the London Medical Schools were once outside the University) and such arrangements would continue. Others may be centred on polytechnics or colleges in the local sector, or even within particular professions themselves. The type of course is critical and there is a very strong argument for running all such courses in conjunction with employment or practice. For if we accept that no one can be judged professionally competent without demonstrating his practical skill as well as his theoretical understanding, then it is essential that both types of learning should be correlated.

Many vocational courses are already effectively planned this way, including those for doctors, schoolteachers, engineers and others. There would be some problems in running all vocational courses in the sandwich mode, but none seems insurmountable, even though the full development may take years. It is also remarkable that most of the recent schemes for the special engineering courses for 'high fliers' are being run as sandwich courses with industrial sponsorship and indeed with industrial involvement in the choice of student. Furthermore, although evidence collected in the early 1970s suggested that, after an initial advantage, students from sandwich courses did less well than those from other courses, more recent evidence collected by the Brunel Institute of Industrial Training shows that sandwich course engineers are still earning more than the average ten years after graduation.

One argument against an expansion of sandwich courses is the difficulty of finding suitable training placements. Certainly, good places are difficult to find under the present system, but this difficulty is not absolute. Let us assume for the moment that those leaving general education courses, whether at school or university, are going eventually into employment – certainly that is our aim. Let us also assume that they will not have learned on their courses all the skills they will need in their employment – both those specific to the particular job, and those general to the field of employment – since these are specialist subjects not required by everyone. They will then require some training. So everyone requires training, and the comparison is *not* between a sandwich student who requires training placements to be found for him and a traditional full-time student who does not. It is between the sandwich system which intercalates periods of training in a place of employment with periods of related but more general education in an institution: and the traditional system which provides all the institutional period in one full-time lump following it with all the training in employment in another full-time lump. No more resources are required. If the idea of continuing education, and if the need for education to derive from experience, are correct, it is difficult to say that the sandwich method of interposing experience and study is not the right way of providing vocational training. A difficulty for the employer, of course, has been that, in providing placements for a sandwich student, he was training someone who might not return as a useful employee: in training someone who had already taken a full-time degree he was training someone who had opted to work in his employ for an unlimited period. In practice, since labour is mobile, the difference was in any case more apparent than real. If responsibility for training were vested in the industrial training boards, or if some form of the transfer fee scheme, advocated in a later section, were adopted the difficulty would disappear completely.

The argument is, then, that it would be possible to increase the number of those entering universities without sacrificing ultimate standards and without harming employment prospects if a system were developed in which: i) all those entering followed the course of their choice for two years only; ii) most of them then went over to vocational training – which might or might not be based on an academic institution, but if it was would be likely to be a sandwich type of course like the clinical training of doctors; and iii) a small proportion continued for a further two years to reach the standard of the traditional honours degree or perhaps one even a little beyond it.

It must be emphasised that the system now proposed ought to be no less flexible than existing arrangements. At present, there is a large outflow of graduates from the universities each year. Many of these find employment that is unrelated to their degree specialisation and then get some training on the job. A system is suggested here in which many of those coming out will be less differentiated, having only had two years of general education. Their next year or years of training can be directly related to their first employment. Alternatively an employer may consider it to the advantage of both the employee and the business that further professional training be delayed until the employee has some practical experience and his interests and aptitudes are clearer. This would result in an alternative form of thick sandwich course: that is, two years of general studies comparable to those of a present-day degree course, followed by at least the equivalent of one year further study intercalated with a year or years of practical experience and related to a particular profession. Furthermore, it may be to the advantage of the employee or his employer that he be retrained on another vocational course at a later date. This would be much simpler to arrange with two-year modules than with the present three- to four-year degree course.

It may be objected that it is unfair to expect students to make career choices after only two years in university; or to ask employers to recruit potential professionals so early. A ready defence is that the majority of young people still have to make such choices when they leave school and a majority of recruits to most organisations are still school leavers. It is interesting to note in this context the arguments recently advanced by the Civil Service Unions that graduates should *not* get preferential treatment in recruitment to administrative grades. Surely the proper way to deal with any problem is not to delay decisions but to make it easier to correct mistakes: some mistakes are inevitable and the later they are made the more difficult they are to correct.

The implications for staffing such a rearrangement of teaching studies is a separate question. One possible difficulty would be staff attitudes to the prospect of increased access by two-year students. There is no threat to research if we accept that staff are entitled to reserve some time for scholarship irrespective of how many students they are actually helping through the learning process. But we *are* asking for a change, in that a higher proportion of teaching work is likely to be with students on the first two years of a course and less with the second two. Many academics feel that it is the later years of a course which are the more interesting, exciting or worthwhile. There is sometimes a sort of academic snobbery in this – it has for example been argued that those teaching for degrees should earn more than those teaching at sub-degree level. Such an argument is not entirely logical since if sub-degree work is really less pleasant it could be argued that the financial reward should be higher, even though the qualifications required may not be so rare. On the other hand many think that it is more difficult to teach the earlier years of a course to students who have not yet developed the capacity for learning on their own. Certainly there has been a tradition in some universities that freshmen should be taught by the professor himself. One hopes that it could be accepted that if Society's need is that more students should be exposed to two years of undergraduate education, and fewer to four years, then no teacher should feel it is beneath him to fulfil such a need.

We should not underestimate the necessary conservatism of teachers (and their representative unions), some of whom may believe that academic freedom includes not only the freedom to hold and express their views in whatever way appears true to them, but also the freedom to decide how many people shall hear their views (1:10 staff:student ratio) and for how long (three years minimum). However, the State, which pays the salaries, must have some right to determine how the Resource it provides should be used, consistent with basic academic freedom of expression and the preservation of scholarship. It is ultimately to the advantage of staff members to divorce the number of teachers from the student load, since this helps to ensure security of tenure if not of role.

Let us now consider the alternative solution, the honours degree course with the weak staff:student ratio. This also has far reaching implications. The first point to make is that such a solution cannot be said to be impossible. The cost of an Open University degree – that is the average of the total annual cost of the Open University divided by the actual number of degrees awarded per year – is no more than one-third of the corresponding figure for a conventional university. This is a very conservative figure, since it excludes the additional costs of residence in the latter, and the additional benefits obtained by the relatively large proportion of OU students who do not actually graduate. To make this point is not to pretend that the quality of experience that is provided for an Open University student is the same as that for the student on a standard full-time university course. The point is that the same academic standard, as measured by examinations, can be reached in a less expensive way.

It might be argued that the Open University deals with a quite different type of student. Whereas the undergraduate who comes straight from school is well prepared and academically sophisticated, but often poorly motivated and immature, the typical OU student is highly motivated and adult, but ill-prepared and unused to study. This surely implies that a different approach to teaching is necessary for this type of student, not that less money ought to be spent on him. If educating mature students were inherently cheaper than educating school-leavers then there could be little argument against postponing university education for all until, say, the age of thirty, as Lord Rothschild once suggested. Since so many of our university institutions are geared to an entry consisting primarily of school-leavers (with Birkbeck College an honourable exception), this possibility can only be left for investigation in the longer term.

In many ways it is surprising that we have in Britain so few other institutions which are intermediate in cost per graduate between the relatively expensive residential university and the relatively cheap Open University. Costs in the polytechnics and other parts of the 'public' sector are difficult to ascertain because of the range of courses they provide: there is no clear evidence that their degree courses are significantly less expensive than university courses in the same subject. It is as if nearly all the types of vehicle available for road transport were either bicycles or in the Rolls-Royce class.

There have been many suggestions for changes in university practice which might reduce the cost of courses. Shirley Williams provided one set with her Thirteen Points. But they have mostly been attempts to chisel the odd one per cent improvement out of an existing system. They have roused fierce opposition from those who have wanted to maintain quality and who already feel that it has been sufficiently endangered by the result of inflation, a shorter working week, expansion and economic crises. What is now being asked for is the conscious acceptance of a differently designed programme, to enable more students to reach degree standard without any increase in the total Resource, while admitting that the quality of total experience might *not* be that of a traditional degree because the resources per student were reduced.

At this stage one cannot do more than offer a few suggestions as to how such a course might be mounted. It would obviously rely considerably on self-learning, so would only suit well-motivated students. It might be necessary to enlist the help of third- or fourth-year students in teaching first and second years. Students might be required to study at home for a larger portion of the academic year – although this might not be possible in some laboratory subjects. There would obviously be considerable reliance on audio-visual material, as in Open University courses, so that the Use costs per student, as opposed to the basic Resource costs, would probably not be reduced.

Two possible ways of expanding access to higher education within a fixed Resource have now been considered and one naturally asks which is to be preferred. The answer must surely be that there is room for both.

Some institutions might continue to restrict their total numbers to the present figures, accepting a larger entry but only allowing a small proportion to take the second two-year part of the course – the differential approach. Other institutions might consider that, provided adequate staff time was reserved for research and scholarship, it would be possible to design courses for higher staff:student ratios. Their total student numbers would go up without a corresponding increase in basic Resource, but all their students would take courses of the same length – the common approach.

The approaches are compatible in the sense that the student on the common course will have reached the same academic standard as the student who has taken four years on a differential course. The quality of his experience will be different as the total amount of Resource provided for him over four years will be no more than that provided for the differential student over two. Some students may prefer to opt for two years in comparative luxury to reach an ordinary degree standard: others may opt to take four years in comparative stringency for an honours degree before they start vocational studies. Only those whose career really required it, and who were expected to make special contributions to the preservation and enhancement of scholarship, would be expected to take the second two years of the differential course with its relatively rich staff:student ratio.

It must be emphasised that the developments outlined above depend absolutely on the acceptance of the idea of a stable Resource as outlined in the beginning. No institution could conceivably agree to take significantly more students with the same basic complement of staff, equipment and buildings, unless there was a cast iron guarantee that its acceptance would *not* under any circumstances be used as a justification for reducing its resources (on the grounds that it was not necessary to take so many students). Similarly no institution could conceivably agree to limit its total numbers to preserve a rich staff:student ratio unless there was a cast iron guarantee that its restriction would *not* under any circumstances be used as a justification for reducing its resources (perhaps on the grounds that other institutions managed on weaker staff:student ratios). If we want diversity then we must accept differences and not use comparison of individual details as a ratchet mechanism to reduce the resources available to everybody. Obviously the way the universities are funded for this Use, and the way students are supported during their studies will help to determine the types of course offered at particular institutions. It is essential to produce an unbiased system which ensures a reasonable balance between the needs of individual students and those of the society which supports them. That is the subject of the next section.

Before turning to that, however, it must be emphasised that although the preceding paragraphs deal primarily with the university sector, much of what has been written applies to the whole field of further education. There is considerable overlap in the subjects covered and the methods of teaching in universities and polytechnics – indeed the differences between individual universities are just as great if not greater than the differences between universities and polytechnics. It might once have been feasible, when there were fewer and smaller universities, to reserve them for scholars and researchers, leaving other institutions to train undergraduates for the world outside. Such discrimination is no longer possible, although one would still expect that in total there would be a greater proportion of continuing honours courses in universities and a greater proportion of vocational continuation courses in other institutions.

DEGREES AND CERTIFICATES

It was implicit in the previous section that a major use of the higher education Resource would be to enable students to read for degrees. Some would obtain ordinary degrees after two years' study at a relatively rich staff:student ratio and then go on to a vocational qualification (which might mean for the few most academically inclined a further two years to reach honours standard). Some would work on a four-year course at a much weaker staff:student ratio.

The basic standard of an honours degree in Britain has been primarily determined by what can reasonably be learned by a specially selected group of school leavers in three years of full-time study of a single academic discipline at a staff:student ratio rather richer than 1:10. It is a relative measure, not an absolute one: for there is no absolute way of comparing standards in, say, history with those in biochemistry. But the standards required at all institutions are similar. It is possible to achieve the standard in different ways, for example by part-time instead of full-time study: but the majority of courses are full-time and take three years immediately after school, and these set the standards.

If we are to consider seriously the introduction of two-year degree programmes, the development of courses for mature students and the possibility of part-time study, we have to ask whether the degree is still a relevant, adequate and necessary measure of university performance. As it stands, it has two unsatisfactory features. The first is that the award is not very descriptive. Perhaps it is true that achievement of first-class honours always betokens high intellectual quality. But the award of a second class fails to distinguish between the candidate who has done brilliantly in one branch of a subject but badly in others and the candidate who is quite good in all. It is worth noting that there are fifteen ways of describing the performance of a student who followed a particular course in the school sixth form – he takes three 'A' Level subjects and is rated in each on a five-point scale: but there are only four ways of rating a first degree, and no distinctions at all in higher degrees. Nor does the degree standard achieved by a student reflect directly the progress he has made during his three years, since the point at which he started is not taken into account.

This really leads to the second disadvantage, that although the degree records a historic achievement it tends to become a mark of permanent distinction. The fact that an individual was judged supremely competent at academic exercises at one particular time does not necessarily imply he will always be so; while the individual who did relatively badly may be an unsuspected late developer whose performance in later life is dazzling. Furthermore, the standard of a degree in a developing subject may well be a contemporary one. As knowledge increases, and new theories are produced to codify it, the requirements for a degree change. There may therefore be little correlation between the possession of a degree in a certain discipline and capability in that subject ten years later.

Degrees have an air of finality and completeness which seems inappropriate in an age of change and continuing education. As a sole signal of university success they may positively inhibit the development of any courses that are not of the conventional kind. There is certainly an argument for replacing them, or at least supplementing them, with subject certificates which would be flexible, simple to accumulate as a result of post-experience study, renewable and explicit. However, degrees have three functions, one of which at least may have to be preserved.

The first is qualification. In certain professions, such as pharmacology, the degree by itself confers a licence to practise. In others it is already an important prerequisite or is being adopted as such to demonstrate the high standard required. This function might equally well be performed by a system of subject certificates: it is remarkable that the Chilver Report on the Training of Civil Engineers recommended that both 'O' and 'A' Level certificates should be considered in judging a candidate's fitness. The Finniston committee did not go into any detail on the syllabus of first degrees but was outspoken on the need for continuing 'formation' by training during an engineer's career.

The second function is initial selection. Potential employers whose requirements include openings for some who are brilliant and some who are merely competent are undoubtedly helped by an education system which grades its students. They might however be helped even more by a system which provided a much more accurate transcript of a student's progress and abilities. Five years after graduation, when the employee has made his mark at his workplace, his degree classification will be forgotten and he will be judged on the evidence of later performance. Unfortunately the candidate who did badly in part of his degree exams may never get the chance to recover in this way.

The third function is incentive. The student is motivated to study the complete syllabus because failure in one subject, the relevance of which he perhaps does not appreciate at the time, would be crippling. Against this one might suggest that students who have no motive to study should not start the course until they have. The major argument for preserving the degree therefore can only be continuity. It represents a contemporary standard to which employers and others have adjusted. If the two-year scheme were adopted the first two years could then lead to an ordinary degree, the two further non-vocational years to an honours degree and the alternative two further vocational years to a master's degree, all without significant change in present arrangements.

At the same time it would seem sensible to introduce certificates of proficiency at each level for the constituent parts of each course. Part-time or post-experience students could then take these on an individual basis. Indeed it seems unrealistic to imagine that the majority of mature students will ever be able, or will indeed wish, to study in other than a part-time way. The system would be much more flexible, providing recognition of individual elements of study instead of only an overall average.

At each level a certificate records two attributes: a state of knowledge, represented fairly accurately, and a capacity for learning, which is implied. Unfortunately the certificate is a rather inaccurate measure of the latter capacity, which is actually the more important. The standard of the certificate is set by what can be achieved in a standard period by the majority of students starting at a particular level. The capacity for learning demonstrated by the individual student will depend on the level at which that individual started, as well as on where he finished. Even then the capacity for self-learning and self-teaching, which is really important, may be masked by the quality of teaching. The student who has been spoon-fed may achieve a high standard of knowledge, but the student who has succeeded in reaching a lower standard in spite of indifferent teaching may actually be capable of great achievements.

We might here take a hint from those exams in music, taken when the teacher believes, from his personal knowledge, that the pupil is ready and certain to pass. The exam then is an unequivocal measure of proficiency only. Capacity for learning can only be inferred indirectly from the time taken to achieve proficiency and the number of instruments in which the student is proficient: and there is not the confusion caused by requiring him to reach a particular level in a fixed time. It may be a little more difficult to preserve national standards in phased courses, particularly when the students include post-experience part-timers as well as those who have just left school. But the university tradition of external examining should cover this, and professional bodies who may or may not accept certain elements as counting towards membership qualifications will exercise a strong influence over vocationally-oriented courses.

Standards in the non-university sector are maintained through the CNAA, which is an external body, strongly influenced by university standards. The uniformity of standards is one of the special characteristics of the British system – as contrasted with the American, for example. But it certainly seems anomalous that a small university can be trusted to set its own standards while a large polytechnic cannot: what is so debilitating about local authority funding? Perhaps the argument was that an independent body of academics in an autonomous institution can be relied on to be dispassionate whereas those in a directly funded institution risk political interference. Perhaps the difference is largely historical and will in time disappear. If, as is proposed later, all institutions of higher education become autonomous, with local authorities providing funds for particular projects but not actually controlling the governing body, would standards be safe? There is always a worry that insufficient funds were provided for the objectives set – but then the university sector has suffered the same way. The scheme proposed here is intended to safeguard scholarship.

The answer can only lie in the universities' absolute control of the numbers attending and resources allocated to the second two years of the honours course. It is possible that the Government of the day might wish to load in more students to the first two years, and standards of ordinary degrees might change as standards may have done in schools where teacher complement was not matched to intake. But as long as final honours standards are completely under the control of the institution and can be correlated nationally and internationally we should be safe. University standards are maintained by a sort of priesthood – all appointments being made by those who are already themselves members of the academic staff, advised by colleagues in other institutions. This can possibly produce a self-perpetuating group, insensitive to the external world, but at least it is independent and, in so far as those outside can read and understand, the published works of all academics are available for criticism.

This suggests that the criteria for granting degrees, certificates or other awards should be these:

A. The institutions should be autonomous in the sense of receiving a block grant for the support of its basic Resource and having an independent governing body as described in a later section.
B. The members of academic staff should be selected by their peers, guided by one or more external assessors and academic referees.
C. The assessment of performance should be made by such staff, monitored by one or more external examiners.

Institutions satisfying these requirements should be free to issue degrees and certificates covering different periods of study. The degree itself may have to be retained as a major component of initial qualification for particular professions: but the certificate may be normal currency for continuing practice and for employment in areas where professional responsibility is not necessary to protect the public.

COSTS, CHARGES AND FEES

The subject of tuition fees always tends to lead to emotional arguments between those who advocate their total abolition on, for example, the grounds that education is a right and must be free to all, and those who argue that they should cover the full cost on, for example, grounds of economic realism. At the outset it is helpful to distinguish between three different quantities:

A. The actual cost incurred in providing a particular service.
B. The fee collected by the institution for the service.
C. The net amount retained by the institution after collection.

There is then a fourth quantity, the net sum actually paid by the student or contractor for whom the service is performed. This may be different from the money collected by the institution if, for instance, part of it is paid by the local authority on the student's behalf. In what follows, the method of determining fees and other charges will first be discussed. This is primarily a question of good management. Having established that, it will be possible in the next section to discuss the question of who should pay the fees. This is a more political question which introduces other agencies than the institutions themselves.

The distinction between the fee (B) and the amount retained (C) is not always appreciated. If, as seems to be present policy, the universities were centrally funded in such a way that their grant was abated by exactly the amount of fee income, then whatever fees were actually charged the net amount retained would be zero. It is also possible to conceive of a system where fees were paid to central government on behalf of foreign students and where the government itself then paid a different amount to the institution educating them; or one where all fees were zero but the government grant to institutions was determined by the number of students enrolled. Such arrangements show that the quantities (A), (B) and (C) above are independent.

The actual costs comprise two elements: the basic costs of each institution – staff salaries and wages, maintenance and replacement of equipment and buildings, which are roughly independent of immediate use; and the marginal running costs – consumables, services and purchases from outside, which can be varied according to immediate needs. As explained earlier, there is a very strong argument for treating institutions of higher education as a permanent Resource of scholarship, whose basic cost is met from central government on a quinquennial plan. It is an essential feature of such an arrangement that support for the basic Resource is *not* then affected by short-term variations in its Use. Of course the long-term pattern of Use is one of several factors taken into account in making the quinquennial plan. But once that has been made the Resource itself remains inviolate. It then follows that the marginal running costs must be covered by the net additional amounts the institution retains for the services it provides in the form of educational courses, vocational training, contract research, and so on.

There is also a strong argument for arranging the fee levels for the various services so that in total they cover the short-term marginal costs. That is, the fees, by whomsoever paid, should approximate to the extra costs to the institution providing that particular service at that time, and the institution should retain the whole fee. Any other arrangement, for example, one whereby some of the fee was retained by the institution to repay marginal costs and some returned to central government by abatement of the basic support grant leads to administrative complication and uncertainty.

The net income from fees is then under the control of the institution itself, as is essential for efficient local management. The institution can match its work to the resources available without penalty or premium. Central government may still control the use of the Resource by regulating its subsidies to those paying fees for the services and by negotiating appropriate levels charged for work it wishes to sponsor directly; but it does not have the opportunity to interfere in internal matters and produce distortions which prevent efficient use of local resources.

An arrangement by which institutions retain fees without affecting the quinquennial grant for the support of the basic Resource is completely consistent with current arrangements for charging for research and short courses. It follows the principle that the most economic use of any central service is obtained when there is general agreement on the level of basic provision allied to payment by the user at marginal rates. Who pays the fees, and on whose behalf, are quite separate questions into which politics enter as well as logic. They will be discussed later after we have considered how the levels of fees should be set.

It is not difficult to evaluate the total running costs of any institution over and above the basic cost of staffing and equipping it. It is very difficult indeed to decide exactly how to allocate these costs to particular types of use. Arbitrary decisions would inevitably have to be made about how the costs of central services like the library or the finance office were to be divided. It seems very unlikely that the result would justify the effort. There would therefore seem to be great merit in claiming the same marginal cost, at least for all non-vocational courses. It is then possible that in a particular institution the net income from one type of course might be subsidising another. One suspects, however, that since the costs of staff and equipment are excluded, being covered by the basic support grant, it is reasonable to assume that the costs of books and travel for the undergraduate arts student are not much different from the costs of chemicals and other material for the undergraduate scientist. Indeed it would almost be possible for the equipment allowance in the basic Resource to be defined in a way that made it so.

Although it may be difficult to disentangle the individual running costs of different undergraduate courses for the first two years, the costs of the second two years of an honours course and the costs of providing special vocational courses at the higher level may be quantifiably different. This has been recognised to some extent in the charging of higher tuition fees for postgraduates. (The recently imposed higher charge to overseas students for laboratory subjects is not quite the same, since here the higher cost of maintaining the basic Resource is also allowed for.) One would therefore expect each institution to have a scale of tuition fees for higher level courses according to the estimates of the extra costs involved.

Having accepted that uniform fees should be charged in one institution, at least for the first-level educational courses, we may consider whether they should vary from one institution to another. The advantages of this would be that extra costs in a particular institution could be allowed for. On the other hand it is not unreasonable to suggest that if a course were particularly expensive in one institution it might be advantageous in the long run to encourage its transfer to another place: any general extra cost, such as the London weighting added to salaries, would be covered in the basic quinquennial grant anyway. It is likely that there would be strong pressure from local authorities, sponsors or fee payers generally to adopt uniform scales (as there has been for standardisation of student union capitation fees). Since in any case the fees only cover a small part of the total cost the administrative complications in allowing individual variations scarcely seem worth while. It is therefore suggested that there should be a national fee structure. If we accept that a Grants Committee is the proper vehicle for advising the Government on the right level of basic support then it would be the natural body to advise or negotiate on fee levels.

Such negotiations could if necessary be carried out annually to allow for new patterns of use – following the demographic curve, for example. But it should be axiomatic that the fee paid by or on behalf of a student should *not* change during his course, except insofar as it follows the cost of living index. To change the scheme of charges once a student has been accepted for a particular course and is therefore committed for several years savours of sharp practice. It can cause considerable distress to a person whose decision to study was based on a careful financial plan by himself, his family or his sponsor.

It is interesting to note that, although the levels of tuition fee charged in the late 1970s were chosen completely arbitrarily, they happened to be of the same order as those which would obtain under the arrangements proposed here. For the cost of salaries and wages, added to that of equipment and the depreciation allowance on buildings earlier proposed, would amount to a figure quite close to the sum of the recurrent, equipment and capital grants made at that time. Even now (1980) the tuition fees charged to home students just about cover the marginal running costs of their education. But the similarity is accidental and in any case the UGC tailors the recurrent grant to its estimate of fee income. That is, it tries to control the total grant plus fee income: this is only justifiable if the immediate objective is to limit student numbers and is completely inconsistent with the present proposals.

Incidentally the Robbins committee in 1963 recommended that the income from fees should be about twenty per cent of the total on the grounds that this would provide universities with reasonable freedom of manoeuvre. In fact the arrangements here proposed would produce fee income in about this proportion.

From the point of view of the institution, the marginal cost of students from abroad is little different from that of home students on the same course. Some may require additional tutorial care, it is true, but the definitions of home and overseas are so arbitrary that it is difficult to generalise. There is therefore no more argument for charging foreign students different fees than there is for making them pay different fares for travelling on British Rail's subsidised services. Any suggestion that certain students are being discriminated against on grounds of country of origin introduces disharmony and is indeed contrary to the basic principles of the Race Relations Act.

On the other hand the Government can properly argue that in determining the size of the basic Resource it allowed only for its use by a reasonable proportion of students from abroad – say 10 per cent. If institutions then took a higher proportion of foreign students the Government could argue with some justice that the education of home students, for which it had a responsibility, was being diluted. In practice, as long as fees were of the same order as the marginal costs, and as long as the Government made clear that the support for the basic Resource was *not* directly dependent on total student numbers, it would not be in the interests of an institution to accept more foreign students than was beneficial to its academic health. It would of course always be open to the Government to develop the size of the basic Resource to accommodate more foreign students if that was its policy and if it could be done bearing in mind the limits discussed in the first section.

An institution could also negotiate a special fee for a particular additional course run at the behest of a foreign government or organisation.

The recent proposal to charge overseas students a 'full cost' fee is unsatisfactory from the point of view of the institutions. It means that there are two levels of charge for the same service: this appears divisive in an institution where good relationships between members learning together are essential. It also means that some of the income required to support the basic Resource is fluctuating and its amount may not be known until long after the decisions about staffing and equipment have been made: this makes good management very difficult.

Of course one must recognise the political pressures to charge wealthy foreigners for a subsidised service and to use our excellent education system as a revenue earner that contributes to our balance of payments. If the Government really wanted to yield to such pressures or take such opportunities it could do so comparatively easily by levying an appropriate charge for student visas or by government-to-government charges. Such an arrangement could be extremely flexible since charges could be used as a bargaining counter in trade negotiations or waived for under-developed countries which Britain wished to help. It would remove political decisions from the sphere of higher education, where they do not belong. The Government could still elect to increase the size of the basic Resource to allow for an increased Use by overseas students beyond the ten per cent suggested in an earlier paragraph, and would itself recoup the cost.

In summary, then, the following arrangements for tuition fees and charges are proposed:

A. The fees for the various services offered by universities should cover the marginal costs, that is those beyond the basic costs of staff salaries, buildings and equipment, and should be retained *in toto*.

B. The levels of fees for degree courses should be negotiated through the Grants Committee. Fees for general educational courses would be uniform throughout the system, but there might be differences between Part I and Part II courses; fees for vocational training might vary from vocation to vocation but would again be uniform throughout the system; the tuition fees charged for a course lasting more than a year should not be changed from year to year (except to allow for inflation) for students already accepted.

C. The Government could state that the basic provision was made on the assumption that the higher education Resource was available for a particular number of students from overseas, and to require institutions taking a higher proportion to demonstrate that home students did not suffer thereby.

D. No fee differential for overseas students would be set, but the Government would charge for student visas or make other government-to-government arrangements if it wished to recoup some of the expense of the basic Resource used for the tuition of overseas students.

E. Fees for part-time courses, short courses, special courses and for other services – such as research and investigations, or use of facilities – would be negotiated by individual institutions to cover local marginal costs with whatever variations the market allowed.

Finally, it must once again be emphasised that these arrangements are designed to achieve efficient operation of the institutions themselves. The political question of who actually pays for students and whether education or training should be free to the beneficiaries is deferred to the next section.

WHO PAYS THE FEES?

In the previous section the tuition fee was considered from the viewpoint of the academic institution, regarding it as the necessary contribution to income. In what now follows it is regarded from the viewpoint of the user – should he pay it directly, or borrow it, or be subsidised in some way?

It has already been postulated that higher education courses should be of two kinds: general educational courses, the content of which is not directly related to a particular career; and vocational courses, which are clearly aimed at particular occupations. The general courses included some which were taught as Part I and Part II at relatively rich staff:student ratios; and others which involved four years' study, at relatively weak staff: student ratios. The following paragraphs argue that the fees for general educational courses should normally be paid by the State on behalf of its students, while the fees for vocational courses should normally be the responsibility of the employer or potential employer.

Life in a civilised society is enhanced by providing basic education for all its members to the limit of their capacity. This means that schooling is provided free to the school leaving age of sixteen or eighteen. By the same token fees for the first two years (Part I) of the 'rich' non-vocational course, or the full four years of the 'weak' non-vocational course described above, should be paid for the student by his local authority as they are now. At first glance it looks as if the four-year student is being unfairly privileged by this arrangement. In fact, he has taken no greater share of the central resource (four years at the weaker staff:student ratio is equivalent to two years at the richer), and he has delayed his employment by two years, and so has lost potential earnings.

On grounds of equity, every home student should be able to claim fees for one general course whenever started, but only for one. A student who wished to do a second general course in a different subject would be expected to pay his own fee to cover the marginal cost. One hopes that many would do so later in their working life when they wanted to enlarge their experience or interests. Similarly anyone who did not qualify for a place, or did not wish to avail himself of the opportunity of going to a university immediately after leaving school, should still be able to claim the privilege of fee payment for one course at any time in his later career. It would also be proper for students wishing to take similar courses on a part-time basis to have their fees paid for them in the same way.

These arrangements for the initial part of a course would be little different from those which apply to school leavers now entering the universities. In passing, the arrangements may be compared with those of the voucher system which has been considered for schools. In that case the proposal was that vouchers covering the *full* cost of primary or secondary education should be issued to parents, who would then be free to take them and cash them at the school of their choice. This is equivalent to a full-fee system and could lead to insupportable instability, since no institution would know beforehand what its future income might be and thus could give no security to its staff. It also has debatable political effects in separating children who should otherwise be on common courses. In the higher education system, the students are in effect given a voucher to cover the marginal cost of their first slice of post-school education. They would have free choice of university, polytechnic or college as at present, while the universities themselves would be free to admit those students whom they think they could accommodate. As has been shown by experience, the net result is a balance in which most students are admitted to an institution of their choice and few institutions are overcrowded.

The arguments for local authority or government support for general courses do not apply to vocational courses where the benefits are more specific to the individual or his employer. The provision of an expensive specialist vocational training for someone who is not going to make his career in that profession seems unnecessary, and it is difficult to see why an individual should have a right to claim that the costs of it be paid on his behalf. The teacher training fiasco of the mid-1970s, when the output of teachers became greater than the posts available, has also emphasised the personal frustrations that build up when vocational training is not matched to likely employment openings.

In view of the fact that part of the Resource is likely to be applied to vocational training of professionals, it could be argued that in addition to tuition fees part of the basic cost of its provision should be furnished by the eventual employers. In the case of the medical profession, for example, student numbers are controlled centrally according to estimated employment prospects in the Department of Health. Why should not the

Department bear all the cost of their training? One contrary argument is that it is difficult to separate those elements of the basic Resource associated with general education and research from those involved in vocational training. Another is that insofar as the State employs a large proportion of those vocationally trained in higher education only a paper transaction would be involved. But the real difficulty would lie in trying to sort out beforehand the proper contributions from a vast range of potential beneficiaries. It would be an administrative nightmare. This is not to say that there would not be great advantages in making an estimate after the event of the total Resource cost of vocational courses provided in the higher education sector. It would not be impossible for a Grants Committee to publish its statistics of expenditure in such a way that the approximate costs of the Resource attributable to vocational training were separate from those of general courses and research, although this would require some rather arbitrary allocation of central costs.

Similar arguments may be advanced over the allocation of capital costs for basic research. The dual support system which has applied in the past assumed that the institution was 'well-found', in the sense of having available accommodation, normal equipment and academic staff. The Research Council grants were then only required to support recurrent costs of such items as consumables and special equipment. Application of this principle has been made difficult by the recent economies in universities, but it is consistent with those advocated here and should surely be preserved. Incidentally it should be mentioned that research grants for fundamental exploratory work are here distinguished from contracts for a particular investigation: the full cost of the latter would be expected to be recovered from the sponsor.

The arguments for central support of tuition fees do not apply to the second two years (Part II) of a 'rich' honours course. The relatively small number of students undertaking this are either destined for 'high-flying' careers, such as the 'A' stream in the civil service, for which this extra educational development has been regarded as essential; or for careers as researchers, scholars and teachers. In a sense, then, their vocations as high-flier or scholar have been decided, so it is logical to treat them in the same way as those on more directly vocational courses.

Accepting that it is the individual and his employer who will benefit directly from such courses it would seem logical for the tuition fees to be paid in one of three ways:

A. By an employer.
B. By an employers' association or industrial training board.
C. By the student himself, from savings or borrowings.

All these methods have advantages and disadvantages and it may be necessary to allow for all of them.

The great advantage of a system in which a person seeks employment immediately after the general part of his higher education is that his vocational training can then be linked to actual practice there. Furthermore, it ensures that the numbers taking vocational courses are matched to expected job openings. It fits in well with many sandwich course arrangements. It does however have certain disadvantages. One is that employers naturally tend to concentrate on short-term needs, although it may be in the national interest to increase the supply of certain professionals against a foreseen long-term requirement. This can, however, be corrected if similar arrangements are made for continuing education. Another is that some firms, particularly those that are small, cannot themselves provide the breadth of experience needed for the practical part of vocational training. A third is that less scrupulous firms may be tempted to 'poach', letting other companies carry the expense of training and then enticing the trained employees away from them by handsome salary offers.

These difficulties would be resolved if professional training were made the responsibility of Industrial Training Boards (ITB). Such an arrangement has itself two potential disadvantages, both of which are evidenced by the present ITB system. One is that Boards might limit their support to relatively few courses – at the present time, for instance, the Engineering ITB will support firms taking sandwich students on engineering courses but not those on metallurgy courses, even though the latter students are destined for engineering firms which need their skills. The second is that many areas of employment are not yet covered by Boards. Neither of these disadvantages is insuperable, although both require changes in Board structure and operation.

It would therefore be necessary at first to allow for employer sponsorship and training board sponsorship to co-exist. One scheme which might facilitate this, and which has advantages of its own, is the transfer fee system. Under such an arrangement each employee would be marked by the total cost of his vocational training, including both the fees paid and the employer's in-house costs. If an employee left a company the corresponding training board would reimburse this sum to that company, less an agreed amount to allow for the employee's contribution to the work of the company after training, and would claim it from the next employer. In addition, the training board itself would be empowered to finance training and be reimbursed by a subsequent employer. Not only would such a system encourage a company to support good training schemes because it knew it would be recompensed if a trained employee left, but the presence on the annual balance sheet of a large sum directly attributable to training would emphasise that the capital of the enterprise included the human resources represented by the skills of its employees. Unfortunately the administrative complications of such a scheme seem almost insuperable at this moment.

As a potential employer of scholars and teachers the education system itself would also sponsor certain students, particularly those on Part II or higher degree studies. There is some argument for making the university a sort of training board for scholarship and thus the sponsor of all students on Part II. It would then be reimbursed by subsequent employers like any other Board. Indeed it might even be open to a university itself to provide the cost of other types of vocational training for which it was subsequently repaid by employers. The State might underwrite such costs up to a certain limit if there was a worry that certain skills were declining.

Naturally emigration and immigration involve problems that need international co-operation. They should not be insoluble, since they are based on recognition of a reality – namely that if someone has been trained at considerable expense to a society or nation a debt has been raised that must either be discharged or consciously waived. The recorded cost only represents the marginal cost of tuition and not the cost of a share of the basic Resource. The idea of making employers or training boards partly responsible for the latter has already been discussed and discarded. An advantage of a system in which only marginal costs are charged is that it encourages employers to sponsor students to get the advantage of the existing Resource and discourages the setting up of expensive and inward looking in-house training schemes.

The discussion above has not introduced any fundamentally new principle. In the cases of doctors and schoolteachers, potential employers already control the numbers on vocational courses in institutions of higher education. Many companies have a tradition of sponsoring employees by paying their fees. If the system became universal, however, there might be a worry that employers or training boards might exert undue influence on course content or on the type of course available. One remembers the outcry which arose when the Chilver Report on the Training of Civil Engineers suggested that the profession should control (sic) the content of university courses.

In practice, provided that there is a diversity of sponsoring bodies, and the basic rights and responsibilities of each side are respected, no difficulties should arise. Academic institutions must have the right to decide which students they accept, to ensure that students do not embark on courses for which they are not prepared; and they must be the final arbiters of whether academic standards have been met. In preparing the syllabus of any vocational courses in universities advice is normally sought from practising professionals, who also give help with specialist lectures and projects. Universities know that unless a course covers certain ground it will not be recognised by the relevant profession and so those graduating from it may not be easily accepted into employment. But they must also be free to include ideas and developments that have not yet been accepted by the profession as part of the necessary preparation for a lifetime of practice.

The only direct control which an employer or board can exert is through the decision to sponsor students on certain courses and not others. However, it is probably no bad thing if certain employers favour certain courses which seem specially suited to their needs, as happens at the moment; other employers with different needs are likely to prefer courses elsewhere. A vocational course which can find no sponsors should probably be allowed to wither, or at least be deferred until people are ready for it.

Although the paragraphs above were written before the Finniston report was published their basic philosophy is not dissimilar. Finniston proposes the creation of an Engineering Authority, one of the terms of reference of which is the encouragement of the supply of engineers. The exact way in which the Authority will interact with the Training Boards is not spelled out, although the idea of training costs being recouped from the Boards is welcomed. One can therefore imagine the Authority working through the appropriate Training Boards.

The Authority proposed by Finniston would also have power to accredit certain vocational courses for engineers which would then receive earmarked funds. The proposals made here would bring some of these funds in from the tuition fees paid by employers. In Finniston's scheme the funds would be completely lost if accreditation were withdrawn. However, it seems possible that those following up the Report will recognise the instability engendered by the removal of accreditation of a complete course and will allow individual elements to be accredited. This would avoid the sudden major change in income consequent on removal of total accreditation; it could also lead to arrangements whereby a student on a course which was not wholly approved could obtain acceptable endorsements later at another institution.

Even when training boards cover most sectors of employment, we will still be left with certain professions, such as the law, where vocational training is undoubtedly necessary but practitioners are generally self-employed. Because there is no immediate employer, it will be necessary for the vocational training to be covered by a loan, either from a specially constituted training board or some other central source, which is repaid over time from earnings.

The question of loans, which was raised by Shirley Williams as the first of her Thirteen Points in 1969, often arouses an emotional reaction. At the time, the idea was opposed, by universities on the grounds that it would discriminate against poorer students (those with richer parents need borrow less) and against women (because of the negative dowry effect). In one sense the division between grants and loans is artificial. However the transaction is titled, the actual fact is that Society provides resources for education and training instead of spending its money on something else. The student who receives this bounty is either asked to repay the money spent on him by discharging an individual debt (the loan system), or he makes a general repayment by contributing to the education and training of the next generation through the rates and taxes which he pays later in life (the grant system). The advantage of calling the transaction a loan is that it draws the student's attention to Society's contribution to his own individual costs. The advantage of the generalised repayment method is that the cost is borne by those deemed most able to pay at the time.

The force of both the early objections to loans has been weakened by social developments in the last ten years. Inflation has squeezed differentials so that the proportion of the population who are able from income to provide the full grant, let alone the fees, for more than one child must be quite small, so most families would have to borrow anyway. The increasing pressure by women for a career, and the need for both parents to work to support a family, is reducing the number of non-working wives and enhancing the value of a wife's qualifications: so the negative dowry will discriminate less against women and may indeed become a 'positive dowry'. A loan system might, of course, discriminate generally against full-time vocational courses undertaken before employment – unless the qualification really was necessary before any form of employment in that particular profession was possible – but that is not necessarily a disadvantage, particularly if it is agreed that vocational courses are best organised in conjunction with experience.

If fees are paid by the employer or training board, one

particular advantage of the loan system – the personal attribution of cost – is retained. The disadvantage that the individual is saddled with repayment is avoided, as the cost is borne by the employer. There is nothing in the system proposed which prevents students who have saved the appropriate fees from applying for vocational courses without sponsorship if they wish to improve their personal qualifications. Similarly students from overseas may pay their own fees or be sponsored by their own government or have them paid by the home government as part of some international agreement.

In answer then to the question, 'Who pays tuition fees?', the following total package is proposed:

A. Tuition fees for a first general course in higher education – which would be either the two-year Part I of a course at a rich staff:student ratio, or the four-year course at a weak staff:student ratio – will be paid by local authorities for home students.

B. Tuition fees for the succeeding vocational course, where this is followed in a higher education institution, will be paid by the employer or a training board, or will be borrowed and repaid from professional fees charged by the self-employed; arrangements might eventually be facilitated by some form of transfer fee.

C. Part II of the traditional honours course at a rich staff:student ratio would be treated as a vocational course for high-fliers or scholars, and the tuition fees would be paid by the DES, or by the Civil Service Department or other eventual employer. PhD fees would be paid in the same way.

Unsponsored students will still be free to pay fees for the courses of their choice, whether a second general course or any form of vocational course, from their own funds. Foreign students could be sponsored by their own government, by the British Government, or by firms, or could save or borrow the fees for any course.

The net result of such a system, of which many elements already exist, would probably be to reduce the number of students taking the relatively expensive vocational courses or

Part II of traditional honours courses unrelated to their eventual employment.

It may be argued that such a system would be depriving those who might at other times have spent three years at university, immediately after leaving school, working at an honours degree in the subject of their choice. Did not the Robbins committee propound the principle that everyone who could demonstrate the potential to benefit from higher education should have access to it? And has not this principle been universally accepted? The principle, however, did not carry the rider that the State should provide the full costs of fees and upkeep for full-time study. Indeed the assumption that taxpayers are prepared to fund an unlimited number of students to follow their own preferences for expensive education, although widely held by potential beneficiaries, is probably false. Many taxpayers believe that to receive special extra education at their expense is a privilege which, if not earned, carries obligations and cannot be claimed as a free right. If the State is prepared to fund the establishment of a higher education Resource, and provided that the Resource is accessible to everyone who could benefit from it and is prepared to pay the marginal cost of their use of the Resource, then it can be argued that no inalienable right has been withdrawn. Surely the important thing is that as many as possible should have the opportunity of two years in higher education and should be able to return later if their careers require further study, or when they are able themselves to pay for the use of the Resource?

A reduction in the total numbers taking full honours degrees would free resources for an increase in those taking Part I, and so increase the proportion of the age group that has some experience of a university. Academic standards are preserved by ensuring that a limited number of students do continue through the full four years of an honours course at a relatively rich staff:student ratio. There might be a decrease in the numbers taking vocational courses immediately after their general course. But this would be balanced by there being more opportunities for those wishing to retrain later in their careers.

The key point is that the cost of vocational courses, which are of direct benefit to the individual and his employer, are borne by them: whereas the costs of general educational courses are shared by society at large. Total costs are not increased, and indeed may be reduced as unnecessary training is eliminated, so that no one should feel unjustly treated. The same principles can be applied to part-time courses, short courses, and indeed continuing and adult education of all sorts. With the basic Resource centrally funded, an individual is only asked to pay the marginal cost of a course which he undertakes for pleasure or advancement. The same arguments do not apply to those further education courses which should be universally available – for example those dealing with citizenship, parenthood, or health – but these would surely be better mounted through the school or further education system rather than through institutions of higher education.

STUDENT SUBSISTENCE AND RESIDENCE

The preceding sections have discussed only the institutional costs of providing for learning and scholarship. We must now consider how the student himself is supported during his periods of study. It is not unfair to suggest that our present system still has many of the characteristics inherited from earlier centuries when higher education was reserved for the sons of gentlemen. Many students are still provided with subsidised accommodation and food, and are looked after to an extent that they are unlikely to enjoy in later life. Not every student receives a full maintenance grant, but for those who do it is relatively lavish. In 1977/78 it was more than one quarter of the take-home pay of a lecturer (at the top of the scale). Yet the lecturer may well support three other people; he also pays rates, must maintain his house, and has countless other expenses that are not borne by the student who lives in subsidised accommodation. In addition the student's recreation is subsidised through his students' union. A junior technician or trainee typist has similar needs for sporting and other facilities, but in many universities such provision for employees is relatively small. In fact one can argue that much of the hostility of the general public towards students, which is manifested in letters to the press after any campus disturbance, is due to a feeling that students, particularly in universities, get much more lavish treatment than their contemporaries.

In looking to the future we have to take account of the following facts:

1. The age of majority is now 18, not 21.
2. Society will no longer accept a system in which members of one particular group – those academically skilled enough to pass two 'A' Level exams – then receive material benefits not shared by their contemporaries.
3. Institutions of higher education are now geographically widespread in Britain.
4. Many more people will want to take general or vocational courses later in life, so the proportion (though not necessarily the numbers) going straight from school to institutions of higher education is likely to fall.

The first fact (allied to the fourth) must mean that all students must now be accepted as adults independent of their parents. The current system, by which student grants are dependent on parents' means, is a recipe for discord and even blackmail – conscious or unconscious. Most academic tutors can provide instances: for example, 'I will pay my share of your grant if you read engineering but not if you read sociology'; or 'I will not pay my share of your grant unless you stop going out with that unsatisfactory boy friend'; or even, from the student himself, 'I did not like to ask father for my grant as I knew it would mean the family couldn't have a holiday'. To continue with such a system, which causes considerable stress at a particularly sensitive time when young people are just emerging from home and finding their own feet, can only be described as sadistic.

By the same token, it seems quite unnecessary to cook, clean, wash-up, decorate for and generally look after students as if they were still children in middle-class Victorian families. Their contemporaries who are already in employment would be expected to look after themselves: why should not they? In time past the communal meal in the college hall followed by coffee in the comfort of the common room was no doubt supposed to foster the sort of discussion that encouraged intellectual development. Now that no student can reasonably be expected to be waited on, is there any reason why the laundromat or kitchen should not be the venue for such conversations?

If a course is to be followed full-time, a student can hardly be expected to support himself on earnings. Nor is it reasonable to expect young people to have savings. As was argued above, it is not right to compel those who have just become adults to be dependent on their parents. The simplest solution would appear to be to make all students eligible for normal unemployment benefit throughout their course. This is, after all, only an extension of the system that already operates during the long vacation. It is simple; it cannot be said to produce undue privilege since the individual would genuinely qualify if he was not studying; and it is free from all the horrors of the parental contribution. Supplementary benefits are also graded according to the situation of the individual and should therefore provide properly for the post-experience student who may have family commitments.

Full-time study takes time which would otherwise be occupied by full-time employment, so it is right to provide unemployment benefit to compensate. But just as a full-time wage earner is free to augment his earnings from part-time or occasional work, so should a student be free to do this without affecting his basic unemployment benefit. It might be necessary to set a limit to the hours worked or the money earned so as to prevent abuse. But students in America and other countries have long been used to working their way through college without apparent detriment to their studies. There would seem to be no real harm in so organising institutes of higher education on this side of the Atlantic that many of the facilities were serviced or maintained by students, who were paid at corresponding part-time rates. In fact one fears that it is only the insidious creed of the total welfare state – 'everything should be done for me by someone else' – that has apparently blinded us to the anomaly of not requiring students to contribute in any way to the basic functioning of the institution at which they study.

At first sight such arrangements might be suspected by the trade unions representing campus employees. The Government would have to make it quite clear that the aim was not to reduce overall expenditure on education or to lessen opportunities for full-time employment. The aim is to extend the Use of a given Resource making it possible to provide new opportunities for school-leavers who do not at present go on to further education, and for those coming into higher education later in life. Open communication, full consultation and unhurried changes are of the essence.

Those who are temporarily unemployed generally live in their own home or with relatives. Is it fair to expect a student to exist on the same basic benefit payment if he goes away to study? Before this question can be answered the more basic one of why students need to go away to study must be considered. The idea of students not being entirely free to be accommodated at any university they choose provokes reactions as heated as any manifested in discussions on fees. It is, however, necessary to review dispassionately the reasons for requiring residence at the present time. They are practical, social and educational.

The practical reason is simply that travelling time is generally wasted time. If a course requires attendance at lectures every day and if study is facilitated by working in the library until ten at night, or on the computer in the small hours, then of course students must live close at hand. But conversely, if practicality were the sole criterion, courses would be so designed that they could be taken by those who did not live within five minutes' walk of the lecture room and relied on public transport. After all, the big civic universities before the war drew students to a very large extent from their hinterlands of Lancashire, Yorkshire, the West Midlands or the Scottish lowlands. Even now many institutions in the public sector (but by no means all) are largely attended by local students.

The social reason was originally the welding together of the elites which were to govern the country and the Empire or to staff the Church and the professions. The common experience of passing three years of early manhood in a cloistered environment has been part of the cement binding together the Establishment, as documented in Sampson's *Anatomy of Britain*. Residence in a community, and not just sitting at the feet of the same sages, was an essential part of this experience.

A universal elite is, however, a contradiction in terms. Certainly in an ideal society every member would aspire to being a member of one particular elite group, whether it be of cabinet makers, oboe players or marrow growers. But each group can only include a small fraction of the total population. In so far as higher education is expanding to the point at which ten or twenty per cent or even more of the population have that experience, it can no longer be the passport to those positions of special influence in professional or public life which represent less than one per cent of total employment.

On the other hand there are quite strong arguments against the socialising influence of residence at the present time. It fosters the idea of students as a race apart, an independent group of people with special interests and special rights. The rise of the student estate as described by Ashby, the political attitudes and influence of the National Union of Students, and indeed the history of confrontation between student bodies and other sections of the population, all develop and emphasise a division that should not exist. If we are really trying to produce a society in which education throughout life is the norm, then everyone will be a student for part of the year! Of course the young will always be more radical in their views than their elders; of course those in higher education are likely to be more articulate than others in putting forward their views; but anything that fosters an artificial division between students and the rest of the population as if they were unrelated and immiscible sectors must surely be wrong.

The educational arguments for residence are threefold. First, it is argued that students learn from each other. The opportunities for unstructured discussion and argument within peer groups that are an essential part of the learning process can best be provided when groups of students live together. An extension of the argument, that it was necessary for students and teachers to live together, started to weaken when college fellows were allowed to marry, and it could hardly be raised seriously in present-day universities. Second, it is argued that students should be free to choose any particular course for which they feel suited on educational grounds and must not be restricted to those provided by a local institution. Although a not unreasonable premise, one suspects that only a minority of undergraduate students actually make their choices in this way; others allow the quality of accommodation and sporting facilities, the siting of the campus, or the social experience of friends, to be the dominant factors in their choice. With the geographical spread of institutions of higher education, very large numbers of students should now be able to find the course they need not far from their homes. Third, it is argued that students should be encouraged to get away from home, where opportunities for study may be restricted, and to escape from the local environment. The present system of grants actually puts a premium on *not* going to the local university. Head teachers in particular seem always to advise prospective undergraduates to go to a university as far from home as possible. Such a widening of horizons may have been essential in an age when the population was static, travel difficult and television unknown, so that many children had never left their home county and knew little about life elsewhere; but these restrictions no longer apply. There is quite a strong contrary argument that too drastic an uprooting from the home environment can cause loneliness and depression. Furthermore the increased chance of finding old school friends in other faculties can enhance interdisciplinary contacts between students at universities with strong local intakes. This is not to assert that young adults should not leave home; only to say that when they do so they need not necessarily go to an institution at the far end of the country.

Perhaps then we should stop thinking about full-time students as a unique form of young adult and think of them as normal members of society who are involved in a particular activity with particular requirements. They have chosen to attend a university course for the time being instead of taking full-time employment. In order to get the full benefit from the course they will need to eat and sleep near the institution, at least during the week. There would appear to be a number of possibilities each of which may be especially appropriate to certain individuals.

Some, who are perhaps not ready to leave home immediately,

may continue to live with their parents and commute daily to a nearby institution which offers a course appropriate to their needs. Some, particularly those who are doing the vocational element of their course or who are returning to university after a period of employment, will already have their own home from which they can commute daily. Some, particularly those without many family ties, will be prepared to move and set up house in the area of the institution of their choice. Their needs are similar to those who find a job in the same area. It seems reasonable to treat these needs as part of the general requirements for housing in the area. By all means group students together to facilitate peer learning, but in a general complex of people with similar material needs rather than in an isolated ivory tower.

Finally, there are those whose home remains distant from the university. This category includes mature students whose family cannot move (for example because the other spouse is working); those already working in another area (including sandwich students); and those who still wish to base themselves with their parents but have no course locally available. These last groups are the only ones for which special residential provision seems justified. It is definitely second-home provision which would not be required for vacations, or perhaps even for week-ends, and need not be lavish.

It is important that the maintenance grant arrangements should neither be such as to bias an individual towards an unnecessarily expensive type of accommodation because its true cost is concealed, nor such as to prevent him attending a course he really needs. Provided the level of unemployment benefit, to which the student maintenance grant is to be linked, is adequate then the balance should be about right. The student living at home should have enough, provided that his travel expenses are covered by repaying extra travel costs in the same way that it is done for various projects sponsored by the Manpower Services Commission. The student who wishes to go away from home would be relatively less well off on such a scheme. Freedom is expensive, however, and it is surely just that anyone who wishes to set up house or to use dormitory facilities in the university might have to work part-time to pay the extra economic cost of the additional facilities he uses.

If the proportion of students living at home (their own home, that is, which is not necessarily that of their parents) is to increase, then it is important that this should be recognised in the provision of campus facilities for non-residents. There should be better accommodation for those who wish to stay late or to rest between instruction periods, or just to meet and gossip, and who are not resident on campus. The provision should recognise that they may be older and more sensitive to noise or chaos than school leavers.

We must accept that what is being proposed here seems rather more frugal than the standard to which some would aspire. One of our main national objectives, however, should be to improve the provision of vocational training for the 16 to 19 year olds who do not go on at present to further education and who are currently helped far less than their contemporaries in Germany or Sweden. It seems wrong to provide extra facilities such as subsidised accommodation for those in higher education while so many school leavers (particularly girls) do not even get basic training.

Having said this, however, it must be accepted that there is still considerable variation in the material standards of institutions in Britain. Some are old and well endowed and have built up their facilities over the centuries. Others are new and essentially incomplete. The former can afford to subsidise cultural and material amenities for which the latter have not yet the funds or the tradition. Eventually, given time, alumni support and the slowly accumulating wealth of the community, the amenities of the less advantaged institutions will improve but at the moment other needs may have greater priority. We can only accept that there is considerable variation between institutions and appreciate our good fortune that past ages have left us such a rich legacy even if it is patchy. Surely nothing is to be gained by destroying what is good and has taken centuries to build just because we cannot increase it tenfold in one generation.

To accept this variation, however, is *not* to admit that there are certain inevitable centres of *academic* excellence. Lord Rutherford maintained that the lean wolf ran fastest: over-indulgence is as dangerous as starvation. So one would always hope and expect that at any time every institution had one or more academic departments or units that were centres of excellence for a particular specialism.

The relevance of temporary centres of academic excellence to student choice will be less for the first part of their courses than for the second or vocational part. It is in the latter that they are most likely to be able to appreciate the intellectual excitement in such centres. By this time, under our proposals they will have made a vocational choice and may well be already in employment. Their employer will guide them towards courses that are highly regarded at the time. These may be in institutions different from those in which they first studied. The employer will have become responsible for the tuition fees and will certainly pay a minimum maintenance grant to the employee even if he does not make up full salary.

For the future, therefore, it is suggested that students should not be considered a race apart, but as normal adult members of society, with the same needs for a home base and the wherewithal to support it. These needs should be met by making them eligible for normal unemployment and supplementary benefit throughout any initial full-time course with the supplementary benefits to take account of exceptional individual commitments. In addition, they would be allowed to retain part-time earnings and be granted travel expenses beyond a basic minimim. Many students would already have, or would set up, their own homes near the institution they wished to attend. Residence on campus would be arranged for those who needed to retain a home elsewhere or were still based with their parents but it would not be lavish and would be charged at economic cost. Those undertaking the vocational part of their course would generally be employed, the employer taking responsibility for their maintenance as well as their tuition fee. Those students not employed would continue to be eligible for unemployment and supplementary benefit but would pay their own fees, as described earlier.

Institutions would make better on-campus provision for study and recreation for those who were not resident. The result might appear a little more frugal than in the past; but there seems no good argument for expanding or even retaining the relatively lavish provision of yesteryear when so little is done for the majority of school leavers, or for those returning to an educational institution later in life.

UNIVERSITY GOVERNMENT: LOCAL

The archetypal university may well have been a free association of teachers, who shared common facilities and supported themselves by the fees they earned individually, rather like a present-day partnership of architects or lawyers. Such a group can be completely autonomous and self-governing, setting its own objectives, and providing whatever services it wants, subject to no other special constraint than the need of its members to earn a living. British universities are still nominally autonomous institutions with their own charters. Apart from Oxford and Cambridge, each one is governed by an independent council or other similar statutory body. Their independence is, however, inevitably compromised by the fact that, apart from the University of Buckingham, they are largely dependent on State funds. In this section and the next, possible developments in the internal management and the external co-ordination of universities are discussed in the light of this fact and of modern trends in employee participation and student participation.

It is first essential to distinguish policy from procedures, executive actions and monitoring. These four distinct elements appear in the operation of any organisation. The first is the determination of overall objectives and basic policy, which is the duty of the governing body. Primarily this involves decisions about staff establishment, buildings and budgeting. The second is the determination of operating procedures – for example, how staff are appointed or how expenditure is authorised. In a university, academic procedures must be ratified by or on behalf of the highest academic authority, usually the Senate. Administrative procedures must be ratified for or on behalf of the governing body. In both cases the procedures must be accept-able, implicitly or explicitly, to those directly involved in their operation, or they cannot be made to work satisfactorily. This usually requires a framework of internal committees. Thirdly, there are executive actions taken by authorised individuals in furtherance of the objectives and in conformity with agreed procedures. Finally, there is the monitoring element of checking that these actions did in fact conform to the objectives and procedures and either confirming them or rectifying mistakes. In what follows it is only the first element, the determination of policy and objectives, which is considered. The internal pro-cedures and terms of reference required for the other three can be laid down comparatively easily according to normal good management practices. The governing body will be referred to throughout as the Council, although it may have different names in different institutions.

The particular difficulty of university government lies in the disparity of the interested groups. One can distinguish:

1. The national government which provides the funds to estab-lish and maintain the Resource.
2. The academic staff who have normally been appointed to tenured posts.
3. The non-academic staff.
4. The students who, although in some respects analogous to customers, are in fact far more intimately bound up with the activities of the organisation than customers of a normal commercial concern.

All of these groups have direct but usually different interests, long term or short term, in university policy. The first three are major power groups in that the operation of the university would stop if government funds or staff labour were with-drawn. Student power is indirect in that the only legal method of disruption available to students – staying away – could have an immediate and catastrophic effect on their own studies but does not much affect any of the other work of the university. It is, however, necessary to reach an accommodation with students over most matters simply because of the physical power they possess, on account of youth and numbers, and the university's lack of sanctions over people who are not employees.

The first complication encountered is that although most of the universities' funds derive from the State, it has always been a cardinal point in Britain that the State should not control academic matters. One of the functions of the university is to set standards against which the actions of others may be appraised critically. There is enough evidence from other countries of the control of syllabuses by the political party in power, or the suppression of research that might cast doubt on the wisdom of official policy, for Britain to cherish the freedom that academics currently enjoy and to eschew State direction.

At the same time, the Government as provider of funds would be quite within its rights to require, after consultation about possible consequences, that the university system follow certain broad policy guidelines – to take more students on two-year courses for example. Indeed if universities were completely insensitive to social needs as perceived by the electorate they could forfeit government support.

In effect the conflict between government funding and academic independence has been resolved in Britain by setting up University Councils on which there is a majority of lay members, and by allocating funds to the universities through the University Grants Committee and not direct from a government department. These lay members of Council should thus consider themselves as representatives of society at large, with the responsibility of ensuring that money provided from public funds is properly spent and that the overall university policies are consistent with its Charter.

The prime responsibility of the academic staff in policy matters is to ensure that the conditions for scholarship and research are preserved. The material conditions include a proper share of available resources and allowance of time, including study leave. Above that, however, the academic freedom to publish and debate the truth as the individual understands it is paramount. The University Senate, representing the distillation of the collective wisdom of the academics, is expected to propose lines of fruitful academic development, and so have a major influence on long-term plans and policy.

Fifty years ago the idea of the non-academic staff bringing influence to bear on the overall policy of the university would have occurred to few. At that time such staff could be engaged or dismissed at short notice: even today they are not described in most university charters as full members of the institution. The concept of employee participation has recently become more generally accepted, as the setting up of the Bullock Committee on Industrial Democracy showed. It is consistent with the theme of this paper that the non-academic staff provides part of the available Resource. Indeed it is a very important part, as the skilled technician, for example, is often a much more difficult person to find than a lecturer in an arts subject. Non-academic staff are therefore likely to be involved eventually in policy making, or at least to acquiesce in the way it is done, because without their acquiescence it cannot be carried out. Unfortunately the historical role of trade union representatives as negotiators with owners does not seem to have fitted many of them fully for this new role as partners in an enterprise, with a share in the responsibility for its success as well as a legitimate claim on its income.

In this context it is instructive to consider the point made in the Ford evidence to the Bullock committee. As summarised, in *The Sunday Times* for 28 May 1978 it read: 'Do the Trade Unions perceive their role as constructive opposition, which would lead to further development of collective bargaining and consultative machinery but would exclude board participation? Or do they see their long term role as one of full coalition partner in the management job, sharing the obligations and responsibilities which go with authority?' British unions have mostly up to now followed the first pattern. German unions follow the second, in which they take responsibility for the honouring of agreements by their members.

Similar difficulties arise with student unions, exacerbated by the facts that student representatives are usually relatively inexperienced compared with officials of employee unions and that the students' time scales are shorter. A student would like to achieve demonstrable progress within his single year of office while a trade union member can work on a longer time span. Furthermore, many student unions have exceedingly cumbersome procedures which require decisions to be reached by majority vote at a General Meeting which may be huge, uninformed, inquorate or unrepresentative: their representatives are then often mandated and given no power of negotiation or individual action. These arrangements could slowly alter as the proportion of the students in an institution who are already employed, or who are returning after experience outside, increases.

In the long term, therefore, one can conceive of a University Council representative of a wider range of interests than at present. It would include representatives of academic staff, non-academic staff and students, as well as lay members from the professions, employers, learned societies and local institutions who were considered disinterested but competent representatives of the society at large which provides the funds. Since it would be such a disparate body and since any decision could effectively be nullified by any of the internal groups, a convention would need to be evolved that ensures that no policy was ratified until the representatives of the groups were unanimous in agreement.

Before reaching this stage – for which most universities are not yet prepared – there is much that can be done to improve their internal organisation. Since outsiders have no prescriptive right to decide *how* the objectives of the institution are met, no lay members need be involved in internal committees. Nor is there any justification for giving academics any pre-eminence in deciding how non-academic sectors of the institution should be run or what non-academic facilities should have priority. In a complicated organisation, where the co-operation of all parties is essential, committees could be developed on the lines of the industrial 'works council', with all types and grades of staff represented. Where employees so desired, they would be represented through internal members of their own union or association. The proper method of operation of such a council is by unanimous voting. Every representative has a veto and no change can be made till all agree. Once agreement is reached it is accepted as binding on *all* parties. Operation of such unanimous voting committees would provide the experience and would develop the responsible attitudes that are needed to fulfil the long-term objective of a really representative university council.

It is indeed surprising that all universities have not already set up such bodies for the involvement in particular of non-academic staff. One suspects that in the past universities have changed so little and so slowly in their methods of operation that the need for formal consultation was not seen. In contrast the need was paramount in industry where change is continuous. Everyone there expects work loads to change and technology to develop so that continual adjustments must be made and continuous consultation is necessary.

NATIONAL CO-ORDINATION

In previous sections it was proposed that institutions of higher education should be regarded as a Resource, publicly funded in a stable manner. Though the discussion centred on universities, much of it is applicable to all sectors. It is now necessary to consider the mechanisms needed for determining and distributing central funds and whether there should be different mechanisms for universities and for polytechnics and other institutions of higher education.

In theory, it would be possible to have a system whereby the basic allocation to every institution was decided in the government Department of Education; indeed, certain institutions (such as the Open University) are at present funded in this way, by direct grant. If, however, the claims of fifty universities, thirty polytechnics and innumerable other institutions are to be equably treated some form of co-ordinating mechanism is required, whether inside or outside the Department. Taking it outside the Department has two advantages. First, it helps to insulate centres of learning from immediate political control, a need discussed in the previous section. Secondly it should facilitate public discussion of the issues involved.

Funds for British universities are currently allocated by central government on the confidential advice of the University Grants Committee. This body was set up in 1919 to advise the Government on the needs of universities. It is largely composed of academics and, supported by its sub-committees, has considerable detailed knowledge of what actually goes on in the university sector. The present UGC system has, however, three disadvantages. The first is its rather narrow base. Although committee members are usually well informed on academic matters their knowledge of non-academic or administrative problems may well be second-hand. No Student, Computer Manager, Librarian, Registrar or even Vice-Chancellor has ever sat on the Committee – though ex-members sometimes become vice-chancellors. There are indeed two or three lay members but they are, unlike their counterparts on University Councils, in a small minority. The result is that the perspective of the Committee is limited: proposals may be made that are administratively unworkable; other proposals may not be made because a predominantly university body does not feel strong enough to take decisions that would be locally uncomfortable.

The second disadvantage is its secrecy. Because the Committee's advice to the Government is not public, it has difficulty in establishing itself as the main advocate of the universities' needs. This role is being increasingly taken over by the Committee of Vice-Chancellors, the Association of University Teachers and other more limited pressure groups. The UGC is becoming thought of as the vehicle for manifesting the Government's view to the universities rather than the universities' view to the Government. The position could be retrieved in the short term by adopting a convention similar to that employed in matters of aviation safety. The British Civil Aviation Authority must consult the Airworthiness Requirements Board before licensing an aircraft. The Authority is not bound to accept the advice but if it does not do so it must make its reasons public. Should not the UGC's advice to the Government also be confidential only if it was accepted? And if not, should it not be made public and the responsible Minister have to explain in Parliament why he did not take it?

The third disadvantage of the present situation is that the

UGC only deals with the universities. There is no comparable body covering the public sector with which it could liaise, and no body overlooking the whole field of higher education which could help to co-ordinate work in the universities, the polytechnics and the other institutions. A binary line, separating universities from other institutions was drawn in 1966 when the Colleges of Advanced Technology (CATs), which had been funded direct by the DES became chartered universities, and the polytechnics, financed through local authorities, were set up to take their place. It was based on the assumption that universities were centres of research and scholarship and all their courses were training for scholars; the polytechnics and other colleges, in contrast, provided training for those destined for the world outside and were to run only vocational courses with strong local links.

It is possible that if a decision had been taken in Britain around 1950 to confine all expansion in higher education to institutions with a purely vocational bias, steadfastly distinguishing these from the traditional universities, a binary division might have made sense. But by expanding existing universities, creating new ones and bringing the CATs into the fold, it was inevitable that the centre of gravity of the universities would shift. A university system that takes in nearly ten per cent of school leavers cannot confine itself to pure research and the production of scholars: it must consider vocational needs, as the polytechnics have always tried to do. Indeed the ex-CAT universities in particular are still more oriented to the application of knowledge than some of the polytechnics.

The spectrum of university interests is now so wide, and overlaps the equally wide spectrum of polytechnic interests so much, that there is almost no subject of study, apart from medicine, that cannot be found on both sides of this imaginary binary line. There are therefore strong academic grounds for considering the whole of higher education as a national resource and correlating all its long-term planning.

Polytechnics, however, and even more the other public sector institutions, are also involved in work at sub-degree level and in part-time studies at all levels. Such work is primarily on behalf of the local populace and needs local rather than national co-ordination. This suggests that the polytechnics and colleges should operate on a dual support system, receiving basic funds for high-level work from central government and funds for lower-level and part-time work, which is predominantly local, through the local education authority or perhaps through an appropriate regional grouping of local authorities. They should be autonomous bodies governed by Councils similar to those postulated for the universities but with two principal sources of funds, local and national.

The duties of the national authority for higher education, or Higher Education Grants Committee, which is now proposed would be twofold. It would have to be able to assure central government that its bid for the support of the basic Resource was reasonable; and it would have to be able to assure the institutions themselves that scholarship would be protected. Some measure of overall direction is inevitable. Certain subjects are either so unpopular or so specialist that it is only possible to assemble a critical mass of students and staff in a few places. Other disciplines may require equipment, libraries or other facilities which are so large or expensive that they cannot be duplicated. The co-ordinating body has to ensure that available resources are not dissipated, accepting that everyone cannot do what they like, where they like, and command unlimited facilities for their activities. On the other hand, institutions have to have some independence from outside control. They must be free to explore new lines of inquiry, to develop new disciplines, and to be critical of existing arrangements. It might be possible to ensure this by so arranging allocations that all institutions have a small amount of 'free' development money above that allocated for known elements of the Resource. The UGC system was developed to preserve just such local autonomy. In summary then, the following system is proposed:

1. There should be a single Higher Education Grants Committee (HEGC) which would advise on the distribution of central government funds for maintaining the basic Resource – that is, providing for staff, equipment and build-

ings – for higher education. It would deal with all institutions involved in such work. Its objective would be to maintain national competence in all academic disciplines. Its recommendations could be publicly debated if they were not accepted. The composition of its membership would reflect that of the governing bodies of the institutions.

2. Local authorities would still be responsible for providing lower-level education for their constituents of all ages. They would also be responsible for the funding of part-time work on a local basis. Funds for the basic Resource for this work would flow through the local authorities to local, regional and, where appropriate, national institutions.

3. In addition employers, which would include central government or local authorities acting in that capacity, could provide special support to institutions giving training on a long-term basis to their employees either locally or, in specialist subjects, regionally or nationally.

Individual institutions would derive their basic funds from all three sources in different proportions according to their particular situations. They would also, of course, all receive funds from users in the form of tuition fees, research grants and contracts for specific services. National institutions would depend largely on the central HEGC allocation. Some specialist institutions would rely heavily on employer sponsorship. Institutions which were more oriented towards local needs would obtain more of their basic resources from local authorities. In each case the governing body would have a duty to be responsive to the needs of the providers of funds and also to protect the independence of scholarship. Each institution would manage itself autonomously under its governing body.

The new system could not be achieved overnight. It could, however, develop out of existing arrangements and it would avoid the need for hard decisions about whether particular institutions were national, regional or local. Such decisions are inevitably arbitrary since in reality education and training form a continuous spectrum, without discontinuities.

CONDITIONS OF ACADEMIC SERVICE

One of the objectives of considering the basic university Resource in terms of staff and buildings is to provide the stability which makes long-term planning and programmes possible. Stability can, however, lead to stagnation. What is required is a stable framework within which change can be planned and facilitated. In the last three decades the great expansion of the higher education Resource has made changes relatively easy: one simply expanded differentially those activities one wanted to promote. If now it is necessary to change the uses to which the existing Resource is put, and in particular to change the pattern of studies in an institution without increasing its staffing, much more flexibility is required. Unfortunately a convention has grown up that academic staff should be appointed to a particular post and should be free to continue in it until retirement. Indeed in many universities this right of tenure is written in to the academic conditions of service. Even the posts themselves may be regarded as 'established' and so be automatically refilled when a vacancy occurs. The resulting difficulty in reassigning teachers or posts to areas where they are most needed causes imbalances of load which are inefficient. Early retirement is an expensive solution and redundancy unacceptable. It is therefore necessary to re-examine the need for permanent tenure and propose an acceptable alternative.

A place must undoubtedly be reserved in any university system for the dedicated scholar who has limited himself to one particular specialist field and made himself the supreme master of it. Sitting at the feet of an acknowledged expert in this class is one of the greatest privileges of higher education. A lifetime of study in a scholarly environment may be necessary to produce people of such distinction. In such cases the idea of permanent tenure of a particular post does seem appropriate. Having said that, one must admit that such people are relatively rare. In general there are sound academic reasons for encouraging mobility.

The first is that novel ideas are often suggested by those who come to a problem fresh from another discipline. Uninhibited by past experience they are forced to think afresh and may make an imaginative lateral jump which had not occurred to those who had become accustomed to looking at the problem in a conventional way. Intelligence, after all, is the ability to see common features in apparently disparate phenomena: it is often best exercised by the man brave enough to launch into a field which is new to him. Such a man would be expected to remain just as fresh intellectually, and just as stimulating a teacher, as one who had been exercising his wits by extrapolating his existing research.

The second reason springs from the danger of overspecialisation. Sympathy for, and understanding of, disciplines other than one's own ought to be the hallmark of the educated man. Most of the graduates who leave higher education for the outside world will have to tackle problems which are essentially inter-disciplinary. Most of them will be expected to be able to apply the habits of enquiry, analysis, logical argument and scholarly exposition, to problems in subjects quite other than the ones through which they were educated. They will find it difficult to do this if their entire life in higher education has been among academics who have confined themselves to a single field.

Furthermore, many exciting developments arise at the boundaries between disciplines, which are, after all, rather arbitrary divisions of the total field of knowledge and understanding. If an institution is made up of specialists whose careers have all been in one department, inter-disciplinary contacts are difficult. Where many of the staff have worked in several departments and know colleagues everywhere such developments are far easier.

There are, however, serious impediments to movement in academic institutions. The first is that any move requires courage on the part of the individual and support by the institution. Not everyone is confident that his pedagogic skills are transferable, or that he has the capacity to absorb and develop a new field. Until such transfers become more frequent, staff will doubt their ability to change. But unless this ability exists in the populace at large any talk of re-training for those outside academe must surely be a dead letter. One can hardly propose continuing education for the rest of the world and assume that academics, who represent the intellectual cream of the country, are incapable of it. The institution, for its part, must be prepared to help by allowing study leave on a generous scale. A member of staff might require at least a year of concentrated study before being prepared to take responsibilities in a new subject, even one not far removed from his previous interest. Working in a university, however, should provide opportunity for a good deal of preparatory work such as attending courses in other disciplines on a part-time basis. Indeed an institution in which it was accepted practice for most of the staff to be attending classes or tutorials in subjects other than their own would be a real learning community.

The second difficulty at present inhibiting staff movement is the lack of incentive. Lecturers are paid by age, receiving automatic increments annually, virtually irrespective of performance. In order to provide encouragement it is necessary to have a system where salary increases are the result of positive actions justified by performance, and not merely the consequence of the passage of time. The normal criteria of academic performance may need to be modified, too, in order to acknowledge the value of breadth as well as depth. In the long run the stimulation of moving into new fields should produce exciting new ideas. In the short run, the academic who changes discipline may lose a year or two in his output of learned publications and this must be properly allowed for by his assessors. This raises the further point that pedagogic skills are often given insufficient weight by academic promotion boards. This is partly because it is easier to assess the value of publication than of teaching. But in an institution where many of the academic staff themselves are being tutored or attending seminars in subjects other than their own, peer judgements would be developed more easily, particularly if the 'student' group included staff from other institutions.

A third difficulty is that any change in tenure arrangements would be interpreted as an attack on academic freedom. If this freedom implies the freedom to express the truth as one sees it and to publish one's ideas for critical discussion, then it is not attacked. For there is no suggestion that contracts would not be renewed. Indeed under present legislation employment can only be terminated for good cause such as demonstrable incompetence or dishonesty. The proposed arrangements therefore introduce no new sanctions which could be used to muzzle free expression of unpopular views.

If, however, academic freedom is thought to encompass freedom to teach whatever one chooses, or indeed not to teach at all, then it has never existed for most academics and can rarely be justified for the others. An institution which accepts fees and grants is inevitably constrained; few of its sponsors provide completely free funds and nearly all academics are required to teach certain subjects under present arrangements. That having been said, however, it is essential that any wider interpretation of tenure such as is now proposed should be based on arrangements that were mutually agreed and acceptable to all concerned.

Combining these ideas, it is proposed that the normal academic contract of service should in future be on a fixed-term but renewable basis. In the first instance it would be for five years and this would constitute in effect the probationary phase. Thereafter it would be renewed on the basis of seven years (or perhaps ten years for the most senior) but not necessarily in the same department. These succeeding contracts might well be preceded by a period of study leave in preparation for a change. They could also involve movement to a higher salary-level as a recompense for the undoubted effort involved in change, a recompense which would not be the norm for those who had continued in the same field.

The proposals would also facilitate the regular rotation of university offices, such as departmental headships, while providing a sufficient term for the incumbent to achieve something during his tenure. The same arrangements, incidentally, might apply to vice-chancellors. The strain of that particular office in present circumstances is one which future generations may not be willing to accept for an indefinite period. If, however, a system such as that advocated in the previous sections were adopted, the post of principal of an institution of higher education might again involve planning, reflection and indeed success, instead of expedients, politics and frustration. That would indeed be a new quinquennium to which one could look forward.

3

The issues: from the graduate employers

DAVID DENNIS

Graduates: educated but not prepared

In common with many colleagues throughout industry and commerce, I spend much of my time grappling with the problems of recruiting graduates for commercial careers. First we aim to attract the highest possible calibre of applicant. Then we attempt to select those who are most suitable, identifying the various combinations of personal qualities which are likely to lead to success and satisfaction in each chosen career. Finally we spend a great deal of time and energy in planning training-programmes to satisfy the wide-ranging requirements of both candidate and company during their first few months together.

If that sounds fairly complex (as, indeed, it often appears to me) then let us consider for a moment how much more difficult is the task facing each student as he or she approaches gradua-tion. He is required to make one of the most important choices of his life with seriously inadequate information about practi-cally every factor relevant to the final decision. Most important, he has little practical experience of the world of work. Vacation employment opportunities are usually of a menial and mundane nature, and even sandwich placements fail, in many cases, to provide sufficient involvement for the experience to be of use in making a career choice.

In addition, our education system has no real tradition of teaching young people to assess their own personal strengths and weaknesses. Too often we stop at the traditional question 'What can I do with my degree?', instead of asking which styles of working, personal relationships and working environments will suit each individual, regardless of degree subject. Finally, our higher education institutions make little attempt to develop the range of personal skills which are necessary for success with any employer and in almost any occupation.

It is on these three areas – practical experience, self assessment and the development of personal skills – that this chapter will concentrate. My purpose is to suggest ways in which our higher education institutions should develop to meet these needs. It is too easy for those in industry and higher education to point to the existence of careers advisers to provide the answer. Certainly, if it was not for the increasingly effective information and counselling services available in universities and polytechnics, the situation would be a great deal worse. However the problem is more deep-rooted.

Our higher education system is, by its nature, geared to objectives and ways of working which are very different from those which apply outside the academic world. It provides few experiences to reduce the huge adjustments necessary for success in employment, and also does little to prepare students in any practical way for the complex nature of these adjustments. We have chosen to accept this situation in spite of the fact that amongst the products of this system are many of our nation's most talented future wealth creators, in whom we have invested heavily for many years. The price of failing to prepare such people well for their careers is therefore great.

Our strategy to 'bridge the gap' must look hard at both our higher education system and at the world of work. Clearly there are implications for our educational institutions involving their purpose, structure and teaching methods. Whilst the purpose of higher education should not exclusively be to serve the needs of employers, many of the methods by which students can prepare for future employment have far wider educational value. Our task is to use the combined expertise of teachers and employers to design courses which achieve the best of both worlds. Not only is such an approach appropriate for the start of the 1980s, it is already urgent. *Higher Education into the 1990s* made it clear that change is being forced upon us. Several of the alternative solutions are consistent with encouraging closer links between education and work. Good planning now could make a virtue out of this necessity and radically improve our long-term economic success as a nation whilst preserving, indeed enhancing, the overall value to our young people of their education.

I do not believe that these problems can be solved merely by running more vocational courses. Vocational education is a traditional battle-ground, the arguments for which are well known: Should education be for life or for work? Should faculty sizes be determined by manpower requirements? To what extent can predictions about future manpower requirements ever be accurate, particularly when the impact of micro-processor technology is largely unknown? Even if accurate forecasts can be made, should they be heeded, or should we meet the individual preferences of students? Is it desirable or practicable for faculty sizes to alter quickly, and how can violent swings of the pendulum be avoided? What emphasis should be given to disciplines which are largely non-vocational? Should not industry recognise a responsibility to train, rather than expect to be provided with fully operational employees?

Clearly, these issues require urgent discussion between specialist employers and the relevant faculties in higher educa-tion. Individual problems will require their own solutions and, in each case, both higher education and industrial training will need to make a different contribution. However, my major concern is with the much wider problems of personal adjust-ment faced by students of all disciplines on entering almost any type of employment.

QUALITIES, NOT QUALIFICATIONS

This issue of non-vocational preparation for work is almost always neglected in discussions of higher education, although the more obvious problem of unemployed school-leavers has encouraged some action at that level. Because 'preparation for work' has largely been equated with 'vocational training', it has been assumed that students reading non-vocational subjects do not need (or cannot be given) any preparation at all. That they need it is clearly evident simply from talking to them. They are largely ignorant of the opportunities, the styles of working and the various combinations of personal skills needed in different occupations. Most important, they have little idea of how to develop or assess their own strengths and weaknesses. They recognise their need for advice, but without knowing how to ask the right questions.

Consequently, the demand is growing for relevant information, about the day to day realities of the available jobs, and the
personal qualities needed for success. There is a clear trend
towards earlier contact with Careers Services and a strong
development of student societies interested in forming links
with the business world, notably the Industrial Society and
AIESEC. The latter is particularly interesting in this context
because, at local, national and international level, it is run
entirely by students. Its major activity consists of arranging
international exchanges for students, providing opportunities
for interesting work experience in a different cultural environment. Nevertheless, most contact on campus between students
and employers is inevitably secondhand, consisting mainly of
talks and discussions, with occasional visits to employers'
premises.

The 'Insight into Management' courses run at weekends by
CRAC provide a further dimension, exposing students to
simulated 'business games', which give a more practical view of
alternative careers. This approach is clearly limited by the time
available (four days to cover marketing, finance, personnel and
public administration), yet the courses are heavily over-
subscribed and provide, for many, their first real experience of
the world of work.

Significantly, the majority of today's students see the main
purpose of obtaining higher qualifications largely in terms of job
opportunities. It is the joint responsibility of the business and
academic worlds to respond far more positively to this trend.

At this stage, let us not imagine we are only discussing
'non-vocational' students. It is equally important that those
studying subjects with a clear vocational direction should be
encouraged to develop personal skills and to go through the
complementary processes of job analysis and self evaluation.
Indeed the academic and social pressures to 'use your degree' are
such as to require an even greater effort to prepare these students
properly for a good career choice.

So the problem which needs to be resolved centres on how to
give this form of preparation, and to determine who should,
most appropriately, shoulder the responsibility. In the course of

this chapter, I shall suggest a number of possible approaches, but what emerges throughout is that both teachers and employers need to be fully involved.

It is strange that these objectives appear not to be ones which the academic world is happy to embrace. Knowledge of the personal skills which are required by our industries, our businesses, our professions and our civil service surely comes under the heading of 'education for life' rather than 'vocational training', and as such should be included amongst the educator's primary aims. For many years, teachers have justified the study of classics, to quote just one example, by pointing out the mental disciplines which such study imposes. Employers will readily agree with this. In recruiting graduates they are primarily interested in the capacity for analytical and creative thinking which any degree demands.

The problem seems to be that our higher education system, whilst accepting the principle of developing 'life skills', has neglected some of the most important ones, and allowed itself to remain static, while the world of employment has steadily changed. Teachers must re-think their approach not only to teaching methods, but to the overall contribution which higher education makes to the personal development of students. If it is possible to catch up with the present needs of employers, then there is a chance of preparing adequately for the more dramatic changes yet to come.

So what are these, as yet undefined, personal skills? Of course, each type of job requires different abilities, but there are a number of important qualities which are needed in the vast majority of occupations. In discussion with my recruiting colleagues in other fields of employment, I find a remarkable measure of agreement over which are the major problems. This applies, by and large, to a much wider section of employment than is generally realised. Whilst industry, commerce, banking, teaching and the civil service have slightly different requirements, they all involve the same basic ingredients. These fall into two main categories, which we can define as 'personal' and 'inter-personal' skills. In the first category there are five broad but related areas: working under time pressure; ranking and dealing with priorities; attention to practical detail; personal accountability through continuous appraisal; relatively low initial status.

In his initial exposure to these criteria, the graduate at first feels that he has entered an alien world. He finds that the volume of work achieved and the order in which it is completed appear to be more important than the quality of his thought or the elegance of his ideas. The nature of the work appears, by comparison with his studies, to be trivial and mundane, success being achieved by somehow keeping a lot of balls in the air, rather than by analysing their optimum trajectory. The result of mistakes is frank (even if friendly) criticism, administered with a directness that can appear threatening. Finally his status (and practical ability) is lower than that of people whom he may rightly regard as his intellectual inferiors.

Closely related is the problem of learning to form new types of relationships with working colleagues. Again five areas of inter-personal skills can be identified: working as part of a team; working within a hierarchy; working with people from all social and educational backgrounds; communicating necessary information to the right people in an appropriate manner; assessing, criticising and training others.

The common thread which runs through these is that the student is no longer self sufficient, nor dependent only upon himself for success or failure. His performance suddenly depends on his ability to work with other people, to adapt his approach to different relationships, and get his own way by persuasion and co-operation rather than by the pure logic of his argument.

By comparison with these adjustments, the acquisition of new knowledge, objectives and procedures is easy – the student has been doing that for years. It is often a necessary therapy for the harassed graduate trainee to be sent off with a pad and pencil to analyse a complex business problem and suggest solutions. This may involve a great deal of investigation and analysis in totally unknown areas, but the result will be beautifully presented, logical and often of considerable value to the employer. The expression of relief and gratitude on the face of the trainee when presented with such a task has to be seen to be believed!

It is my own belief that these criteria are crucial to success and personal satisfaction in most careers, but it would be foolish to suggest that every student can develop them in equal measure, or that they are required in the same proportions by each employer. So whilst educating students to cope with these adjustments is vital, it does not assist individual career choice.

An informed career decision requires two types of knowledge: of the job and of one's self. Employers' literature normally does little to help. We are very good at 'selling' the company, but extraordinarily bad at describing the real content of a job to anyone who has little relevant experience with which to make comparisons, or who is unfamiliar with the organisation concerned. Yet it is 'job content' which has been top of the list on every survey into student career-choice which has ever been undertaken. Furthermore, many students have never considered objectively where their own strengths and weaknesses lie, except in terms of academic success. Ask them at what sort of personal relationships they are most successful, and you may be suspected of asking a vaguely improper question!

The majority reach the age of twenty-one without anyone – teacher, tutor or parent – having sat them down and asked them to think about themselves in terms relevant to future job satisfaction, such as:

Will I enjoy working on my own, or as part of a team?
Will I work best with many superficial relationships or a few deep ones?
Do I want to be responsible for other people?
Will I prefer the security of a large organisation or the relative independence of a small one?
How will I cope with swiftly changing priorities?
What degree of routine will I be happy with?
Will I be motivated without clearly quantifiable measures of success?
Will I enjoy travelling away from home, and how often?
How important will material rewards be?

The answers are by no means clear for each individual, and they certainly change with age and domestic circumstances. Yet even if definitive answers cannot be given, at least we should encourage young people to consider these questions. It is criteria such as these, I would suggest, that we all use privately to assess the satisfaction that we obtain from our jobs.

I have outlined, so far, two major problem areas: firstly, a lack of preparation for the adjustment from higher education to employment; secondly, a lack of job knowledge and self knowledge on the part of the student, both of which are prerequisites for a sound career choice. These problems can only be overcome by changes within higher education, and a more positive approach by employers. Our failure to communicate these ideas is perhaps the most serious indictment of the way in which we arm young people to cope with their adult lives. The sort of self-knowledge required for career choice is the same as that which each of us needs to develop, one way or another, in order to survive socially, in marriage, and in every activity. It is education for 'life' in its fullest sense.

Employers have a responsibility to design training programmes which make easier the complex adjustments from higher education to work. Too often employers lack sensitivity, accepting the distress and confusion suffered by graduate trainees as a 'natural' phase, when clearly much can be done to alleviate the problems. If we cause a graduate to lose confidence and doubt his ability to contribute, then sure enough he will be of little use. Initial training should provide an intelligent mixture of practical experience, project work and theoretical training, to allow a smooth transition to the new environment. A graduate, above all, needs to be reassured that the considerable intellectual skills that he has spent some years developing will be well used in his job. With good training he is more than capable of adapting to achieve new objectives, but he needs time to adjust.

WORK EXPERIENCE

Of the possible solutions to the problems outlined above, I deliberately start with work experience. First, because it provides the most direct answer, allowing the student to come to terms with the necessary adjustments whilst providing an opportunity for him to assess his personal suitability for at least one career. Second, because it cannot take place without the co-operation of teachers and employers, which is vital to any solution. It also has the practical advantage that forms of work experience are already available to students at various stages of their development, both within and outside the course framework. Improvements in this area are, therefore, refinements of existing practices rather than innovations. Bearing in mind that circumstances dictate urgent action, such an approach may be our only short-term solution, born of necessity, but to the long-term benefit of all concerned.

This urgency stems from the predicted numbers in higher education during the 1980s and 1990s. *Higher Education into the 1990s* gave a range of predictions, all of which involved some increase in numbers to the mid-1980s and then a major contraction, at least into the mid-1990s. The problems of such a trend are enormous. Many solutions involve a departure from the Robbins principle; other solutions involve reductions of one sort or another in the quality of education that can be offered. However, the Document also makes it clear that delaying entry for a proportion of students (up to two-thirds at most) would allow numbers to be 'smoothed out' over the decade of peak demand. A combination of a year's delay for some, and periods away during the course for others, would achieve a similar effect.

Here is the opportunity to explore a variety of patterns for new courses involving a mix of academic study and work experience. Since the Industrial Revolution the worlds of education and work have drifted further and further apart, both physically and in character. The proposals which follow are just a few of the possible methods by which they can be constructively reunited.

For a long time, students have supplemented their grants by accepting boring vacation work. This is not to say that the experience has been completely worthless. An observant student can use even the most repetitive and menial occupation to learn how people behave at work, how they relate to their managers and how they can be motivated. It is also possible for him to assess his own suitability for a particular working environment and management style. However, it is rare for such vacation employment to provide sufficient insight into the content of more senior jobs within the organisation, or any real idea of the pace or pressures with which a graduate would have to work. This can only be achieved by a more structured approach to the employment experience.

A: A year in-between

Let us consider the first of the Document's options, involving a year's delay in taking up a place. Applicants to Oxford and Cambridge have done this for many years during the equivalent of two academic terms between taking entrance examinations and starting the course. Variants of these arrangements are widely accepted in many other universities, polytechnics and colleges. The way in which this time is filled is entirely up to the individual, and many students have used it constructively to fill some of the 'gaps' in preparation for work which have already been discussed.

If the 'year in-between' were to become the rule rather than the exception, then it would benefit from more planning and control. It should be designed, with the help of school or college staff, to complement planned areas of academic study, or deliberately to provide contrasting experience. Where possible the student would experience employment in more than one field in order to compare different jobs. In addition, each period of employment needs to be long enough to allow sufficient involvement and individual contribution. It might be desirable for universities and polytechnics to recommend, or even insist upon, particular types of experience before joining certain courses. In the case of sandwich courses, such pre-course employment could be planned to complement later placements.

B: Sandwich courses

We should free our thinking from the traditional 'thick' and 'thin' structures, and allow the definition 'sandwich course' to embrace varying mixtures of academic study and work experience.

Where course content relates closely to a particular field of employment, students could spend time regularly attached to a local employer. Rather than rely entirely on project work controlled by the university, polytechnic or college, it should be possible for certain employers to develop a much closer relationship with the faculty concerned, contributing practical experience to course design, and perhaps becoming involved in the assessment of performance.

Vital to any form of work experience, if it is to be of use, is that its content and structure should be planned to enhance the benefit of academic study and vice versa. Each placement should be designed to open up the world of work by layers, like peeling an onion. Three broad stages can be envisaged, the first consisting of formal training including attachments to the various functional areas of the business (e.g. production, marketing, personnel). A second stage, using project work, would build on this general knowledge in specific areas, chosen to complement, where possible, a particular course option. Within business studies and other vocational courses, the possibilities are obvious and little more imagination is needed to relate, for example, language courses to exporting companies, or the broad range of social sciences to industrial relations. The third stage should provide real responsibility, putting into practice the experience already gained. This could take one of many forms depending on individual circumstances. Within a large organisation, the student could act as personal assistant to a middle or senior manager, or, depending on his skills and temperament, might gain more from working as part of a small technical team. At all times, the student should be involved with senior employees, learning what is required in a demanding job, and what frustrations and satisfactions can occur along the way. Academic staff concerned with such placements should themselves experience as much as possible of this type of programme. Similarly, employers who provide these placements would benefit from a personal knowledge of course content and teaching methods.

Let no one imagine that the commitment required by employ-

ers in order to achieve the real benefits of work experience will
be insignificant. Many more places are needed over and above
those currently offered. Only trained personnel can design and
implement suitable programmes and monitor them closely.
Time must be spent in understanding clearly the educational
objectives and how they relate best to the employer's structure
and activities. Line managers must be trained to provide guidance and criticism which is constructive and appropriate to each
student's needs. A similar flexibility will be needed on the part
of teachers and course designers, in order to ensure that individual work-experience attachments are 'milked' of their full
educational value, by good preparation, follow up, and discussion. This approach requires building a long-term relationship
between an employer and a course tutor. At present this is only
the case in a few highly vocational areas. For example, Marks
and Spencer offer scholarships to clothing-technology students
at Hollings College, Manchester, and provide periods of relevant work experience within the company and at suppliers.
New thinking is required to extend this approach to arts, science
and social science courses.

Those employers able to contribute resources are presumably
also good businessmen. As such, they will wish to see a return
on their investment. Many of the benefits are, inevitably, long-
term and difficult to quantify. A better prepared graduating
population will make more successful career decisions, be
quicker and cheaper to train, and will make a real contribution
earlier. But there are also short-term benefits to employers – and
not just for the major companies. A small business might find
that a close relationship with a relevant faculty will, from time
to time, provide a graduate recruit. Occasional vacancies of this
nature can, otherwise, be hard to fill. During a well-planned
period of work experience, both employer and student have a
good chance to weigh each other up. Those students who have
fitted in well are likely to consider joining the employer
permanently on graduation. The employer has therefore invested in the best possible selection technique, and can be as
confident as is ever possible of taking on a successful trainee.

Recruitment and training represent a major investment on the part of any employer. By the end of his first year, each graduate has probably cost his company well over £2000 in addition to his salary. A high early drop-out rate in many areas has cast doubts on the effectiveness of many current selection methods. It also represents a significant waste of money. It might even be possible for employers to justify work experience schemes purely in terms of cost effective recruitment. I would not imply that they should enter these schemes merely with the intention of creaming off the best graduates for future employment, but if that possibility leads to more and better placements, then it will be no bad thing. I have so far made no mention of the valuable contribution which the student may make to the employer during his work experience. The injection of fresh (even naive) thinking may allow old problems to be seen in a new light. Students may well be entrusted with project work of the 'desirable' rather than 'essential' type, which might otherwise be neglected altogether.

What emerges from this discussion is the need for a more radical approach to an established practice. Not merely to encourage more students to become involved in work experience, but to achieve the full integration of practical and academic teaching. The preceding pages have outlined a principle and some basic objectives. The detailed methods by which these are developed must be individually worked out by teachers and employers. Our first priority is that the fullest discussions should take place with a double purpose. Firstly to break down those suspicions and misunderstandings which still exist, and secondly to develop jointly a new approach which will turn good intentions into practical solutions.

THE TEACHING ENVIRONMENT

In dealing with work experience, I have touched on the broader area of teaching methods and the working environment within higher education. In this final section, I shall examine to what extent the various factors which constitute the teaching environment can contribute more fully to the preparation of students for the world of work.

School leavers of eighteen seem to find the transition to employment less of a 'cultural' adjustment than those who have first progressed to higher education. The conclusion may be drawn that higher education in some ways leaves students less well prepared for work than they were three or four years previously. It may be helpful to examine the contribution which school on the one hand, and higher education on the other, make to the development in young people of the ten skills ('personal' and 'inter-personal') previously discussed. The table below shows my own rough estimate (in assessing higher education, I am assuming a traditional three-year Honours degree in either Arts or Sciences).

	Very poor	Poor	Reasonable	Good
Personal skills				
Time pressure		HE		S
Ranking priorities		S	HE	
Practical details	HE		S	
Accountability		HE		S
Low initial status		HE	S	
Inter-personal skills				
Team work		HE	S	
Hierarchy	HE			S
Work relationships		HE		S
Presenting information		S	HE	
Training/criticising others	HE	S		

S = School; HE = Higher Education.

Of course, it is impossible to quantify such matters accurately, and my estimates take no account of different courses, different teaching methods and different domestic environments, all of which have a marked influence. Nevertheless, a strong overall pattern emerges. In only two cases does traditional higher education improve upon school, and then not by much. In the other eight cases, schools do better than higher education, and in seven cases out of ten provide a reasonable or good preparation. This has come about not by any conscious effort, but as a by-product of educational objectives in each case. Schools, by their nature, restrict individual freedoms more, and require pupils to be disciplined in their interaction with each other.

Students, being older, are given far more freedom, both in what they choose to do and in how they organise their time. They have few constraints on how they interact with staff and other students, and can choose to be almost entirely self-sufficient if they wish. This is not in itself a criticism; indeed, this environment builds a number of personal qualities much appreciated by employers. Students learn to think for themselves, find those ways of working which suit them best and become self-motivating. The answer is not, of course, to make higher education more like school, but to examine ways of making it more like work, in areas which do not detract from educational standards, and which may even enhance them.

A variety of teaching methods are currently employed in higher education, each requiring different skills from the student as well as the teacher. A lecture demands very little from the student, except the capacity to concentrate hard and write notes rather fast. However a wide range of personal skills are used when the teaching method involves active participation from each student. The tutorial, where two or three students and their tutor discuss previously prepared work, opens up the possibility of developing several useful personal qualities: written and verbal communication; the ability to work as part of a team in constructive discussion; listening to and evaluating other points of view.

The seminar can add significantly to this list of skills, because it requires each student to make a presentation to a small group of his peers. Such an approach can be used to develop the ability to persuade others; a positive attitude to criticism, implying a measure of accountability; some time pressure involved in the presentation; the ability to lead a discussion; the confidence to criticise the contributions of others; experience of working in a simple hierarchy.

A high content of seminar work within a course will, therefore, be of considerable benefit to the student when he enters employment, as well as providing a more interesting way of learning. However, a successful seminar is not easy to run. Students and tutor need considerable training and experience if the greatest benefits are to be obtained. The tutor, in particular, needs to be adept at handling group dynamics as well as at monitoring and influencing the content of the discussion.

If a student is exposed to a variety of teaching methods coupled with periods of work experience, then a firm foundation is laid which will assist in many of the necessary adjustments to future employment. The student will not only have gained knowledge and confidence in various working relationships, but will also have had a chance to compare his own performance in each. He may have discovered that leading and controlling a seminar group is one of his strengths, or that he is better in a one-to-one relationship. He may have been able to assess several different working environments and have begun to favour some in preference to others.

A catalyst is needed to set the seal on this process, for few students can carry out useful self-analysis unaided. Historically, this has been the role of the careers adviser, who may be the first person ever to advise the student to consider what style of working is likely to suit him, and to worry less about how to use his degree subject. To attempt this process in the final year of study is inevitably too little and too late. Half the value of work experience and well thought out teaching methods will be wasted if the student is not made aware in advance of the questions that he should be asking himself. Careers counselling (or rather 'life' counselling) should take place both before and during higher education, so that the student is conscious of the self knowledge that he can gain at each stage.

This is not a job only for those involved in higher education. The seeds should be sown way back in early life both at school and at home, but it is indispensable during the critical late teens when young people first develop the maturity to use experiences consciously in order to look into themselves, evaluate their reactions to different situations, and draw conclusions about how to organise their lives. They learn how to use their strengths, and cope with their weaknesses. The expertise to provide the student with a wide range of personal skills and teach him to assess his own qualities may not at present exist in sufficient depth among academic staff in higher education. Many academics do not yet see these areas as part of their role at all. Instead they see their objectives in terms of examination success and the development of academic excellence. This represents too narrow a definition of 'education' and the result is graduates who are similarly restricted in their understanding of the world, themselves and each other.

Careers advisers, on the other hand, have developed, over many years, an increasing awareness of the need for students to undertake this process of self-evaluation. During counselling interviews, much time is devoted to encouraging the student to ask the right questions about himself as well as to seek information about various fields of employment. The efforts of careers advisers are becoming increasingly effective in this area, and more and more students are approaching their careers service earlier in their academic careers. With such a groundswell of undergraduate opinion in its favour, it is timely to launch a major initiative. As students demand more and better counselling, the already highly pressured resources of our careers services will become woefully inadequate.

The present economic climate is hardly one in which to suggest an increase in the numbers of careers advisers or more funds to improve the service that they offer. Nor would this, on its own, provide an adequate long-term solution. Ultimately we need to embrace the concept that academic study and the development of self-knowledge should go hand in hand; both fully integrated into the fabric of education. It is the responsibility of all academic staff to contribute to the personal as well as the intellectual development of students. This philosophy must underpin every decision which is made about course content and structure, about teaching methods, and about the educational environment itself. The complementary skills of the academic and the careers adviser need to be used in conjunction througout each student's education. Employers also have a role to play. Managers in industry, commerce and the civil services constantly employ a wide variety of skills which can be helpful to the student and the teacher: assessing strengths and weakness; counselling; training; developing personal skills.

At present employers visit higher education institutions mainly in order to interview potential recruits, and occasionally as guest speakers at student societies. I would suggest that ways can be found to use employers' skills more imaginatively. For example, the development of seminar skills, amongst students and teachers alike, would form an interesting project for a training officer, on loan from his company, for one term or for a whole year. A course of lectures or seminars concerning the practical development of good communication would be of relevance to all students. Managers on secondment would also participate in informal discussion with students which would increase mutual understanding. They could also act as counsellors where needed.

We are entering an era where companies are increasingly aware of their social responsibilities and in many cases would see 'sabbaticals' for middle-management staff as benefiting the community, the company and the individuals concerned. Such an intimate relationship between the worlds of work and education would require sensitive handling, with a period of experiment to achieve initial understanding and co-operation. Each set of circumstances has its own solutions. The 'employer content' in an engineering course would be very different from that appropriate to a history degree. Nevertheless, the non-vocational preparation for work which I am advocating has many common features which apply whatever the academic discipline.

CONCLUSIONS

I am aware that I may have been clearer in identifying the problems which concern me than in proposing all-embracing solutions. In this area there are no easy answers. The problem is threefold:

to develop in students the basic range of personal skills needed by all employers to provide insights into the real job content of different types of occupation

to encourage self-knowledge amongst students to enable them to make choices from an informed position.

The first two problems reflect a lack of experience and knowledge of a kind which cannot be overcome without practical exposure to the world of work, backed up by a complementary teaching environment. The third problem is fundamental to our approach to education. I make no apology for placing responsibility squarely with the teachers, but not just with those in higher education. They should only be required to refine a process which has already been well developed throughout school-life. However, even in this, employers who are prepared to become fully involved in work experience can make a contribution, encouraging students to analyse their own reactions to different pressures and environments.

Each of these three factors deserves urgent attention because it hinders the progress of intelligent young people, and not only in their career development. We are failing to prepare them for life, for the world as it really is, at home and at work. We are failing to show them the opportunities which are open to them. Worst of all, we are failing to teach them to look at themselves as they are, to see the truth, both good and bad, to accept it and to plan their lives accordingly. Each step that we take to improve this situation is in the interest of all parties concerned. That the solutions require a joint approach between employers and teachers is therefore not only true, but highly appropriate. The necessity for imminent changes in higher education gives us the opportunity to build new bridges. Let us not argue for too long over the details of each design, but get down to some solid construction.

SIR MONTY FINNISTON

Lifelong learning for the professions

To benefit society generally means contributing to the standard of living whether this is to be found in the provision of products, or systems or services; the product may be the fridge, the motor-car or the golf club; the system, the telephone, the electricity supply or the bus; and the service, education, health or the police. Even today one's leisure has to be worked for by somebody in the sense that golfers require clubs and balls, tennis players require racquets, and indoor entertainment requires chess sets, television, radio and so on. The products of leisure are the products of work.

To make these products requires skills, both mental and manual, but education, which is the process, formal or informal, by which one learns, is the provider of these skills in both a general and a specific sense. If this in itself were not enough, the fact is that the product demand is continually changing by reason of consumer preference (however this is generated) or by the inventiveness of the producer. The innovations require additions to and changes in skills, so that the educational process is ever-continuing and ever-changing from primary school to higher education to retirement. A good example of education which finds its role in industrial society (and which will be discussed later) is engineering, on which a Government Committee of Inquiry, which I had the privilege of chairing from July 1977 to January 1980, has just recently issued its Report. However, I begin with a general account of the kinds of learning which run throughout lifelong learning but which are an essential requirement for study in higher education.

Learning to live

The primary feature of learning, for higher education just as much as schools, is that it requires communication between teacher and student. This requires language, and the teaching of language is the first and essential condition in learning to live. Without language the process of learning would be entirely the result of one's own effort; by definition this must be a process certainly slow, probably errant in many of its interpretations of experience and limited to that experience and to oneself. To communicate means to be able to absorb from others knowledge and experience without these exercises having to be repeated by the learner. This communication is by sight and sound but the medium is the language.

The teaching and the use of the English language demand the first priority in schools and higher education. No subject takes precedence over language. Not in the sense of being able to appreciate Shakespeare or the Bible or whatever may be the fashionable best-seller; that gain is one of the added pleasures of language which is aided by additional and sophisticated analytical and emotional development which comes with experience – what the young do not have and cannot therefore be expected to appreciate. It is the use of language to gain access to somebody else's mind and to be understood in that process that is the basis of living. Understanding develops with learning – and learning develops through language. A sightless world would lose much but a dumb world would lose more, since this would remove all links between individuals or make communication so much the harder and less effective. The question therefore arises: 'Is English as a language being taught satisfactorily in schools? Further, do universities, colleges and polytechnics acknowledge their responsibility at their level of study and even for later in life, recognising its importance to living?'

The impression is that they do not. Conversations of the ordinary (so-called) public recorded for radio and television are sometimes incomprehensible not just in the sense of dialect but in presentation, in just putting words together in a grammatical frame and (as I shall expand on later) in logical sequence. Letters and reports from people established in society are not unknown in which clichés and phrases masquerade as sentences of sense, and sentences can be of tortuous incomprehensibility. (Bernard Levin may be addicted to long sentences interspersed with incidental phrases, but at least if one breaks the sentence up one can comprehend his intention.) One's ability to communicate is not just for the chit-chat of conventional social exchange but in the decision-making processes with which everyone is faced in living, in discussion of policies, in consultation in industry, in the disclosure of information, in the interview for the career, in teaching and in learning. These and all living engagements require command of language. Command of language enhances the learning of other skills and disciplines. If it is absent there is confusion or, worse still, intolerance, and silence through inability to communicate is inhibiting and expresses itself in apathy. Intolerance and apathy are not ingredients of living.

The ability even of children to assimilate language should not be underestimated. Professor Hall, of the Center for the Study of Reading at the University of Illinois, in studying the psychology of language, has come to a preliminary finding that, where strong ties exist between language which is used, and the situations in which it is used are in a familiar context, i.e. where a child can interact as an equal, that child shows all kinds of competency in his use of language. The same child at home or at school where he is not treated as a near equal might come across as not knowing very much at all. If these theories are correct, many teachers and parents will have to listen in a new way.' Those who write texts and tests in language arts may have to rethink and rewrite their materials. There is an implication in this research that children do not like to be treated as children, and in a modern world where teenagers have disappeared and young adults spring up at the age of twelve, perhaps new attitudes to the use of language by teachers in teaching have to be developed.

Teaching the use of language as such is not sufficient of itself to stimulate learning. To this must be added the order which reason and logic bring to language. There can be no objection to emotion, wit, humour or the splendid phrase. Such features may facilitate learning, although it is always wiser to appreciate the worth of the cake rather than the immediate pleasure of the icing; but these features should be used to supplement reason and logic, not substitute for them. The second essential in education for living is being able to communicate logically or, in a wider but much less specific sense, rationally. Adversary discussions in public debates may be a tribute to command of language by the disputants but not to the sense of rational debate. Reason finds expression in the use of logic.

I have been told that in the olden days when public schools set the standards which others followed or aped, the teaching of Latin was a substitute for the teaching of logic because of the ordered way in which that language was constructed. In today's society, to learn logic through Latin is not an attractive option, although learning English through Latin might be, but I am not advocating this. What I do advocate is that mathematics should be taught as a compulsory discipline not only because commerce, industry and domestic life demand at least numeracy (a part of mathematics), but also because mathematics is the epitome of logic even if couched in symbolic language.

The teaching of mathematics both in its logical and in its numerical aspects should be related to the world of learning to live; it should be applied rather than pure; its teaching may be generalised in formulae but it should be taught in such a fashion as to translate these formulae into numbers applying to problems of living; in some aspects it should even be taught by rote, despite the fact that the individual does not at the time of teaching understand the mathematical justification. In a recent visit to an apprentice school, I asked the supervisors what they thought of the present generation compared with ten years ago. The answer was not favourable to this generation. The supervisors pointed out that the majority of applicants for apprentice places were asked seven questions, the seventh relating to the conversion of fractions into decimals. The surprising result was the large number of apprenticeship seekers (nearly one-third) who did not know how to effect this arithmetical change. I do not argue that this particular ignorance is shattering to the individual, but it is an unnecessary ignorance. It can simply be removed by teaching fraction conversion to decimals as an outcome of one of the basic mathematical operations of addition, subtraction, division and multiplication. It is better to be aware than to be ignorant.

The present shortcomings of mathematics education are widely held to be due to shortages in the supply of qualified mathematics (and science) teachers, but the problem is exacerbated by variations in the content of what students are taught in their 'A' Level mathematics syllabi. There are, for example, over sixty different 'A' Level mathematics syllabi in this country. Even Mr Heinz did not consider that he needed more than fifty-seven varieties to satisfy the market. Simplification in teaching at the expense of the subtleties and niceties of theory is to be preferred. Are we being too clever as teachers at the expense of the child?

There are two further features to consider. The first is that the computer has come to stay, but with computation based on the binary and not the decimal system, although the latter still obtains in the normal conduct of affairs. The binary system will have to be taught as a regular part of the curriculum at some time. It must not be assumed that children are incapable of assimilating the niceties of Boolean algebra as the basis for computer operation. One should not underrate the capability of an individual at whatever age to assimilate learning, perhaps with lesser understanding of the subtleties.

The second point is that the learning process is not a time-determined process. The examination system may lead to that conclusion, but learning is a continuing process. There is a time or age at which teaching of a subject can be more effective later rather than sooner. If one does not appreciate the subtleties of a particular piece of knowledge at 11, perhaps by 14 the penny might drop and if not at 14 at 17, and if not at 17 then when one is a parent or grandparent. These two features, the absorptive capability of the young and the continuing assimilation of knowledge with age, have in some way or other to be accommodated within the teaching process. Nowhere is this more marked than in the teaching of mathematics, and science or technology, and related disciplines. If time is not a rigid constraint should we not be asking, 'Are we pumping in too much knowledge too fast, too soon in our educational system?'. We are accustomed to the concept of cost-benefit analysis in decision-making processes. Have our curricula been subjected to comparable study of personal development benefit analysis? Are teachers in higher education subjecting their teaching to the same kind of accounting?

It is not being argued that there are subjects other than those which have been or will be mentioned which should be excluded from the domain of learning as part of living. But there is a time for everything. It was William Hazlitt who said, 'That which anyone has been long learning unwillingly he unlearns with proportionable eagerness in haste'. Check this against your own personal experience. How well would you score if you were to be examined in the knowledge that you had when you left university or school? I doubt whether, twenty years on, many outside the academic institutions would show up too brightly against present-day standards of examination. Parents with children of school age will know the feeling.

The third of the 'musts' in learning to live is a knowledge of science. In a sense it does not matter which of the scientific disciplines is the one in which individuals wish to engage – physics, chemistry, biology or, indeed, engineering. The importance of a knowledge of science and of the scientific method, which in turn is dependent upon logical analysis, is paramount. We live in a world which depends upon the applications of science through technology and engineering for its standards of living and which in turn constitutes a basic element in providing work.

Physics and chemistry have obvious applications in learning to live. The physics of heat, light, sound, electricity, magnetism, abound in today's products in the machinery of engineering, whether this be in motive units such as the automobile, the train or the aeroplane, in the electrical products of the motor and generator or in the electronic products of television, radio, hi-fi or the laser. The outcome of a knowledge of chemistry is to be found in such products as pharmaceuticals, fertilisers, insecticides, antibiotics, detergents, even food. Biological sciences have contributed to our understanding and control of health and

of animal husbandry. The future output of sciences in this area
will provide us with new materials based on the permutations
and combinations of genetic compounds with far-reaching
consequences outside the biological disciplines.

Since drafting this chapter my attention has been drawn to an
article in the *Observer* of 6 April 1980 by Dr John Rae,
Headmaster of Westminster School, entitled 'Teach British to be
Pirates not Prefects'. He argues that 'the Victorian public
schools treated science as second-rate and over-emphasised the
intellectual skills of analysis and criticism. Their ethos imposed
stultifying conformity, their snobbery encouraged contempt for
the world of industry and trade'. But we have an economy now
where industry and trade are the major wealth generators
contributing thirty per cent of the gross domestic product
(GDP) through manufacture and where the export of goods and
services contributed by manufacturing constitutes sixty-six per
cent of all exports; where another three per cent of the GDP
comes through agriculture which is in fact now essentially an
industry based upon the use of machinery and chemicals and
science; and where a further ten per cent of the GDP resides in
the traded services all of which depend upon manufactured
products whether this be ships, aircraft, computers or electronic
equipment. The quicker we get our trade and industry back into
better shape the more fully will the standards and expectation of
standards of living of the population be satisfied.

Teaching science is to teach people how to progress through
man's control of the natural environment – earth, sea and air –
how to convert raw materials into useful products for living and
how to do this in controlled fashion based on design and
experiment, logical analysis and intellectual application. If this is
not one of life's objectives for oneself and others, what is? It is
not that one is seeking for expertise at an early age in any of the
sciences but rather in inculcating a sense of understanding, and
thus ridding the individual of superstition, myth and fear of
nature and of man's works through technological application. I
was brought up on physical sciences and yet the television series
'Life on Earth' by David Attenborough, and his book based on
these programmes, gave me an understanding of (but not an

expertise in) animal life which would otherwise have been missing. The intellectual satisfaction alone is justification; that it might stimulate other activity in other spheres is exciting. The real world is not divided neatly (if that is the word) into the disciplinary compartments which the educational system and the teaching profession find administratively convenient.

Science is the one area where manual skills for practical purposes can be taught. I have great respect for those who can manipulate materials to give them shape and (in the process) function, and I have admiration for the craftsman who imaginatively translates mental concepts into artefacts. The fact of modern life is, however, that, for mass markets (and the standards of living of any nation are determined by the availability of products or services to the mass market), manufacture is not a product of individual craft but of machines in which craft has been incorporated. The Industrial Revolution replaced man's brawn by machine power. Today machine power has been given a quasi-intellectual capability by the microprocessor. Instructions can be programmed by the intelligence of the human being which the machine then implements at one remove from the operator. In the world of industry the machine is taking over more and more the manual skills of the individual, aided by the transfer of the lower end of man's intellectual abilities to the machine. (The exception to this in industry is the maintenance engineer, the repair man, the fitter; he is engaged in one-off jobs, not mass production. In fact, the less he has to do the better the processes and the products of mass production!)

Certainly, it is necessary to teach that the making of things is essential to living, but I do not believe it is necessary to insist that accepting this principle demands that manual skills be taught in the same way as intellectual knowledge and understanding are imparted. Learning to do things in a personal, manual sense is essential to an appreciation that the artefacts of living have to be fashioned and that one does not live by concepts alone but by designs translated into things.

To the skill of making things there is also the antecedent activity of design. Perhaps design as a curriculum subject just requires an encouraging environment; if so it is likely to be found in the workshop rather than in the classroom, and in the workshop I would include the science laboratory or its engineering counterpart. For example, the introduction of the computer – and computer aided design – should make it easier to excite children's minds for designing. Such experiments are proceeding throughout the country. I have visited schools with projects in which whole classes participate not just in design but in manufacture of the products and in marketing and selling them to families, relatives and friends as well as the outside world. This shows a marked appreciation of both industrial and commercial activities, which are more than designing or making, but a synergism of these supported by a complex of activities which go towards learning to live.

This leads me to a fourth taught subject which may surprise – that is the use of games as a learning medium. Whatever may be the importance of games, particularly games with a physical content to improve the condition of the body, it has a further justification in that it introduces the concept of competition. An environment of competition determines success or lack of it and in learning to live, achieving success is a desideratum. I am not, of course, meaning the development of techniques for winning at all costs. However, judging by modern international industry, the devices and techniques of the unacceptable face of capitalism – and of communism for that matter – would certainly not lead one to believe that the Marquis of Queensberry rests placidly in his grave. Undoubtedly this will to win is important both to the individual and the community which he serves. There are no good losers; losers are just non-winners.

Games and the teaching of essential subjects should have one further ingredient – the creation of confidence. The transfer of this attitudinal trait into later life and career is essential to success. Many of these subjects, English, maths, science, logic and even design, are, of course, a base for development in the higher reaches of the educational system. There would appear to be a strong case for the standards achieved in English, maths, science and logic, and even those optional subjects which might be the choice of career activity of the student, to be set at higher levels than at present. It might be argued that the examination system is intended to do this, but the examination system discriminates only between levels of achievement. What the teaching process in secondary schools leading to the examination does is to set the standards of achievable learning. What one would desirably seek (and what, for example, at one time the Scottish educational system insisted upon in the study of technical subjects) is to leave the first year at university to advance the teaching and learning of maths, physics and chemistry to a standard which enabled the subsequent study of other disciplines based on these basic subjects to be taken to an advanced level.

The world we live in is organised to accommodate various aspects of living and human beings have to accommodate themselves to work within the rules and authorities of the institutions. True, the conditions of organisation may and should change with new circumstances, new technology, new concepts and new values, but what is surprising is the lack of knowledge by children and – even more salutary – by adults of the operations of the institutions which, if not exactly ruling their lives, at least condition them. How does government work? What internal controls are there in the trade union movement? How is education organised? What authority do teachers have? What relates the unions to the class-room? What is this curious creature the National Union of Students which pronounces on matters of policy outside the domain of its experience, knowledge or influence? In this regard, knowledge of industry, its workings, its structure, its relationships with society, and so on, is also part of this information and instruction programme.

Many of these institutional features are argued about in the media and elsewhere but the basic understanding is lacking. It would be an improvement if in learning to live within the institutional framework of society one knew something about this framework from some time within the 14 to 16 age range. One might, then, as one grew up be disposed to participate in democratic changes to the institutional structures where these did not suit the changing circumstances of living. Has higher education any responsibility here also?

This leads to the most important and most difficult of all

conditions to satisfy in society: the problem of values in
individual and group conduct – whether this latter be in the
family, in the neighbourhood community or in the wider
contexts of region or nation. Values are set by society and
assimilated either by tradition, fashion or imitation. There was a
time when religious instruction provided a basis for individual
conduct related to society at large but in many respects the tenets
of religions have been questioned by the findings of science. I
mean here the physical and not the social sciences which have
been disappointing in their findings and have not given the lead
one hoped for. The methodology of science which demands
observation, experiment, test and theory to advance knowledge
and understanding further, does not lend itself satisfactorily
or unequivocally to dogmatic assertions or tenets of faith as
unquestionable truth.

Many of these problems have been with us from time
immemorial. Others have become more pronounced with technical development. There have been concepts which are generi-
cally huddled under the term 'human nature' as if they were
genetically determined and were not capable of individual
control. But new problems in which values will determine
action are constantly being generated as society advances its
control over the material aspects of life. Abortion, genetic
engineering and nuclear developments are but three on which a
decision of what is acceptable to society and to individual
conscience will have to be established.

In many cases such as these, reasons of logic do not satisfy and
cannot in fact arrive at any conclusive decision on the pros and
cons of various lines of action. In the absence of such guidance
society becomes confused (none more than adults who see the
foundations on which their social duties and responsibilities
were based, founder) and the issues become centres for disrup-
tive activity. Since the more obviously thoughtless acts of disorder
in society are attributable to youth – hooliganism, vandalism,
crime against people and property – the earlier in life rules of
conduct of individuals in and towards society can be inculcated
the better for the individual and society in youth and later in life.
The Jesuits had it right in principle. There must be a place in

education for moral teaching from the earliest age, and through-out life for information and education of society and of the moral codes which underpin it.

Career choice: chance or design

So far the emphasis has been on education in schools, but before one enters higher education there is the problem of determining one's career. On this subject more personal guidance is required than at present obtains in schools or at home. Since one is learning to live, the essential question one has to ask is, 'What am I going to do?' The guidance one receives at present is random, comparatively casual – after all there is no responsibil-ity on the part of one who gives advice – and likely to be biased either because of ignorant rejection of alternatives outside the knowledge of the adviser or because of bias towards conformity or tradition.

It would not be an exaggeration to say that more detailed attention is paid to recruiting individuals to a particular com-pany than guidance given to somebody at the start of their career to ensure the appropriate choice has been made. It seems to me that individuals at school should be subjected to constant education in the sense of acquiring increased knowledge of *all* kinds of conditions of employment. Why medicine and en-gineering should rank first or second in the list of hierarchical preferences in Germany and the United States, while in Britain, dependent as it is upon its manufacturing industries and hence its engineering, engineering ranks much lower in the scale of career choices is a mystery, made even more so by the fact that the talent for engineering in the broadest sense in Britain is mani-festly as great if not greater than in other countries. Why are medicine, accountancy and law so popular as professions when they are not taught in school? Is it because they are *not* taught in school they are so popular? It is said that school children are put off industry when they visit factories. How many would be put off medicine if they were to visit a casualty department or operating theatre as part of their induction to their future career? Are there subtle snobberies at work?

The choice of job opportunities for the intending professional and even for the skilled is less severe than the total unemployment figures would suggest and with a little more backbone put into generating national industrial competitiveness the figures would be even smaller. Reading the professional lists of disciplines for which expertise is sought one is constantly surprised at the almost unlimited opportunities for living and learning. We have in this country forty-five universities, including the Open University, and thirty polytechnics. Nobody could claim shortage of places. One may argue whether the differences in quality at the universities may not lead to an over-demand in some universities, polytechnics and colleges and not in others. Such weaknesses in particular disciplines can be corrected with broad planning. One may even question whether the choices people make of particular subjects do not tend to weight the scales in favour of the humanities rather than the sciences and engineering. Even that can be corrected by increased demand-pull by industry. The one point being made here is that the system of tertiary education in this country does not lack places to absorb numbers which some educationists go so far as to claim points to a superfluity of universities for certain subjects.

Once entered into a place of higher education one is faced with the different mode of teaching and learning (professors are not school-teachers) and age changes the responsibility students have for their own improvement. One of the worrying features is of course the proliferation of knowledge and ideas and change. It is of interest to note that the Committee of Inquiry into the Engineering Profession had the greatest difficulty in coming to a conclusion on curricula and their content in the engineering disciplines. It could not devise a 'standard' curriculum which would be applicable to all engineers, with the remainder being taken up by the optional subjects more appropriate to the specialisation of a particular individual. Was there in fact a core curriculum to be devised? How much of the course should it amount to? How standard was it? This raises for higher education the problem which was discussed for secondary, namely that there might be too great an effort to push too much into the individual at these educational ages. If the learning process is going to be stopped when one leaves higher education, then there may be some case for attempting to put quarts into pint pots although the rejection rate of individuals would be high. But since in a world of change much of the knowledge of today would be obsolescent before one retired and since it will have accrued to itself features not present at initial graduation, the implication is that learning is a life-time study and this applies whether it is accountancy, law, science, engineering or teaching.

THE PROFESSIONAL

For many, entering university, polytechnic or college is a prelude to entering a profession with the intention of following a career. It is of interest to examine here the nature of a profession, and then turn to its links with higher education, using the case of a profession which has lost caste but is essential to the conduct of society. In past years to be an amateur carried a social-class value distinguishing between the individual practising a particular skill and being paid for it, and the individual who engaged in the same exercise for enjoyment. Today, the cachet professional is one which is sought after, the word giving an added status certainly to the individual himself who can use it to describe the service he can give through his skills independent of whether he belongs to an organisation of those practising similar skills.

The recent Committee of Inquiry into the Engineering Profession was faced with the problem of determining what was meant by a profession (in this case of engineering) and found refuge in a most unlikely place – an Appendix to Command Paper 4463 (HMSO 1970) prepared by the Monopolies (note Monopolies) Commission on 'The general effect on the public interest of certain restrictive practices so far as they prevail in relation to the supply of professional services'. The three essential conditions perceived by the Monopolies Commission in their definition of a profession were as follows:

1. Professionals are required to be expert in a particular area of activity for which an advanced and extended formation is necessary and practice in which requires a high level of

theoretical foundation; (formation means preparation for service and includes academic learning and practical and experiential training).

2. Professionals have custody of a clearly definable and valuable body of knowledge and understanding.

3. Professionals accept responsibility and accountability for the decisions they make against recognised values and standards of conduct.

The Committee of Inquiry concluded that certain classes of those identified as engineers fulfil these key characteristics of professional occupations.

To enter a profession certain minimum standards of skill are required for qualification and this minimum is continuously being upgraded. If development of the particular discipline is not proceeded with or furthered by continued learning to improve, then the activities of the individual are more adequately described as 'occupational' or 'vocational' rather than 'professional'. This is not to denigrate the vocational. If head counts are the basis for democratic influence, society itself is in large measure dependent upon the vocational rather than the professional – and indeed it would be an impossible world for the professional to engage in his activities were it not for the support given by the appropriate vocational. The postman, the dustman, the policeman (on the beat) and the transport worker are not professional in the terms of this chapter but they certainly are occupational activities and they require some skill, however minimal, to discharge their responsibilities with efficiency and satisfaction to the society they are serving. It is interesting that in a capital-intensive industrial society it is these semi-skilled people whom industry tends to replace with machines. With professionals, on the other hand, machines are developed to augment the human skills.

Conditions for professional attainment

To define by exclusion is unsatisfactory, so what is it that one demands of a professional? It is that the individual attempts and successfully provides a solution to problems for which his particular skills are essential. This has three implications. Firstly, that the solution to the problems demands a knowledge, understanding and appreciation, both in the analytic and in the synthetic sense, of that body of knowledge relevant to the problem. Secondly, that it demands intellectual (and where appropriate manual) capability in the individual to use that knowledge. Thirdly, and as important for the determination of professionalism as either of the two preceding conditions, that that body of knowledge is continually extended to improve the effectiveness of the professional in his particular activity. Professionalism in an age of change cannot be a static condition which once achieved is never to be updated in the light of new knowledge, experience or experiment. The fact that the professional does not do the research, but that it is encouraged in others of his own profession or even outside his discipline to enlarge and enhance the evolving parts of his own profession, is an essential element in the pursuit of professionalism.

There is a further feature which contains (in the sense that it overviews) the three preceding conditions. This feature is one of general principle and not specific to any one profession. In a changing and complex world it raises problems covering all professionals not just as members of their specific profession but as citizens of society. I refer, of course, to morality – a context in which professional solutions to the problems can create confusion and conflict in the professional when such solutions are questioned in conventional terms of right or wrong or in humanistic terms of value. This arises because the conduct of a profession is not an isolationist activity. The service the professional contributes is to and through society and therefore he has to be responsible for his actions to society. There are problems, for example, of constraints on human rights and so on, which are part of the society in which professional opinion is neither better nor less well-founded than other individual opinion. But there are also problems of specific concern to particular professionals such as contraception, foetus life, transplants, genetic engineering – problems created by professionals in advancing their profession, but raising issues outside the professional skills.

Professionals might not like to be called problem solvers

(there is a tendency for professionals to encourage a mystique about the skills of their profession), but it is difficult to describe the essence of their activities as other than that. The doctor or dentist is faced with a sick man or woman; the sickness even if confined to the teeth or gums may have a variety of symptoms which have to be analysed; a diagnosis has to be made and a solution offered. The engineer has to meet a specification; he designs a machine; the design poses various problems and to resolve these he has to provide solutions to make the machine operate. In the various options open to him he has to take the one which effects the greatest efficiency in a machine, but if the machine breaks down in operation he has to determine the cause and provide a further solution. Most professions have similar if not identical problems which repeat themselves so that solutions become instinctive reactions. Where problems are unusual the solution is usually referred to specialist professionals. Professionalism has its limitations.

This leads to the second of the conditions, namely the intellectual content of the problem solving. Here there are two aspects. The first is educational in an academic sense and the second experiential in the practical sense. In education the development of the professional has until now been centred upon the tertiary system of education – universities, polytechnics, special colleges of study, schools of further education and so on. The Committee of Inquiry into the Engineering Profession noticed a number of features about the education of engineers, which I believe would apply equally to many other professions in greater or lesser degree. One was that in a world of change, of increasing complexity and in-depth understanding of a particular discipline, there was increasing difficulty in assimilating the new knowledge on grounds of sheer growth alone and in particular for the uncorrelated facilities for teaching and training to accommodate. The Committee made several points on this. First, it recognised the different relationship between the professional engineer and his employer compared with the individual relationship between doctor and dentist and patient. With the wide spectrum of activities classified as engineering – mechanical, electrical, electronic, chemical, civil, etc. – the Committee recommended that the content of curricula, whether in academic study or training in industry, should be constantly reviewed and accredited by outside bodies consisting of educationalists, engineers of repute and experience and employers responsible to a statutory Engineering Authority. This was intended to ensure that the individual was being supplied with what was considered to be beneficial to society by maximising the benefit to the individual. Of course not all professional education can do this or would wish to do it, since there is the view that what is best for a profession is what those in the profession determine – the self-governing principle. But are professionals wholly the best judges of themselves? In a market for products the Consumers' Association would deny this. In a market for services the public might also have a view of what that service should be, particularly in the establishment of a code of conduct, which raises questions of negligence and incompetence. In the education and training of professionals the answer must be the affirmative, since almost by definition to be educated is to learn from the best.

Second, the Committee recommended that the curricula for degree courses should relate to and accommodate the anticipated requirements of a main body of professional expertise, but that those selected for an elite (in this case after one year in an establishment of higher education) should enter a different stream with an enhanced curriculum to bring out these qualities to the greater benefit of the individual and of the society he would cater for in his career. The selection would not just be made on the basis of intellectual ability (although this would loom large in the weighting of an elite) but on judgement of character and initiative. People considered the elitist approach undemocratic or worse. The fact is that the world is not of equal ability or potential skill, and recognition of this is not to be deplored. The Honours system and its classification long recognised this.

Third, how do professionals ensure that their knowledge is kept up-to-date? When one considers that the period from the start of a career to retirement encompasses some forty years during which time the world has moved on very considerably, the whole question of continuing education of post-graduate and post-experience is raised. It is obvious that newcomers to a profession – that is, those just graduating or qualifying – are in a considerable minority and that any profession is dependent upon its existing stock of practising professionals for the immediate prosecution of its activities. Not to cater for that majority seems an odd oversight of cost benefit as well as democracy. In the case of engineers we identified aspects of expertise an engineer may wish to develop after graduation and before retirement:

1. An awareness of what others are doing in his own or in related fields.
2. A knowledge of specialist technologies and techniques not covered in his initial formation.
3. A knowledge of new technologies and techniques which have arisen since he qualified.
4. Details of new demands upon the engineering dimension and their implications (e.g. health and safety regulations, product liability laws, etc.).
5. Managerial skills, for example in financial control, marketing or industrial relations.

In its Report the Committee of Inquiry recommended to the Government that registered engineers (and the qualifications required for registration are a separate matter which I do not propose to deal with here) should be granted a statutory right of release to paid study leave (paid by employers) to improve themselves in their profession.

Universities, polytechnics and colleges are very concerned about the demographic decline in population in this country in the mid-1980s and the effect this will have on filling places. The answer to this fear is that higher education institutions must play a greater role in society not by catering for those between the ages of 18 and 22 in the main or for the still smaller numbers engaged in research, but to spread their knowledge more widely to those already engaged in and practising with knowledge and experience which may, however, be obsolescent, obsolete or lacking in relation to new developments. This of course will require considerable changes in attitude and teaching methods in universities or other establishments but the difficulties of change are not an excuse for avoiding change.

One problem which the professional man has to face is his dependence upon other professionals. A major example of this is in medicine where much of the effectiveness of modern medicine is due to the developments in drugs and antibiotics, many of them produced synthetically through the skills of the industrial chemist, someone far removed from the doctor. It is too much to expect (and quite unnecessary for) the doctor to be expert not only in prescribing drugs, but also in the evaluation of the subtleties of the drugs in which he is concerned. Yet there must obviously be some relationship between the doctor, chemist and drug manufacturer beyond a consumer/contractor relationship. When controversies like Thalidomide and the more recent case of Debendox obtain, there is need to strengthen the consultative and learning processes part of his equipment and expertise. These communication links between experts can best be forged in the higher education institutions as the medium through which the exchanges take place. It also imposes commitment upon the professional bodies who seek to improve standards in their profession to be committed to such total life education.

Codes of conduct

When we come to the code of conduct of the professional there is room for infinite discussion. I would however suggest three features of professional life which should condition one's actions or determine one's decision on the various options which are open. The first is that no professional should withdraw his labour for whatever reason. In this respect he will differ from those trade unions who assume the right to strike (and the right to work at one and the same time). The withdrawal of one's labour is a negation of the purpose of professional activity which is to use one's expertise to the greatest benefit of the client or customer, not to withhold it for whatever reason. If a profession is catered for by a trade union, it is the rules of the union which must bend to the rules of conduct of the profession. The Report of the Committee of Inquiry stressed this point.

The second is that the boundaries in which action or decision can be taken should be defined by law (if possible), in this case the law of the land and/or rules set down by the professional body itself. Lord Redcliffe-Maud in his Wilfred Fish Lecture on 'Professional Responsibility' said 'What matters most is not the system but the professional integrity of the individual member of the profession and his readiness to agonise when his professional conscience is in conflict with what the state tells him to do or to accept'. In my view it is too burdensome for the relationship between a professional and society to be subjective. It faces the individual with a responsibility which is better resolved by corporate decision of fellow professionals and more likely to be sustained in public criticism or discussion if related to the corporate view of the profession as a whole. The attempts of the Royal Society to define the role and place of genetic engineering for bodies medical or otherwise who discuss matters of society and professionalism is an example of this, as are the considered studies of the Council of Science and Society, the Science Policy Foundation and similar bodies. In a wider context such meetings as Pugwash or for the Helsinki Agreement on human rights would have been less effective had it not been for the intervention, advice and leadership of professionals influencing political decision. Subjective opinions if felt strongly should be brought into public debate by fellow professionals for decision and not left to arbitrary individual action. This professional debate with, in and for society demands an outward looking and participative attitude to problems not just of the profession itself but relevant to the wider responsibilities of the profession. 'Conspiracies against the laity' are better denied by involving the laity.

Thirdly, the professional should always be concerned with improving the status of his profession, not just as a matter of self esteem but for society in general. Such improvements are not induced by self-satisfaction or apathy, and even less by obstructive, even destructive, elements of behaviour which operate in present-day society and which have led to present dissatisfaction with, for example, some features of the social services.

Continuing formation

It is interesting to note the kinds of improving knowledge and skills that engineers might develop following their initial education. Awareness of what others are doing in his own or related fields; knowledge of specialist technologies and techniques not covered in his initial education and training; knowledge of new technologies and techniques which have arisen since he qualified; details of due demands upon the engineering dimension and their implications for example in health and safety regulations, product liability laws etc.; and managerial skills, for example in financial control, marketing, or industrial relations. Although this was set out for engineers, there would be very few individuals at professional level, even in disciplines other than engineering, who could not justify continuing education on similar or equivalent grounds.

If continuing formation (i.e. a post-graduate/post-experience educational/training package) becomes the rule rather than the exception, then one can imagine that before the end of this century there will be considerable changes in the organisation of schools, universities and polytechnics. There will be changes in two senses. The first is that the type of student will tend not to be the young undergraduate or sixth former but the older individual already experienced in industry or in work generally. Second the type of courses and teaching methods to be developed for such people will differ from those appropriate to the younger undergraduate. For example, the modular system might well develop still further to suit the short-term sojourns of post-graduate and post-experience students; the seminar and the colloquium might be modified to facilitate group teaching; the use of the media and, particularly, the television (either through the Open University or through normal channels) might incorporate general or special courses; and there should be a considerable increase in the use of home study based on the cassette and the audio-visual tape.

One cannot but emphasise that learning is a lifelong process. There is no point in stuffing knowledge, much less forcing understanding, into minds either incapable of assimilating knowledge or, worse still, misinterpreting or misusing it. The world does change and it changes because new ideas, new concepts, new knowledge and new information come to it through a variety of processes and experiences. Furthermore, these extensions of knowledge are deriving more and more from international origins which enlarge the breadth and depth of change. Of course some of this extension of knowledge will be obtained through day-to-day contact with one's colleagues and experience but structured teaching still constitutes the most satisfactory way for assimilating new knowledge and under-standing. To maintain or even advance one's expertise, and thus advance the interests of the company one serves and hence the nation, is also considered a condition of membership and as part of the code of conduct of professional organisations.

It was for this reason that the Committee of Inquiry came to the conclusion that the Government should introduce the statu-tory right to paid study leave for all statutorily registered engineers, including those currently practising to become regis-tered with an Engineering Authority on criteria and lines to be devised by that Authority. Notice the term 'statutory right to paid study leave'. In France employers spend the equivalent of two per cent of their annual payroll on continuing formation provision; all employees, not just engineers, have a statutory right to paid leave for the purpose of study, the period of leave entitlement being related to length of service. Some German Länder have adopted similar right of release laws and the European Commission is considering an EEC directive on this.

In this connection, since experience resides in those who are practising in industry, their conversion to the role of teachers to communicate their experience, knowledge and understanding is also likely to become an essential change in support of education for practice in industry. In the more progressive firms, particu-larly those concerned with communication in the electronics field, these kinds of in-house teaching services are almost the norm. It is most impressive to see shelves of tapes dealing with specific subjects in which individuals can have tutorials to themselves with visual display units rather than face to face teaching. In today's context, learning can be frozen and put on record in the book, the tape, the audio-visual cassette, the microfilm and so on, for reference at any time in the future. And where there is doubt or question the pupil can record his question and receive his explanation by the same routes.

The professional institutions number among their members some of the leading exponents of their particular discipline – individuals not just intellectually knowledgeable of their professional disciplines but also experienced in their applications in the multifarious and, in some cases, unquantifiable pressures of decision-making which can significantly affect the lives of people and industries. Such men must be aware of the changes being brought about in the society in which they live, and should (as many do) be expected to feed back into the educational system this knowledge and experience. To this extent the professional institutions and the academic institutions, whether at secondary or at tertiary level, require greater inter-communication. How this is to be effected is a matter of choice. The recently sponsored engineering degree courses at Bath University encouraged by GEC are one example of an industrial intervention. If for 'industry' one read 'professional institution' some comparable schemes could be devised. The Institution of Chemical Engineers, for example, has shown great merit in their association with universities and polytechnics and in influencing the direction and course of curriculum content.

Whatever form education may take, it is not an isolated activity sufficient in itself although one cannot deny that one can engage in education on grounds of self-interest. What is certainly true is that the society in which we live is based for its advance in the eyes of the vast majority of its people upon an improvement in their living conditions. This can only be achieved by applications of intellectual and manual skills; and these intellectual and manual skills can only be generated through education, whether this be formal or informal. If formal, then all the resources of the educational system of industry and of man's activities have to be directed towards communicating the accrued knowledge and experience.

Teachers too have to learn

The classic derogatory cliché 'those who can do and those who cannot teach' has been well paraphrased by Patrick Nuttgens in a paper 'Learning to Some Purpose' in which he says, 'the ordinary mind deals with things; the educated mind with ideas'; and in this same paper, 'the privileged world of leisure, discussion and speculation' ranks far above 'the imperfect, flawed and confused world of industry and work' in the minds of the middle classes'. It is these attitudes which require modification in the light of this country's economy, which depends upon doing things in order to maintain a standard of living and to enjoy these privileges of leisure, discussion and speculation.

This last statement brings in one further feature. By definition a teacher must at least be equal in knowledge (not necessarily in intellect) to communicate with the student; if the teacher has less knowledge, then by definition the student can gain nothing from the teacher. This implies that if teachers are to maintain this lead in knowledge they themselves must undergo the education and retraining just as the student has to continue revitalising himself through further education and training. The question which arises therefore is, 'Do we organise this re-education and training of teachers to full effect?' Or, much more to the point, 'Do teachers insist on it as much as they should, or are they satisfied that their age difference at primary and secondary school and their authority in tertiary education is a sufficient criterion for wallowing in their obsolescent knowledge?'

The answer rests in the principle of continuing formation. What is right for a professional to sustain himself at the peak of his ability as a practising professional must be right for the teacher as a professional, with the additional proviso that since the teacher is preparing the student to learn to live, the responsibility for his or her professionalism is doubly important. Perhaps the profession of teaching has to be opened to include those with knowledge through practice, by secondment, or some other method, to meet the obligations to the on-coming generation.

CONCLUSION

It may be felt that this chapter has raised more questions for higher education than it has answered and that these questions are part of the confusion of society today and particularly of the British. The British have always recognised that education is vital for the civilised progress of the nation (which means both material and cultural values). What it has not recognised as clearly is that such progress has to be weighted towards the education of professionals for the industrial and commercial worlds which sustain the standards of living, material and cultural. For a wide variety of reasons, national and international, this objective (a major change in the life of the nation) has to become the leading objective. If Britain, which has meagre natural wealth and is dependent upon the efforts of its manpower, cannot sustain economic virility, then the culture of the arts, sciences or humanities will either not develop or, much worse, decay.

In such an environment the teaching/learning process to sustain industry and the economy (which does not mean only academic knowledge but practical experience of the industrial activities of the nation) has several features. The first is that such learning is a continuing process from childhood to retirement; secondly, because of the limitations of the intellectual processes and capabilities of human beings, such learning has to be selectively condensed and parcelled out to suit the age and condition of the student; and thirdly, the content of that learning, because of change, has constantly to be updated.

A changing world of increasing intellectual breadth and depth of knowledge might be expected to justify experiments in absorbing this new knowledge and its application in living by individuals and communities. Such experiments should recognise that learning to live is a selective process and living to learn equally requires selectivity. Somebody once said, 'There may be many things which we do not know which we do not need to know'. Improved quality of teaching and learning rather than increased quantity is the proper direction for experiment. What to leave out rather than what to put in. This applies at all levels and stages of education – school, higher education and in career.

A major consideration of learning to live is the choice of career initially. This has to be made at a time when there is little experience of the world by the student; hence greater attention to career choice should be provided by society. The period for learning need not be conditioned by the time limitations imposed by school and university; the reaches of higher education should extend through the lifetime of individuals and as a result benefit the living standards of society. To extend the educational facilities to meet a life-time study will need a change in the use made of educational institutions and industrial organisations.

To support these objectives there must also be a corresponding up-dating of teachers and teaching methods. The exploding developments in communication techniques afford an extension to the teacher and student for learning to live.

NORMAN EVANS

Conclusion

This book stands as a contribution to the discussions about the future of higher education and an attempt to widen those discussions. A combination of reductions in financial support for higher education as a whole, and of demographic factors which are going to make a great difference to the composition of student bodies, are dictating just as much as demanding some of the terms of the discussion. Both developments raise questions which have been interesting to some all along, but which have not really troubled many who are responsible in institutions for policy. This is because, generally speaking, although finances have not been as easy as they were in the expansionist 1960s (outside teacher training), until the last year or two few have really feared that some universities and polytechnics – quite apart from the newest colleges and institutes of higher education – might be closed for lack of funds and/or lack of students.

There are two lines of policy which these present developments put under scrutiny. First there is the Robbins principle of having a sufficient number of higher education places so that all qualified applicants can study for a first degree. Second there is the binary principle, which divided higher education into two parts: that rather quaintly called the public sector (all those institutions which are maintained, as technically they are, by local education authorities, and some voluntary colleges which were formerly teacher training colleges) and the universities. Each of these principles has been debated in the book. Whether or not the kinds of alterations put forward here become the basis for the policy decisions which have to be made very soon, there can be little doubt that both Robbins and binary are going to be revised. There are already indications that the present Tory Government may be thinking of some kind of forum so that both the universities and the maintained institutions can meet with their pay masters and discuss the higher education which together they are all providing. Reductions in educational expenditure could easily mean a review of the arrangements whereby automatic financial support is given as a matter of statutory right to all students studying full time for a first degree. And Robbins needs reformulating to determine who is qualified, to study what, under what conditions. Such decisions will only make sense, however, if there is some other principle or set of principles on which those decisions are made. Another round of ad hoc tidying-up to cope with the immediate issues will incur very considerable risks of irrevocable damage to some institutions as well as to the system, which then could obstruct the very development of policies. Model E was precisely the policy option intended to avoid that kind of catastrophe. The example of what happened to teacher training is too recent and too sour and dour to be ignored. The chapters in this book have suggested the factors which need to be taken into consideration and about which there need to be policy developments. In particulars, they are not all consistent with one another: that was the design and intention of the book. The contributors were free to explore their own chosen concerns within the overall brief, and it is interesting to survey the gaps. One of these is the relative lack of discussion of science, except in the chapter by Sir Monty Finniston. In general, however, one thing does emerge clearly: that the higher education of the future is going to be significantly different from what it has been in the immediate past. The basis for that assertion is that, while matters have not been approached in these terms, what many of the discussions here have raised is a different relationship between institutions of higher education as resources for learning which act as guardians and creators of knowledge, and the individuals who want to make use of these resources as students, and who are also paying for the maintenance of those resources through taxes. This is the significance of the degrees of responsiveness institutions show to the society which supports them. What kinds of students? What kinds of study do they require? And what can be done to facilitate their study? These are the questions to which higher education needs to respond. It is only in the context of the questions that the larger issue can be faced about the service of higher education to the nation. One way and another, the contributors to this book attempt to face these issues. They originate in the supply and demand side of higher education which the Robbins formula settled for fifteen years but which now needs reformulating in terms which can accommodate changes anticipated during the next fifteen years.

Behind the higher education system stands the government system, and with it the binary issue. Institutions of higher education can only respond to what they may understand as the changing demands being made upon them, or alternatively what they take to be the changing requirements which they would wish to meet, within the provisions made for them by central, and to some extent, local government. Essentially that means money. It has been no part of the argument of any contributor to this book that there ought to be more money devoted to higher education. However desirable that might be, mainten-ance of its level at present at best and some reduction at worst is taken for granted. The present distribution of finance within higher education can do with some reconsideration and some of the contributors have commented directly on this. But the point here relates directly to students. Whatever happens to the binary system of financing higher education, something is seriously wrong with arrangements which put part-time students at such a severe disadvantage compared with full-time students, at the very time when all the evidence suggests that the development of part-time studies is one way of meeting the needs of the future. By themselves institutions can do nothing about this. This is part of the responsibility of government.

One of the reasons for wanting a reformulation of the Robbins principle is that in 1963, when it was put into use, higher education and studying for a first degree were extraor-dinary. The competition for places had become intense, leaving many well-qualified school-leavers without the opportunity to pursue their studies as they wished. The Robbins formula was designed to make studying in higher education less extraor-dinary. So one of the most significant developments in higher education over the past two decades has been the way, and the consequences, of its becoming more ordinary.

As more and more young people from more and more families have entered universities, polytechnics and colleges over the last twenty years, being a student, studying for a degree, has become a familiar experience of educational life as the general public understands it. This is the meaning of the figures: in 1963 there were 216,000 students following full-time and sandwich first-degree courses; in 1978 there were 512,000. Numerically that looks impressive. And for sheer expansion of provision indeed it is. So from being the experience of a very small proportion of any age group, an elite higher education has become a fairly ordinary matter for a sizeable proportion of the population, despite the fact that now only some fourteen per cent of each age group in our population attend such courses.

When a commercial commodity ceases to be special and becomes ordinary, an important change takes place in the relationship between provider and purchaser. The producer or provider has to solicit custom; prices tend to fall, and if the commodity does not sell it is dropped and replaced by another. As more people have this experience as part of their general rising expectations of life, it tends to influence their attitudes to non-commercial matters. For example the professional services of medicine, law, accountancy, and architecture are no longer necessarily accepted on the terms on which they are offered. Clients' views of the services they receive and the actions they feel entitled to take on the basis of those views are leading to increasing numbers of controversies concerning complaints of sub-standard professional practice. Education features fairly prominently now within this changed relationship between client and professional and that includes institutions of higher education.

In its ordinary guise the basic requirement of higher education is for the institutions and the system itself to adjust to their public, which includes not only students but industry and commerce, and employers. Students require more consideration of their context. If, as we have to assume, patterns of life are going to show significant variations from past models of work, holiday, marriage, children and retirement, producing different rhythms in employment, unemployment, underemployment, and early retirement with inbuilt assumptions about retraining as the working background for the life of families in whatever form they may develop, then institutions will simply have to change their ways if their services are to be used adequately. That means considering curricula, methodology and patterns of provision – what is offered for learning, how the teaching is conducted and arrangements to enable students to study. This is the burden of H. D. Hughes's contribution. The theme runs through George Tolley's curriculum section. It is implicit throughout Stephen Bragg's radical scheme for revision of the system.

Employers in industry and commerce similarly require more consideration of their context. David Dennis makes their case for the development of social and personal skills which at present receive slight attention in most places. But beyond that there is another way in which institutions of higher education need to take account of developments in industry and commerce. David Dennis gets near the point when he considers the advantage of industrial and commercial personnel contributing to the teaching of the appropriate subject in first-degree courses. This is not a passing reference. It is a fundamental requirement of service-industry employers that he is asserting. It poses a problem for institutions: how should they respond? Sir Monty Finniston develops this further by suggesting a closer relationship between the professions and higher education which could be equally appropriate for all professions, not just those in the applied sciences. In order to prosecute their activities successfully many industrial and commercial concerns have had to develop their own education and training facilities to a very high level. In some cases it is arguable that, such is the academic quality of their staff, they would be capable of teaching significant parts of first-degree programmes entirely from within their own resources. They have become educational institutions in their own right simply because they have had to do so. To this extent higher education and employers are now in an overlapping, not sequential, context. And to the extent that this overlapping is not acknowledged or acted upon, it looks as if higher education is insisting on trying to remain extraordinary when the ordinariness of it seems to have been established.

There is another way in which the context of the employer touches higher education and overlap is implied between the work of academic institutions and the economic and commercial life of the country. The proliferation of institutions and their degree courses has introduced differing conceptions of first-degree studies. Whereas commonly degrees were thought academic, now there is explicit reference in many prospectuses to degrees being vocational or professional. Both are likely to be given further emphasis through requirements for retraining staff either to continue in their existing occupation or to take up different occupations during mid-career, using degree studies as the appropriate vehicle.

All these points relate to conceptions of academic standards and the tension caused by the extra becoming ordinary. In some ways it is easy to understand how this is so and in some ways it is necessarily so. Historically universities have not only been the seats of learning but the essential bases from which the search for greater knowledge has been mounted. The guardianship of academic standards is one of their most cherished duties. Some trends at least can be seen to muddy which can appear a quite straightforward matter. They are the changing nature of first-degree studies over the years, and the development of under-standing about learning itself.

In the immediate post-Robbins period arguments raged about more necessarily meaning worse. It was an inevitable conse-quence, it was held, that standards in first degrees would decline as the numbers of students increased so dramatically. This is a very difficult matter to prove or disprove from empirical evidence. Beyond the kinds of general points which Stephen Bragg makes, and the priesthood of academics kept pure through the system of external examiners, it is difficult to go further without close and specific scrutiny of attainment levels across the work of several institutions. But the simple point to make is that the development of first-degree studies told as a story running through Fielding, Parson Woodforde, George

Eliot, H. G. Wells, Max Beerbohm, Kingsley Amis and Malcolm Bradbury, means among other things that standards of attainment change in ways which retrospectively may seem quite notable. So the academic standards being guarded are changing all the time.

The issue of the proliferation of institutions leads to the same point by a different route. As more people are involved with the teaching, whatever the system of academic validation, what actually happens between teacher and taught will show greater variations than when the numbers involved were smaller, with the consequence that attainment levels may well appear to be different, if it is assumed that they are all strictly comparable. In all probability they are not. And it is one of the arguments of this book that part of the problem with higher education as we find it is that there is too much of one kind of higher education, whereas what we need is more of another, and more differences within it. There is no doubt that this complicates notions of academic standards.

The third influence bearing on questions of academic standards is greater understanding of how learning takes place. Again there is one simple point to make relating to academic standards, drawn from psychological studies. Different combinations of reading, hearing, seeing, doing and thinking can produce significantly different levels of attainment in different individuals who are studying the same materials. This means that attainment levels reached by a number of individuals all using the same route or routes to learning may show variations which reflect not so much the capacity for learning of those individuals but their performance measured by an externally imposed system of learning. It may be the teaching and learning method which is being measured as much as the ability of individuals to master material. Once again this complicates the notion of academic standards. These factors acquire a greater significance when they are applied to an increasingly heterogeneous student body.

The possibility of changing the scope of some courses raises the question of what constitutes first-degree levels of attainment. It becomes a curriculum matter of the skills and abilities as well as the knowledge a particular study is intended to foster. It concerns not only the content of courses, but the way they are taught as well. These matters raise difficult and complex issues which touch on the integrity of academic study, so it is not at all surprising that the changes sought by some of the contributors here are not easily effected. Stephen Bragg faces some of them quite directly. In different ways Charles Carter and Harold Silver approach the same questions, and so does George Tolley.

The implications are not at all comfortable, for they could begin to suggest that higher education is going to have to attend to the academic standards of courses which are at sub-degree level, as part of its principal responsibility. The polytechnics and colleges, and the institutions from which they grew, have had long experience of doing just that. But within the sphere of higher education for good or ill, the tendency has always been, with rare exceptions, for institutions to try and shed the lower-level work and concentrate on first-degree studies. The idea of more higher education but of different kinds could mean a painful adjustment for many institutions to doing what formerly they had taken pride in avoiding – teaching at sub-degree level. It could mean altering the emphasis on research. That does not necessarily diminish the importance of research for institutions. Nothing can be of greater importance than sustaining its quality. But it does mean taking full account of the views offered here by Stephen Bragg, Charles Carter and Harold Silver. If changes can properly be considered for some part of higher education provision, then research as an essential activity comes into the reckoning. Thinking of more higher education but of different kinds means that higher education may come to describe a wider range of academic activities than at present. The quality of research must necessarily be sustained. The attainment levels appropriate for a Bachelor's degree must necessarily also be maintained within contemporary academic conventions. Sub-degree work or two-year courses of higher education, whether in the terms suggested by Charles Carter or by Stephen Bragg or in any other, necessarily means expecting different attainment levels at the end of shorter courses, and courses which may begin at lower levels than the present three- and four-year courses. When related to possibilities of part-time study it may mean designing series of self-contained courses which can be studied in succession over a relatively long period, culminating in a first degree, but which include preparatory courses of a kind rarely provided in institutions at present.

This would be a literal extension of present higher education provision. As such it could require a different and perhaps more painful adjustment. Whether it is acknowledged or not, the basis for much first-degree study at present tends to be an assumption that, among the students who are studying, there are the likely successors of the academic who is teaching the course. Academics teaching courses which had a lower beginning or ending level of attainment would not be able to make that assumption in the same way. It could just as easily be the case that the teacher's successor was his present pupil; but the course could not be designed on that basis. Some teachers could find this extension an enjoyable and rewarding development of their work. Others could find it threatening and view it as a serious encroachment on academic standards. The contributors to this book would say that is a mistaken notion, but they would not dispute that it is highly significant.

The willingness of the various kinds of institutions, universities, polytechnics and colleges to undertake developments such as these will test the capacity of higher education to respond to the world which gives it life. The test could be severe. There is no end to the questioning of what is now offered, and the adaptations which could then be required, once the need to seek additional categories of students is assimilated to academic policy. Several possibilities are suggested here.

Just as complicated a matter are the various offerings by institutions for study. There are two separate but related aspects to this: the content of courses which can be studied and the modes of study. Part-time study would inevitably alter the relation between the institution and its surrounding population, something which Tolley hints at. In theory an allocation of different functions to different kinds of institutions could have a similar effect, but so far experience of this kind does not seem very encouraging. If these potential students are to be positively encouraged, both content of courses and patterns of study will have to take careful account of their circumstances. Opportunities for part-time study are a critical factor, but even that needs systematic development rather than assuming there is one form of part-time study. For some, regular evening classes meet their requirements for fitting together study, occupation and domestic living. For others a mixture of formal teaching, correspondence tuition, modes of distance learning and blocks of full-time study during holiday periods might be preferable. For others, periodic study could be an attraction, whereby study could be undertaken over a period of time rather than following a course through continuous study for a set length of time. Since many of these arrangements would need to be made with the particular needs of a relatively local population in mind, what suited one area would not necessarily suit another. Developments of this kind, in a larger number of institutions than offer them at present, designed as a community service to enable men and women to study, could have a considerable effect on student recruitment.

This does not mean duplicating the efforts of the Open University. For many, the experience of working with other people on a regular basis is far more attractive than the highly developed sophisticated tuition-systems which the Open University has pioneered in this country so very successfully. It is probably true for most people that learning is a social business as well as an academic undertaking. Modes of study need to take this into consideration.

To some extent what is offered for study is influenced by how it is to be studied. Some of the variations of part-time study preclude some courses which are normally studied at present on a full-time basis. But even assuming that problems such as these have been overcome, what is offered will need to take full account of the working experience of potential students if it is to be positively attractive. For most potential older students, enrolling in courses of higher education is likely to be related to factors of social and employment mobility. Relevance as voiced by the 18+ students in the late 1960s takes on a different significance in this context. Most of these older students are likely to want to feel assured that what they study is going to be useful in helping them achieve whatever goals they may have in mind for themselves.

This is where the knowledge and skills they may have acquired informally become so important. What they study needs to take account of what they know already. This could easily mean designing courses anew for particular groups of students, rather than working on the assumption that all that can be offered is contained in the prospectus of courses currently being taught. It could also mean finding ways of giving due recognition to attainments in knowledge and skills which they brought with them and acquired before undertaking their formal study, which could be verified academically in formal assessment terms to count towards graduation. Any indications that an institution was making these kinds of facilities available would imply a willingness to fit courses to people rather than assuming that people will fit themselves to courses. This again could have a considerable influence on the willingness of potential students to enroll.

The knowledge and skills already acquired by the time of application also means ways need to be found of extending the present exceptional admissions arrangements, without in any way lowering the standards of entry, so that the lack of formal matriculation is not seen as an automatic bar to entry, as tends to be assumed by so many people at present. Just as there is more than one customary way of learning, so there ought to be more than one route of entry which is customarily used. Every one of these matters could affect the perceptions held of higher education by constituencies of potential students who are not coming forward at present. It is these kinds of new and additional students who hold the key to the questions about student recruitment. And student recruitment holds the key to unlocking the uncertainties which are so seriously affecting higher education.

The various points put forward could begin to form the basis for devising means of meeting more readily the needs of students in our rapidly changing society. None of them would be easy to work out in practice. However at the lowest calculation, the survival of many institutions may depend on developments such as these.

In some ways asking for institutions of higher education to change to take account of these factors can seem an improper demand. Any suggestion that academics should adjust their views about what is appropriate for study within the field of their own expertise can be interpreted as an invitation to abdicate from the responsibility of guarding the integrity of knowledge. If what was implied by any of these developments was nothing more than an on-demand service for students, then indeed that would be a danger. But it is not. What is being argued for is that the alterations in the content of courses, which take place most of the time in so many disciplines as a result of the extension of knowledge achieved through research, should be made to produce ranges of courses which more obviously take into account the circumstances of the working population and so of potential mature students. The needs of the older students are becoming every bit as significant as the needs of the traditional 18+ students.

One of the difficulties of taking the needs of mature students as seriously as those of younger 18+ students, is that generally speaking teachers in higher education have less experience of teaching older students. Universities have a fine tradition of adult education, specialising in this provision. Frequently the Adult Education Department draws extensively for its teaching on full-time teachers from the various departments and faculties of the university. However, this experience is spread relatively thinly throughout universities, and work with experienced adults cannot properly be claimed as part of the mainstream of most universities' work. Polytechnics are usually more experienced in this kind of teaching. Their origins in further education with its long-standing service to industry and commerce make that clear. The colleges and institutes of higher education, too, have significant experience as teacher training institutions with mature students. But whatever the range of experience institutions can point to in working with older students, it is highly unlikely that, in most, there is a sufficient number of academic staff employed throughout the institution to ensure that the needs of the older student can be considered with the same confidence as those of the more traditional undergraduate student. And this is a serious matter. Adult students are not simply older students. Their motivation and ability to study may be at sharp variance with younger students. Often they reach attainment levels far in advance of their younger student contemporaries. Their experience of work and domestic life can mean the stakes are far higher for them. But they can also need different kinds of academic and personal support. Teaching adults can be a different kind of teaching.

One way of approaching this problem is to appoint as academic staff men and women who themselves have been engaged in teaching these kinds of students within industry and commerce. It is this kind of liaison that Sir Monty Finniston is calling for. Unfortunately financial restrictions make fresh appointments almost entirely dependent now on retirements, and even these vacancies are often not filled. If the teaching experience required cannot be found in that way, there is another – the retraining of the present academic staff. Most universities and many other institutions now have some provision for staff training. Perhaps the top priority now for training units should be specific preparation for working with older students. This would be no more than applying to higher education policies which are now ordinarily accepted in industry and commerce: that employees are likely to require retraining at least once during their careers in order to remain competent employees. Sir Monty Finniston points out that this applies to all kinds of teachers as well as to everyone else.

In some ways, to those who are on the outside of higher education looking in at it, asking for these kinds of changes seems the most ordinary thing in the world. For some of them what is improper is that it is not happening as a matter of course. This takes the emphasis back to the perceptions of higher education held by different groups of people. And it refocuses attention on what for so many appears to be the relative lack of response by institutions to the changes taking place around them.

Amongst other things, the contributors to this book have

been writing in specifically practical terms about different kinds of response. They are not indulging in flights of fancy to produce a book of dreams. Their experience of institutional responsibility holds them to propositions which can become daily practice. But it is important to notice that the search for greater responsiveness takes them to government as well as colleges and universities. Stephen Bragg's radical revision of the financing system represents an attempt to bring overall control, institutional development and student support into a logical relationship along one clear line of responsibility. Government can exercise its proper responsibilities for controlling overall levels of expenditure. Institutions can exercise their proper responsibilities for the academic work they undertake. Students can exercise their responsibilities for deciding what, when and how it is most appropriate for them to study. Charles Carter's preferred solution to development within some form of unified control of the system is for government to assign functions for institutions. This is not unlike the DES approach to polytechnics in the 1960s and later to the re-organisation of teacher education in the 1970s. Harold Silver, on the other hand, sides with Stephen Bragg, though from a different starting position and wants institutions to have some boundaries laid down for them and then be left to work out their own salvation. On student grants H. D. Hughes reinforces the points made by Stephen Bragg and Charles Carter; and in a sense the financing of students is the obverse side of the curricular issues on which George Tolley, David Dennis and Sir Monty Finniston concentrate. It is no good altering the courses of study if the potential students for whom they are designed are not enabled to study them.

What is absolutely clear, however, is that local and central government have their part to play in enabling institutions to adapt themselves to the future. Many of the changes called for by the contributors to this book can only come about if Whitehall and Town and County Halls develop their own approaches so that in their turn they become more responsive, in creating the circumstances to enable the institutions to get on with the job. There are three matters which require urgent consideration to achieve that end. At national level some improvement is long overdue in the systems of administration of higher education so that the present separate groupings of universities, polytechnics and colleges and institutes of higher education are brought together as a coherent whole. At the institutional level some steps need to be taken to enable institutions other than universities to develop their academic work with the same sense of direct responsibility which characterises the development of universities, within a system of administration which can be relied on to avoid unnecessary waste. For the individual student some alterations to the grant regulations are necessary to support and encourage part-time study on strictly comparable terms to that available for full-time students. This is a weighty list of issues for the DES, the government and local authorities to confront. But nothing less than facing them directly will suffice if higher education is to be enabled to adapt itself to its times. Shuffling off behind a series of unco-ordinated ad hoc measures will not do. If it is proper, as it has to be, for government to make demands on institutions, institutions are entitled to expect government to make comparable demands on itself.

Government alone is in the position to make one alteration to the existing scheme of things which conceivably could be the most powerful single influence for change, enabling higher education to undertake the tasks which lie ahead. In the context of this book it may seem too easy and perhaps surprising to single out the revision of the system of student grants. Institutions are powerless in this matter. Yet unless something is done there could be the bizarre sight of universities and colleges trying to respond to the changing needs of the population through encouraging part-time study, while the Treasury and finance committees of local authorities appear to obstruct the developments which they themselves could be calling for, through pricing part-time study out of the market. If something is done, then institutions need no longer be caught in the lock-step of assumptions that education is for the young, work for the middle-aged, and compulsory leisure is for the elderly. They could begin to adjust their academic provision to the way in which leisure, work and education are blending into a life-long pattern. Part-time study, periodic study, occasional study, study in institutions and study at home could take their place alongside full-time study with different modes of study being used for different stages of study.

Changes like these, which could follow from a revision of student grant regulations, could have a far wider significance than facilitating different patterns of study. It could begin to alter the relationship between students and colleges. By focusing greater attention on individuals as potentially students through deliberately trying to take account of their circumstances attention would also be focused on individuals as learners. Implicitly the balance could be altered between the activities of students as learners and of institutions as providers of courses and teachers. Institutions would be better able to respond to society.

There is another alteration to the existing system which government alone can determine: the provision of two-year courses. Charles Carter raises the issue in one way. H. D. Hughes approaches it from another direction. It is fundamental to Stephen Bragg's thesis. If making part-time courses available to students on the basis of a mandatory grant-aid entitlement might enable institutions to respond more readily to society and make possible a fuller exploitation of existing resources, then introducing two-year courses, again with mandatory grant-aid provision for students, might prove equally cost effective. It would provide a finishing point with a qualification for those – and they are not a few – who at present spend three years obtaining a degree, whereas they might well prefer to end their studies after two. Two-year courses might simply offer a shorter course at the same level as present degrees (this was the intention of the Dip HE). They could, nevertheless, end in the award of a first degree, as Stephen Bragg proposes. They might be given to those with lower entry qualifications, as is suggested by H. D. Hughes. Whatever the variant, they would extend the capabilities of institutions for responding to the circumstances of potential students. A combination of the two, part-time courses and two-year courses, with provision for part-time study, might make a considerable difference to recruitment. Whole new constituencies of students might be attracted. Existing resources might be fully exploited. The money would be seen to be well spent.

Ours is becoming a learning society. Bookshops and lists of titles from publishers, television and radio programmes and their ratings, do-it-yourself shops of every kind, travel agencies and their bookings; the dividing line between entertainment and learning is now almost impossible to draw. More individuals are wanting to know more about more things; they are wanting to learn. Society's most precious resource for learning remain higher education. We need a better match between the two.

Notes on the contributors

STEPHEN BRAGG has been Vice-Chancellor of Brunel University since 1971. His previous twenty-six years of working life were spent as an engineer in industry. He has been particularly interested in improving links between industry and universities, and was an industrial member of the Univerisity Grants Committee. He is currently Chairman of the Managing Committee of the Central Services Unit for Careers Services in Universities and Polytechnics. His technical interests continue with membership of the Airworthiness Requirements Board and the Standing Committee on Structural Safety.

CHARLES CARTER is Chairman of the Research Committee of the Policy Studies Institute, a private 'think-tank' mainly supported by Foundations. He was formerly Vice-Chancellor of the University of Lancaster from 1963 to 1979. He is an economist, and has held Chairs at Belfast and Manchester and was for many years Editor of the *Economic Journal*. His interests are particularly in problems of the application of science to industry. He is a Fellow of the British Academy, and Chairman of the Northern Ireland Economic Council.

DAVID DENNIS is responsible for graduate recruitment with Marks and Spencer. After graduating from King's College, Cambridge, he joined Marks and Spencer in 1970, taking over his present position after eight years' experience in commercial management. He is now particularly involved in the selection of graduates and the development of better liaison between the higher education institutions and the business world.

NORMAN EVANS is Research Fellow at the Cambridge Institute of Education. Before that he was Principal of Bishop Lonsdale College of Education, Derby, having served ten years as Headmaster of Senacre Secondary School, Maidstone. Senacre was one of Kent's Newsome experimental schools, having pioneered a Work Experience Programme for 15 to 16 year olds in 1959. The years at the College spanned the James period, bringing diversification of general degree studies, and negotiations to create a unique voluntary college of the Derby Lonsdale College of Higher Education. At Cambridge the work has been a DES-funded project on 'The Preliminary Evaluation of the In-Service B. Ed. Degree'. An abiding interest has been attempting to fit the curriculum to pupils and students, rather than the other way round. A current concern is seeking ways to bridge the gap between formal educational provision and non-traditional learning.

SIR MONTY FINNISTON set up his own industrial consultancy company in 1980. From 1977 to 1979 he was Chairman of the Committee of Inquiry into the Engineering Profession. He started his scientific career in 1933 as a Lecturer at the Royal College of Science and Technology, and during the Second World War served in the Royal Naval Scientific Service, after becoming Chief Metallurgist at the United Kingdom Atomic Energy Authority at Harwell where he was a pioneer in the development of nuclear power. In 1959 he became Managing Director of the C.A. Parsons Company's Nuclear Research Centre, which became the International Research and Development Company in 1962. On the formation of the British Steel Corporation in 1967 he was appointed Deputy Chairman and was Chairman for three years from 1973. Amongst his present appointments he is Chairman of the Policy Studies Institute, Chairman of the Council of the Scottish Business Schools, President of the Design Industries Association, President of the Association of British Chambers of Commerce, and Chancellor of Stirling University. He is a fellow of the Royal Society of London and the Royal Society of Edinburgh.

H. D. HUGHES is President of the Workers' Educational Association, and a member of the Advisory Council on Adult and Continuing Education. From 1954 to 1950 he was MP for Wolverhampton South-West and he was Parliamentary Private Secretary to Ellen Wilkinson, Minister of Education, from 1945 to 1947. He was Principal of Ruskin College, Oxford, from 1950 to 1979. He is a Vice-President (and former Chairman) of the Fabian Society; an Honorary Fellow of Sheffield Polytechnic; Panel Member of the Civil Service and Post Office Arbitration Tribunals; and Council Member of the National Institute of Adult Education. He was a member of the Russell Committee on Adult Education from 1969 to 1972.

HAROLD SILVER has been Principal of Bulmershe College of Higher Education, Reading, since 1978. He has held posts in colleges of commerce and technology, and was for seventeen years at Chelsea College, University of London, first in Humanities and then in its new Centre for Science Education, where he held a chair in Education (Social History). His main current research interests are in nineteenth-century British and American social science and education, in the role of education in British and American anti-poverty campaigns in the 1960s and 1970s, and in the nature of diversity in higher education.

GEORGE TOLLEY is Principal of Sheffield City Polytechnic. Educated and trained as a chemist, he has occupied senior positions in industry and for a long period was active in the plastics industry, being a former Chairman of Council of the Plastics Institute. His academic career has included posts as Head of the Department of Chemistry of Birmingham College of Advanced Technology (now the University of Aston), Principal of Worcester Technical College and Senior Director of Studies at the RAF College, Cranwell. He has served for a number of years as a Member of Council of the Council for National Academic Awards and is currently Chairman of the Committee for Business and Management Studies of the Council. He is Chairman of the Board of Management of the Further Education Curriculum Review and Development Unit, and is Honorary Secretary of the Association of Colleges for Further and Higher Education. He is a former Vice-Chairman of the Committee of Directors of Polytechnics. Dr Tolley is a priest of the Church of England and an Honorary Canon of Sheffield Cathedral.

Index